Meanings

Meanings

THE BIBLE AS DOCUMENT AND AS GUIDE

KRISTER STENDAHL

FORTRESS PRESS   PHILADELPHIA

Library of Congress Cataloging in Publication Data

Stendahl, Krister.
  Meanings: the Bible as document and as guide.

  Bibliography: p.
  Includes indexes.
  1. Bible—Criticism, interpretation, etc.—Addresses, essays, lectures. 2. Christianity and other religions—
Judaism—Addresses, essays, lectures. 3. Judaism—
Relations—Christianity—Addresses, essays, lectures.
I. Title.
BS540.S67 1984   220.6   83–5601
ISBN 0–8006–1752–5

K125H83   Printed in the United States of America   1–1752

Contents

Contents

Preface

It is with mixed feelings that I present this collection of essays, published in more or less accessible places over three decades—from *Kerygma and Kerygmatic* in 1951 to *Christ's Lordship and Religious Pluralism* in 1981. At many points I now see weaknesses that I did not see in my eagerness at the time. In some cases I have changed my mind and my methods. In all cases the literature to be consulted has grown and made earlier entries obsolete.

A more humiliating aspect of the collection is perhaps a certain repetitiousness. It becomes obvious that I have a few favorite themes and passages of Scripture that come to my mind again and again.

It also hits me hard that I have thought of myself as sensitive to the question of inclusive language. After all, I began to write on the themes of *The Bible and the Role of Women* (Philadelphia: Fortress Press, 1966) in the early 1950s. Now I see that inclusive language did not enter my consciousness until I was awakened by the women of the Harvard Divinity School in the 1970s—and most of these articles were written before then.

So I had to choose. Should I let it all stand for the record—warts and all? Or should I adjust everything to the truth as I see it now? I have chosen the former line. The *Introductory Notes* do at times indicate some second thoughts.

The repetitiousness to which I referred earlier may even have a special function in this volume, and I hope the reader will not become bored with it. One of the purposes of this collection of *Meanings* is exactly to show how certain biblical themes and passages speak about different situations and problems that we face in the church and in the world.

I owe much thanks to my teaching assistant Julian V. Hills. He helped with the manuscripts in many aspects, both small and large —typing to teaching me English, from clarity of phrase to clarity of thought.

The Day of Sancta Lucia, 1983

Acknowledgements

"Biblical Theology: A Program" was first published as "Biblical Theology, Contemporary" in the *Interpreter's Dictionary of the Bible*, vol. 1 (Nashville: Abingdon Press, 1962), and is reprinted by permission.

"Kerygma and Kerygmatic" was first published as "Kerygma och kerygmatisk" in *Ny kyrklig tidskrift* (1951), and is reprinted by permission.

"One Canon is Enough" was first published as "The Gospel as Center and the Gospel as Totality of the New Testament Witness," in *Evangelium—Welt—Kirche*, edited by Harding Meyer (Frankfurt am Main: Verlag Otto Lembeck und Verlag Josef Knecht, 1975). It is reprinted by permission of the Centre d'études oecuméniques, Lutheran World Federation, Strasbourg, France.

"Quis et Unde" was first published in *Zeitschrift für die neutestamentliche Wissenschaft*, Beiheft 26 (Berlin: Toepelmann, 1961), 94–105, and is reprinted by permission of the editor of Beihefte zur *ZNW*. It was published in the *Festschrift* to Joachim Jeremias.

"Messianic License" was first published in *Biblical Realism Confronts the Nation*, edited by Paul Peachey (Nyack, N.Y.: Fellowship of Reconciliation, 1963), and is reprinted by permission of the publisher.

"The Sermon on The Mount and Third Nephi in the Book of Mormon" was first published in *Reflections on Mormonism: Judaeo-Christian Parallels*, Religious Monograph Series, edited by T. G. Madsen (Provo, Utah: Religious Studies Center, Brigham Young University, 1978), 139–54. Used by permission of the Religious Studies Center, Brigham Young University, Provo, Utah.

"Prayer and Forgiveness: The Lord's Prayer" was first published in *Svensk Exegetisk Årsbok* 22–23 (1957–58): 75–86, and is reprinted by permission of the publisher, *Svensk Exegetisk Årsbok* of Teologiska Institutionen in Uppsala, Sweden.

"Sin, Guilt, and Forgiveness in the New Testament" was first published as two articles in German in *Die Religion in Geschichte und Gegenwart*, 3rd edition (1957–65), J. C. B. Mohr (Paul Siebeck), Tübingen. The essay first appeared as "Sünde und Schuld IV: Im N.T." and "Sünden-vergebung II: Im N.T." and is reprinted by permission of the publisher.

"Hate, Nonretaliation, and Love = 1 QS ×, 17–20 and Rom. 12: 19–21" was first published in *Harvard Theological Review* 55 (1962): 343–55. Copyright © 1962 by the President and Fellows of Harvard College. Reprinted by permission.

"Paul at Prayer" was first published in *Interpretation* 34:3 (July 1980), and is reprinted by permission.

"The Church in Early Christianity" was first published in German in *Die Religion in Geschichte und Gegenwart*, 3rd edition (1957–65), © J. C. B. Mohr (Paul Siebeck), Tübingen. It first appeared as "Kirche II: Im Urchristentum" and is here reprinted by permission of the publisher.

"The New Testament Background for the Doctrine of the Sacraments" was first published in *Evangile et Sacrement—Oecumenica* (Strasbourg: Centre d'études oecuméniques, Lutheran World Federation, 1970), 41–60, and is reprinted by permission.

"Immortality Is Too Much and Too Little" was first published in *The End of Life*, edited by John Roslansky (Amsterdam and London: North Holland Publishing Co., 1973), and is reprinted by permission of Gustavus Adolphus College. The paper was originally presented at the eighth annual Nobel Conference (1972) held at Gustavus Adolphus College, St. Peter, Minnesota.

"Judaism and Christianity I: Then and Now" was first published in *Harvard Divinity Bulletin* 28:1 (1963): 1–9, and is reprinted by permission.

"Judaism and Christianity II: A Plea for a New Relationship" was first published as "Judaism and Christianity: After a Colloquium and a War" in *Harvard Divinity Bulletin*, New Series 1:1 (1967): 2–9, and is reprinted by permission.

"Christ's Lordship and Religious Pluralism" was first published as "Notes for Three Bible Studies" in *Christ's Lordship and Religious Plural-*

ism, edited by G. H. Anderson and T. F. Stransky, C. S. P. (Maryknoll, N.Y.: Orbis Books, 1981), 7–18, and is reprinted by permission of the publisher.

Biblical quotations, unless otherwise noted, are from the Revised Standard Version of the Bible, copyright 1946, 1952, © 1971, 1973 by the Division of Christian Education of the National Council of the Churches of Christ in the U.S.A. and are used by permission.

1

Meanings

The longer I have lived, the more I have come to like plurals. I have grown increasingly suspicious of singulars. I have come to question the incessant theological urge toward oneness. Come to think of it, that is perhaps why I happened to become a biblical scholar. For the word "Bible" is after all the English for *biblia*, the Little Books. Perhaps that same suspicion of mine explains why I am so fond of the Trinity, a most daring attempt at not sacrificing richness and diversity on the altars of theoretical monisms of various kinds.

I have chosen a plural word—Meanings—as the title for this collection of essays, written over a period of some thirty years. A more specific reason for the title can be found in the first essay (on "Biblical Theology," below, pp. 11–44). There I argued for a hermeneutical model in which the distinction between "what it meant" and "what it came to mean," or "what it might come to mean," is of decisive importance. I suggested that biblical theology in its strict sense should be restricted to "what it meant," that is, the descriptive task.

I came to this conclusion for various reasons and by a conscious critique of tendencies that I saw both in the ecumenical biblical theology movement and in various existential attacks on the attempts at descriptive historical work. In restricting the primary role of the biblical scholar to the descriptive task, it was my intention to liberate the theological enterprise from what I perceived as "the imperialism of biblical scholars" in the field of theology. The more clearly one sees "what it meant," the more obvious it becomes how impossible it is to live without the ever-ongoing work of systematic theology. Biblical categories stimulate and guide, but do not confine the task of contemporary theology be it in the academy or the churches, in seminars or in sermons. The mystique of the Hebraic over against the Near Eastern or the Hellenistic would become demystified and seen as the first stages in an often creative and always necessary development. The home turf of biblical scholarship—even when rightly called theology—is where one answers

1

the question "what it meant," that is, what Paul or any "biblical" writers thought that they thought. I saw it and I still see it as that simple. I guess my philosophical preconception here is that the search for "meaning" has no meaning if not in the form of "meaning for whom?" There is no method, however existential or structuralist, by which one can detect "The Meaning" (singular and timeless) of a passage, saying, or book.

When James Barr wrote the article on biblical theology in the Supplementary Volume of the *Interpreter's Dictionary of the Bible*,[1] he said:

> Stendahl's article was thus quite unrepresentative of what was then generally going on under the name of biblical theology: it was a program of what he would have liked to have been done, rather than a statement of what was being done . . . It is not so clear, however, that the article was deliberately *intended* as an attack on the contemporary movement . . . Only in hindsight may we suppose that it "struck a blow at the very heart of the movement as it was originally conceived."[2]

Barr was certainly correct in his observation that I conceived of the article as a "program," and as a suggestion of "where to go from here." Perhaps I, of all people, should not have used a dictionary article for such a purpose, but rather stuck to a more descriptive task. Yet, I am puzzled by Barr's uncertainty about my intention. I thought it to be clear enough, not only with hindsight. Brevard Childs certainly reads me right at that point, even if I would have liked him not only to appreciate my attack on the movement, but also to recognize more fully how indispensable the descriptive task is for theological purposes.

My "program" for sorting out "what it meant" and "what it means" strikes me still as indispensable. Its first advantage is that it guards against apologetic softenings and harmonizations, against conscious and unconscious modernizations in the interest of making the Bible more acceptable and conterminous with religious and ethical sentiments and concerns of the contemporary reader. A tough test case is perhaps the essay "Hate, Nonretaliation, and Love" from 1963 (below, pp. 137–50), in which I try to show how Paul's famous words about heaping coals of fire on the enemies' heads are just as gruesome as they sound.

Another advantage in the program of "meant—came to mean—means" is, of course, its fostering great respect for the diversity within the Scriptures and its explicit critique of all attempts at homogenizing the various theologies to be found within the Bible. The four "portraits of Jesus" in Matthew, Mark, Luke, and John become distinct, and have to be seen and meditated upon one by one. It is important to resist the temptation to make transparencies of them, place them on top of each other, and put them all in the projector together. That becomes blur—holy blur, yet blur. The essay *"Quis et Unde*—Who and Whence? Matthew's Christmas Gospel"* demonstrates the importance of disentangling the Christmas story in order to see the Matthean material in its own terms (below, pp. 71–84).

A case of special importance is the use of the Bible of the earliest Christians (what the church came to call the Old Testament) in what became the church's New Testament. It is perhaps not accidental that I wrote my dissertation on that very subject and thus became sensitized to a very specific case of what things "came to mean" in a community excited by the life and work, the death and resurrection, of Jesus.[3] Over the years I have become increasingly fascinated by the problem of how Jews and Christians have the Tanak/Old Testament in common—and yet it is a very different Scripture to each of them. However, any meaningful discussion of that subject must begin with a mutual willingness to search for the intentions of the original traditions and authors. Such a search will no doubt discern different levels of meaning already in the texts themselves, for in using traditional material authors may well present a purpose and a point of their own. After all—or should I say "before all"—the creation story in Genesis 1 seems to function as a mighty substantiation of the Sabbath as built into the cosmos itself, God resting on the seventh day. What a marvelous "meaning," perhaps not irrelevant to a time like ours when we have become conscious of the ecological limits to manipulation of the creation.

Brevard Childs's hermeneutical call for a recognition of canon and Scripture, as constitutive for exegetical work, strikes me as valid *if* seen as a conscious asking for the levels of meanings which can be ascertained in the minds of a community for whom the whole of the Hebrew Scriptures, or the whole of the Christian Bible has become Scripture. But as his *Introduction to the Old Testament as Scripture* shows, such an understanding also requires access to the prior levels of meaning in the constituent parts of the whole.[4]

It has always struck me as odd when my essay on biblical theology is criticized as too cool an approach: a dogged insistence on historical description, asking only for the intention(s) of the original, as if nothing else mattered.[5] I thought I had made it clear enough that my insistence on "what it meant" had *two* important functions. To be sure, it is useful for a better understanding of the worlds of life and thought in the specific historical settings of the original texts. Such an enterprise opens up significant possibilities for biblical studies in the academic community.[6]

The main burden of my argument, however, was that it is exactly in the church's use of Scripture that the respect for the descriptive task is essential. It is so in a more strict fashion than is usually recognized. It may well be that I did not make myself clear enough. If I did not, then there is a very simple explanation. It seemed so obvious to me that all my work grew out of my being a preacher and a minister of the church. I thought and still think, that I was meant to be a priest (as we say in Sweden). It was my preaching in the mid-1940s that brought me back to doctoral work in Bible studies.[7] It was my curiosity about what those Pharisees I had to preach about in the gospels for each Sunday were really like that led me to the school of St. Matthew.[8] It was in counseling Lutheran students as chaplain at Uppsala University that I came to see the drastic difference between what Paul had meant and what his writings had come to mean for Augustine and Luther and my church.[9] It was the Swedish debate about the ordination of women that sharpened my hermeneutics — and the essay on biblical theology was written the year after my study on the role of women.[10] What propelled me was the interest in finding the *right* model for relevancy. It was the search for such a model that led me to insist on the distance between the then and the now, the "meant" and the "means." It is my hope that this volume of collected essays will serve as an extended test of one way to see and foster the interplay between the descriptive task and contemporary needs in both church and society.

I was once asked by someone who had looked at my bibliography why I had been so preoccupied with two topics: Jews and women. I think, in retrospect, that the answer is not hard to find. The Christian Scriptures contain stuff that has proven calamitous to both Jews and women. The nonapologetic thrust of descriptive biblical theology allows us to face that problem squarely. It suggests a hermeneutic suited for the "public health" task of theology, that is, a hermeneutic of suspicion, by which the nondesirable side effects, or even effects, of the biblical material can be discerned and counteracted. But such a task requires the honesty of not "prettying up" the original.[11]

What major shifts have occurred in the field of biblical, and especially New Testament, studies during the three decades which these essays span? I would identify one which I think is of sufficiently broad scope to merit serious attention: the shift from "history" to "story." Biblical

scholars of my generation and those who were our teachers were mes-
merized by history and historicity. The theological moves were cast in
the language of history ("history of salvation"; or attempts at distinguishing between *Geschichte und Historie,* "historic and historical," etc.).
The natural question was how the Bible as history might relate to the
Bible as Holy Scripture.

Now there is the Bible as story, theology as story. For both philosophical and literary reasons, the focus on language and on forms of literary criticism demand the center stage.[12] Perhaps the odd idea of a
"language event" is a transitory hybrid from one perspective to another
(just as Lutherans speak of a sacrament as a visible Word—since the
Word *has* to be the primary category).

It is tempting to speculate about deeper cultural forces at work in this
shift. Could it be that preoccupation with history comes naturally when
one is part of a culture that feels basically happy and hopeful about the
historical process? Hegel's panhistoric philosophy belongs to the ascend-
ancy of Western imperialism—it was even said that other parts of the
world were lifted "into history" when conquered, colonized, or con-
verted by the West. Now the Western world is not so sure, or so opti-
mistic, about where history—our history—is going. Because of this
the glamour, the glory, and the Shekinah have moved away from
history.

There is a striking analogy to such a move from history to story and
wisdom. I refer to the major move by which Rabbinic Judaism—a
child of the very tradition that is often credited with having given "the
idea of history" to the world—cut loose from the frantic attempts at
finding meaning in history after the fall of Jerusalem (cf. 2 Baruch; 4
Ezra) and placed the center of religious existence in Halakha, that is, the
life style and wisdom of Torah. To be sure, the historical consciousness
remained—although not at the center of their theology—as stories, as
Haggada of less than binding authority.[13]

With such speculations aside, it is important to ask how the hermeneutical program which shapes our examination of "Meanings" might
be affected by a move from "history" to "story." It is quite clear that
my original program was conceived within the problematic of the Bible
as History/the Bible as Holy Scripture. However, now I want to assess
it within another duality: the Bible as a classic/the Bible as Holy
Scripture.[14]

There is something very appealing in phrasing the issue that way. For
it comes so much closer to how most people experience the Bible. The

Bible is a classic, whatever else it might be. I use the word "classic" to mean a piece of literature that is recognized as having a durable significance beyond its own time and place of origin. There are the works of Homer and Shakespeare. And in a pluralistic world one would recognize as religious classics such works as the Koran and the Gita.

It could be argued that for many people not only outside but also inside the Christian church (whatever "outside" and "inside" means in a "Christian" culture), the Bible functions exactly as a classic, perhaps a "classic plus," but often without conscious, or clear, distinctions between a classic and Holy Scriptures.

And yet, not only in the church but also in Western culture at large, there is an awareness of the Bible as Holy Scripture (regardless of any specific view of inspiration). Everyone knows the Bible, the Christian Bible or the Jewish Tanak, as the Scriptures of communities of faith. In short, there is a sense of the Bible as normative (whether one accepts those norms or not). Such a consciousness does not quite figure in peoples' minds when reading Homer or Shakespeare.

It is this element of the normative that makes the Bible into a peculiar kind of classic. This is of course true in an intensive sense within the Christian community (and what a sliding scale of intensity there is). But I find it important to remember that the normative character is present also in the minds of most people who read the Bible "only as a classic."

When biblical scholarship has become greatly enriched by learning the methods of literary criticism (new criticism, structuralism, etc.), it seems that this sense of the "normative expectation" has been lost or overlooked. To ask poets (or artists) what they actually meant or intended with a piece of art is often an insult, and they are apt to answer: "It is for you to answer what it means to you." That is fair enough.

But is it not legitimate and meaningful for a reader of the Bible to seek guidance from the Scriptures? And if so, the *intention* of the original sayings, or stories, or commandments can hardly be irrelevant. Let me give only one example, the *lex talionis* (Exod. 21:22–25; Lev. 24:20): "eye for eye, tooth for tooth, hand for hand," words that must strike most contemporary readers as ferocious. Self-serving Christians often quote these words as an example of that spirit of vengeance that is supposed to characterize Judaism as compared with Christianity, the religion of love and forgiveness. But attention to "what it meant," to the intention of the legislation, to descriptive historical exegesis, all make it abundantly clear that the point made was the quantum jump from "a life for a tooth." Thus it is a critique of vengeance, not a sanction for vengeance. Such examples could be multiplied seventy times seven—and more.

This all leads to the conclusion that it is exactly the Bible as Holy Scripture that requires the services of the descriptive biblical scholars and their simple reminder "that from the beginning it was not so" (as Jesus said). This is as true about the Bible's commandments as it is about its theological constructs, or about its human self-understandings.

Actually, the more intensive the expectation of normative guidance, and the more exacting the claims for the holiness of the Scriptures, the more indispensable is the attention to the meaning of Scripture at the time of its conception and to an examination of the possible intentions of the authors. When the Bible is enjoyed in a far-more-relaxed mood as a classic, people like to find its support, or sanction, for their thoughts and actions. The low intensity of the normativeness often makes such use of Scripture less careful, and people even think they give honor to God and Christianity by such use of the Bible. Also in such situations the call to historical honesty by access to what Scripture meant is necessary and salutary, lest vague biblical authority become self-serving, trivializing, or even harmful.

The following essays often move from the descriptive task to the development of meanings for church and society today. In so doing the essays try to demonstrate that it is exactly by a sharper awareness of the original issues that new light and guidance can be found for our own times. While I find it difficult to define the way in which one should speak about biblical inspiration, I do find that the Bible has been a constant inspiration for my imagination and for my perception of the world in which I have been placed, a world of plurals in which I learn from the Scriptures to be increasingly fascinated by that which is other than myself—as is the Bible, in a wide variety of ways. As is God.

NOTES

1. My essay had been the entry under "Biblical Theology: Contemporary" in the *Interpreter's Dictionary of the Bible*, vol. 1. (Nashville: Abingdon Press), 413–32. Written in 1959, it was published in 1962. James Barr's article is in the *IDB*, Supplementary Volume (Nashville: Abingdon Press, 1978), 104–11.

2. The quote within the quotes is from Brevard Childs's *Biblical Theology in Crisis* (Philadelphia: Westminster Press, 1970), 79, cf. 26.

3. *The School of St. Matthew and Its Use of the Old Testament* (Lund: Gleerups, 1954; 2d edition with a new introduction, Philadelphia: Fortress Press, 1968).

4. *Introduction to the Old Testament as Scripture* (Philadelphia: Fortress Press, 1979), 27–83; on "The Hebrew Scriptures and the Christian Bible," 659–71.

5. For a typical example of such a criticism see the Series Foreword by Walter Brueggemann and John R. Donahue in Paul D. Hanson, *The Diversity of Scripture* (Philadelphia: Fortress Press, 1982), x. For a more penetrating criticism of my "theological naiveté," see David H. Kelsey, *The Uses of Scripture in Recent Theology* (Philadelphia: Fortress Press, 1975), 202–3.

6. I elaborated this dimension in articles such as: "Religion in the University," *Daedalus* (Summer 1963): 521–28; "The Future Role of the Universities in the Education for Religious Ministries" in Krister Stendahl, et al., *Religion and the Academic Scene* (Ann Arbor, Mich.: Office of Ethics and Religion, University of Michigan, 1975); "Biblical Studies in the University," in *The Study of Religion in Colleges and Universities*, ed. Paul Ramsey and John F. Wilson (Princeton, N.J.: Princeton University Press, 1970), 23–29.

7. The questions of Bible and preaching have stayed with me over the years, and more recently I am actually teaching biblical preaching at Harvard Divinity School. For a sample of how my hermeneutical program works for sermons, see my "Preaching from the Pauline Epistles" in *Biblical Preaching*, ed. James W. Cox (Philadelphia: Westminster Press, 1983), 306–26; cf. also *Holy Week*, Proclamation 1, Series A (Philadelphia: Fortress Press, 1974).

8. See above, note 3.

9. *Paul Among Jews and Gentiles* (Philadelphia: Fortress Press, 1976).

10. *The Bible and the Role of Women* (Philadelphia: Fortress Press, 1966). The Swedish original is from 1958.

11. See my "Ancient Scripture in the Modern World," in *Scripture in the Jewish and Christian Traditions: Authority, Interpretation, Relevance*, ed. Frederick E. Greenspahn (Nashville: Abingdon Press, 1982), 201–14. For a superb example of what an accomplished NT scholar can do if withstanding the apologetic tendency to pretty things up, see Elisabeth Schüssler Fiorenza, *In Memory of Her: A Feminist Theological Reconstruction of Christian Origins* (New York: Crossroad, 1983).

12. This shift has many facets. There is the literary dimension as found in Northrop Frye, *The Great Code: The Bible and Literature* (New York and London: Harcourt Brace Jovanovich, 1982). There is the movement represented by the Society of Biblical Literature journal *Semeia* (1974–), edited by J. Dominic Crossan, and foreshadowed by the pioneering work of Amos N. Wilder (see *Semeia* 12–13, 1978). The depth of the philosophical and theological shifts is perhaps best expressed in David Tracy, *The Analogical Imagination: Christian Theology and the Culture of Pluralism* (New York: Crossroad, 1981). Tracy significantly uses as one of his main categories "The Classic."

13. See Jacob Neusner, *Ancient Israel After Catastrophe: The Religious World View of the Mishnah* (Charlottesville, Va.: University Press of Virginia, 1983).

14. This theme is elaborated more fully in "The Bible as a Classic and the Bible as Holy Scriptures," *Journal of Biblical Literature* 103 (1984).

ON BIBLICAL THEOLOGY,
THE KERYGMA, AND
THE CANON

2

Biblical Theology:
A Program

Introductory Note: Each essay included in this volume will have a short introductory note, giving the setting of the original paper and some more recent reflections. The chapter "Meanings" serves as an extended note to this first essay, published as the entry "Biblical Theology, Contemporary" in the *Interpreter's Dictionary of the Bible*, vol. 1 (Nashville: Abingdon Press, 1962), 418–32. The original article includes an extensive bibliography.

A historical survey of major contributions to the field of biblical theology makes it more than obvious that there is no one definition of this field on which biblical scholars can unanimously agree. It is true that a closer analysis of contemporary contributions to the field may well show that some of the older definitions are obsolete, as well as bring to light certain common tendencies in aim and method; but it will not eliminate the tensions between different conceptions of what a biblical theology is or should be. Such diversity was to be expected, since very different theological and philosophical presuppositions are necessarily involved.

And yet, in spite of these differences, recent biblical studies have gravitated with an unprecedented enthusiasm toward topics and problems which undoubtedly fall within the biblical theological field. This seems to be due to the fact that a new stage has been set for biblical theology, as a result of a new emphasis upon its descriptive task. Since consideration of this task has proved far more suggestive and creative than is often recognized, there is good reason to consider the nature of the new descriptive biblical theology and then to move toward its implications for other aspects of theology. This can be done only by way of hermeneutics. Thus we arrive at the following outline:

A. The descriptive task
1. A new stage set for biblical theology
2. What it meant and what it means
3. Three approaches to NT theology
   a. Barth
   b. Bultmann
   c. Cullmann
   d. Conclusions
4. Is a descriptive NT theology possible?
5. The descriptive approach and the OT
6. "Sacred history" and the unity of the Bible
B. The hermeneutic question
1. As raised by a descriptive biblical theology
2. Alternative answers to the hermeneutic question
3. The significance of "canon" for biblical theology
4. The preacher and biblical theology

THE DESCRIPTIVE TASK

A New Stage Set for Biblical Theology

The alleged biblical basis for what has been called "liberal theology" in its classic form (the use of the term "liberal" in this sense, referring to the dominant theology ca. 1900, does not imply that many more recent types of theology are not just as "liberal" in their method and presuppositions)—that is, the view that the OT is a witness to the evolution of a more and more ethical monotheism and that the gospels are biographies of Jesus as the even-more-refined teacher of the Golden Rule, the fatherhood of God, and the eternal value of the individual—the alleged biblical basis of this view was not shattered by the conservatives, but by the extreme radicals of the *religionsgeschichtliche Schule* ("history-of-religions school"). They could show, on the basis of the comparative material, that such a picture of Jesus or of the OT prophets was totally impossible from a historical point of view and that it told more about the ideals of bourgeois Christianity in the late nineteenth century than about the carpenter from Nazareth or the little man from Tekoa. What emerged out of the studies of the *religionsgeschichtliche Schule* was a new picture of the men, the ideas, and the institutions of biblical history. Those elements and traits, which did strike modern man as crude, primitive, cultic, and even magical, were now given equal and often greater emphasis than those which happened to appeal to enlightened

12

Western taste. The "peril of modernizing Jesus"—to use Henry J. Cadbury's phrase—was fully recognized. Johannes Weiss and Albert Schweitzer made a forceful plea for a most abstruse and appalling eschatology as the actual setting for Jesus and his followers; H. Gunkel, H. Gressmann, and S. Mowinckel placed the OT back in the matrix of Near Eastern myth and cult. Johannes Pedersen applied V. Groenbech's studies of human self-understanding in old Nordic religion to an extensive study of OT anthropology, where cherished distinctions between soul and body, magic and religion, cult and ethics, individual and collective, were thoroughly intermingled and lost much of their meaning. It became a scholarly ideal to creep out of one's Western and twentieth-century skin and identify oneself with the feelings and thought patterns of the past. The distance between biblical times and modern times was stressed, and the difference between biblical thought and systematic theology became much more than that of diversification over against systematization or of concrete exemplification over against abstract propositions.

What emerged was a descriptive study of biblical thought—empathetic in the sense that it was beyond sympathy or antipathy. This was actually a new phenomenon in biblical studies, and yet it came as a mature outgrowth of the historical and critical study of the Scriptures. It differed in three ways from earlier contributions of historical criticism:

1. The straitjacket of doctrinaire evolutionism—in Darwinistic as well as in Hegelian terms—was considerably loosened. While development and stages were recognized and noticed, the later stages were not preconceived as progression (e.g., from priests to prophets) or regression (e.g., from Jesus to Paul). Each period and each ideology was given enough attention to be granted a careful description on its own terms.

2. The question of fact—that is, whether, for example, the march through the Red Sea or the resurrection of Jesus had actually taken place as described—was not any more the only one which absorbed the historian. Now there was more concern about what the function and the significance of such an item or of such a message as "He is risen" might have been to the writers and readers (or hearers) of the biblical records. Form criticism and *Sitz im Leben* became the catchwords for students of the documents of temple, synagogue, and church.

3. The question about relevance for present-day religion and faith was waived, or consciously kept out of sight. This statement will be, perhaps, the strongest reminder of how biblical theology was swal-

lowed up or threatened by a history of biblical thought or a history of biblical religion. This historicism or antiquarianism, with its lack of interest in relevance, has been challenged on many scores by modern writers. And yet it remains a fact that modern biblical theology would be quite inexplicable were it not for the fact that the *religionsgeschichtliche Schule* had drastically widened the hiatus between our time and that of the Bible, between West and East, between the questions self-evidently raised in modern minds and those presupposed, raised, and answered in the Scriptures. Thereby a radically new stage was set for biblical interpretation. The question of meaning was split up in two tenses: What *did* it mean? and What *does* it mean? These questions were now kept apart long enough for the descriptive task to be considered in its own right.

What It Meant and What It Means

To liberals and conservatives alike, this distinction was not sharply in focus prior to the *religionsgeschichtliche Schule.* We may be justified in taking Harnack's *What Is Christianity?* as the most influential popular summary of liberal interpretation of the NT. It is not accidental that Harnack, as Bultmann points out in his Introduction to a reprint of the work (1950), "failed to realize the importance of the so-called *religionsgeschichtliche Schule* and never truly became sympathetic with it." Albert Schweitzer had brought this aspect of Harnack's interpretation to bear upon the problem now under consideration when he said in *The Quest of the Historical Jesus:* "Harnack, in his 'What is Christianity?' almost entirely ignores the contemporary limitations of Jesus' teaching, and starts out with a Gospel which carries him down without difficulty to the year 1899."

The apologetic intentions of the "liberals" should not be forgotten. In the light of later development, "liberal" came to stand for the "leftists" in the theological assembly. By the turn of the century this was not so. The liberals understood themselves as the mediating party who, often with a deep concern for Christianity and its future role in our culture and with a genuine piety, refused the radical assaults of David F. Strauss and others. But the way in which they carried on their apologetic task made them poor historians of religion. Their methods were basically the same as those used by the conservatives. Both were convinced that the Bible contained revelation which could be grasped in the clean form of eternal truth unconditioned and uncontaminated by historical limitations. The difference was only one of degree. While the orthodox interpreters found this revelation in the whole of Scripture and systematized it by harmonization and by interpreting the less easily fitting by those passages which were hand in glove with their own systems, the liberals arrived at the pure revelation by way of more or less drastic reductions. This reductionist approach was often carried out by literary criticism, but once the *ipsissima verba* ("very words") of the prophets or of Jesus were established, these words happened to square well with the ideals of the modern age. Thus the tension between the past and the present meaning had been overcome before it could create any problems for interpretation. And this happened because the liberals were convinced that the teachings of the Bible were meaningful for modern man—just as the orthodox claimed the same for a vastly more challenging amount of biblical teaching. For the liberals the nucleus of revelation had to be that which could be hailed as relevant and acceptable to modern man.

The resistance to the *religionsgeschichtliche Schule* was openly or unconsciously aimed against its disregard for theological meaning and relevance. By and large, Gunkel's *Schöpfung und Chaos in Urzeit und Endzeit*, Mowinckel's *Psalmenstudien*, and Schweitzer's *Quest* appeared on the scene with no immediate relation to the ongoing theological discussion. Schweitzer's work did actually contain an Epilogue in which the author made a cautious attempt to draw out the ramifications of the thoroughgoing eschatology of Jesus for theology as well as for the life of the believer, but the return is rather small. When facing the shocking distance back to the Jesus of the gospels, Schweitzer finally takes refuge in an expectant mysticism where the Christ of faith comes to us as "One unknown," yet one who in an ineffable mystery lets man experience who he is. In the German edition this final sentence of the whole volume symbolically ends with ellipsis dots.

This ellipsis formed, however, a challenge, the response to which is the vigorous interest in biblical theology starting in the 1920s and showing no slackening tendencies toward the end of the 1950s. Once freed from the anachronistic interpretations of their predecessors, and forced to accept the hiatus between the ideas and ideals in the biblical material, the theologically minded student of the Scriptures slowly found a new and deeper relevance in what the *religionsgeschichtliche Schule* described for him as the pre-Westernized meaning of sayings and events. In the broader context of cultural climate this tendency had its obvious similarities in the taste for the primitive, with its crude vigor in art, music, and literature. It was akin to Rudolf Otto's reevaluation of religious phenomena in his study of holiness. This tendency had

15

striking parallels in the field of historical theology, where, for example, Luther's own words and intentions were sharply contrasted with the teaching of seventeenth-century Lutheranism, the sympathies of the scholars always siding with the former. But it was primarily the experience of the distance and the strangeness of biblical thought as a creative asset, rather than as a destructive and burdensome liability.

Without this new and nonmodernizing look at the Bible, Karl Barth's programmatic commentary on Romans or Rudolf Bultmann's *Theology of the New Testament*—or his book written in 1926 on Jesus—would be inexplicable. O. Cullmann's *Christ and Time*, as well as his more recent *New Testament Christology*, are the typical examples of a somewhat different result of the same ideal of historical distance. In OT studies, W. F. Albright's *From the Stone Age to Christianity* and G. E. Wright's *God Who Acts*, as well as W. Eichrodt's and G. von Rad's OT theologies, are all inspired by the same tension between the mind of a Semitic past and the thought of modern man. Yet most of these writers launch strong attacks on the "historicism" of the "historian of religion." By these terms they do, however, usually refer to other elements in the *religionsgeschichtliche Schule* than the one to which attention has been drawn here—namely, the descriptive element, and its awareness of the distinction between what it meant and what it means.

Three Approaches to NT Theology

This distinction between past and present meaning has its specific problems for OT theology, and we may consequently be wise in first trying to clarify the issue in relation to NT theology. We may for this purpose go to three contemporaries who exemplify three different types of NT theology: Karl Barth, Rudolf Bultmann, and Oscar Cullmann. They are all aware of what we have called the distance between the centuries. In particular, Bultmann's relation to the radical tradition—over against the liberal—in biblical studies is obvious, for example, in his references to D. F. Strauss. The question raised by the distance should thus be faced in its most radical form: Do these old documents have any meaning for us—except as sources for our knowledge of a small segment of first-century life and thought, or as means for a nostalgic visit to the first era of Christian history? If they have a meaning in the present tense and sense, on what ground do they have this meaning?

Barth. In the Preface to the second edition of his commentary on Romans, Barth argues for the exegesis of Luther and Calvin over against that of men like Jülicher and Lietzmann. The former are the only ones who really have tried to "understand" Paul, since, for example, Calvin, "having first established what stands in the text, sets himself to re-think the whole material and to wrestle with it, till the walls which separate the sixteenth century from the first become transparent, that is, till Paul *speaks* there and the man of the sixteenth century *hears* here, till the conversation between the document and the reader is totally concentrated on the subject-matter, which *cannot* be a different one in the first and sixteenth century." The concentration on the subject matter (God, Jesus, grace, etc.) bridges the gap between the centuries, and it does so since they cannot but be the same. This identity in the subject matter guarantees the meaningfulness of the Pauline writings. They must speak about what Calvin (or the modern interpreter) knows as the subject matter. This is apparently so since God, Christ, and all of revelation stand above history. Thereby the tension between the first century and ours is resolved, or rather transformed, into a theological category of "otherness."

It is also significant to note that Barth speaks as if it were a very simple thing to establish what Paul actually meant in his own terms. To say that the Reformers interpreted Paul by equating the problem of the Judaizers and the Torah in Paul with the problem of work-righteousness in late medieval piety and that this ingenious translation or application of Pauline theology may be 80 percent correct but left 20 percent of Paul inexplicable (and consequently distorted in a certain sense the true picture of Pauline thought), to say this is to call attention to a problem which could not be detected, let alone criticized, by Barth or any truly Barthian exegete. Thus biblical theology along this line is admittedly incapable of enough patience and enthusiasm for keeping alive the tension between what the text meant and what it means. There are no criteria by which they can be kept apart; what is intended as a commentary turns out to be a theological tractate, expanding in contemporary terms what Paul should have said about the subject matter as understood by the commentator.

When the term "biblical theology" is used of works where this method is applied, it does not designate anything basically different from systematic theology, except that its systematic task is so defined as to make the Bible central in its work. Thus it may be convenient for classification within the realm of systematic theology to speak of this theology as "biblical" rather than philosophical. But from the point of view of biblical studies such a theology is not automatically "more biblical" than other types of systematic theology.

Bultmann. On the last page of Bultmann's *Theology of the New Testament* we find a statement (in italics below), apparently made in passing, which is worth noting in relation to the question of whether or why the biblical documents have any meaning for the present. Bultmann places the reader before an alternative: "Either the writings of the NT can be interrogated as the 'sources' to reconstruct a picture of primitive Christianity as a phenomenon of the historical past, or the reconstruction stands in the service of the interpretation of the NT writings *under the presupposition that they have something to say for the present.*" Bultmann sides with the second alternative, and in so doing he takes for granted that the NT has such meaning. For Bultmann, as for Barth, the common denominator of meaning is the subject matter; but for Bultmann there is only one subject matter which is valid: the self-understanding as it expresses itself in the NT and as it is experienced through human history until the present time. This gives to Bultmann's NT theology a strikingly uneven character. In dealing with the message of Jesus, the kerygma of the early church and its development into the second century, his method is by and large descriptive; but in the exposition of Pauline and Johannine material—and this is almost half the whole work—the tone and even the method are different, since these writings lend themselves so much more easily to anthropological interpretation.

Yet nobody could blame Bultmann for not having given reasons for what he is doing. Most of his later writings have centered around his plea for demythologizing, and it has become more and more obvious that this to Bultmann also implies a dehistoricizing of the NT. His attack on the historicism of NT interpretation (i.e., the use of the NT as a "source" for our knowledge of a historical past, be it the historical Jesus or the life and teaching of early Christianity) is centered in his emphasis on the NT as a message, a kerygma. The intent of NT theological utterances is not to state a doctrine (as for orthodoxy) and not to give the material for a concept (as treated by the historians). It is to challenge man in his own self-understanding, and consequently "the act of thinking must not be divorced from the act of living." When the NT kerygma witnesses to historical events (as in 1 Cor. 15:3–8), these "events" are of little significance as events; what counts is to re-create their effect on man's self-understanding. Thus—in Bultmann's own view—his NT theology becomes "theology" explicitly only where it clarifies the "believing self-understanding in its reference to the kerygma." As such—and only as such—the NT has "something to say to the present." Only on such terms does Bultmann find it possible to do justice to the intent of the NT.

Cullmann. In Cullmann, perhaps the most productive contemporary writer in the field of NT theology, we find a very different approach to biblical theology. If history is mute to Bultmann for reasons of hermeneutics and philosophy—a view which colors Bultmann's exegesis to the extent that he interprets NT eschatology as implying the end of history in Christ—Cullmann finds the key to NT theology in its understanding of time. Most discussions of Cullmann's *Christ and Time* have centered around a criticism of his distinction of linear time (biblical) versus circular time (Greek) and his idea of Christ as the center of time. If these interpretations were refuted, the thrust of Cullmann's argument is still unchallenged when it urges us to recognize how the categories of time and history, rather than essence, nature, and eternal or existential truth, are the ones within which the NT moves (cf. Cullmann's "Le mythe dans les écrits du NT," *Numen* 1 [1954], 120–35). On the one hand, Cullmann has thereby recaptured the mood of thought of the NT writers and stays within it long enough to work out its implication for different aspects of NT thought. On the other hand, it is not quite clear how Cullmann understands the relation between such a descriptive biblical theology in its first- and second-century terms and its translation into our present age; his hermeneutic discussions have nothing of the radical penetration of Bultmann's. His work is basically confined to the descriptive task. When Bultmann could say about Cullmann—as he does about E. Stauffer's NT theology—that he "transforms theology into a religious philosophy of history," Cullmann's answer would be that NT theology *is*, whether we like it or not, a religious philosophy of history, and that he finds it difficult to see how this historical dimension can be translated away in any presentation of the gospel to the present age.

Such a discussion between Cullmann, Stauffer, and Bultmann would, however, be totally fruitless, for the following reasons: (1) All three take for granted that the NT has "meaning," but while Bultmann discusses from the vantage point of his own motivation for such a meaning, Cullmann (and Stauffer) have not clarified their answer to why or how they consider the NT as meaningful for the present age. Because of this lack of clarification, their works are read by many—perhaps most—readers as being on the same level of present meaning as Bultmann's or Barth's highly "translated" interpretations; and there are indications that they do not mind such a use of their works. A close study of Stauffer's NT theology makes it quite clear, however, that its method remains strictly descriptive; this is the more obvious in his extensive and impressive use of noncanonical intertestamental material as equally significant to picture the mood of NT thought. Cullmann's Christology follows suit in this respect. (2) Consequently, Bultmann's critique of such an approach should be the opposite to what it actually is. He could charge his opponents with not having seen the need for transforming or translating the NT religious philosophy of history into a contemporary theology, a need which he himself has epitomized in his quest for demythologizing. This would force his opponents to clarify why they consider such a dehistoricizing translation unnecessary or arbitrary. (3) Bultmann's case for the end of history in Christ and Cullmann's for ongoing history as the essence of NT eschatology have to be tested on the descriptive level. On this level a meaningful discussion can be carried on. If Cullmann seems to be much closer to the truth, Bultmann's interpretation may remain valid as a demythologized translation. But the "validity" of such an interpretation hinges then on the validity of the hermeneutic principles of the interpreter and is of no direct consequence to the descriptive task of biblical theology.

In the present state of biblical studies, Cullmann's (and Stauffer's) contribution reminds us of Schweitzer, who felt himself compelled to present as forceful an eschatological picture of Jesus as he found in the sources, in spite of the fact that he did not see too clearly what its theological ramifications might be. This is the same as saying that these works carry the signs of hope which belong to every vigorous contribution to descriptive biblical theology, in spite of its hermeneutic unclarity. The pitfall for both the scholars and the common reader is the ambiguity by which the descriptive method is allowed to transcend its own limitations. (Stauffer later moved on to a quite different methodology, by which he claims to have established a new basis for the "historical Jesus.")

Conclusions. It thus appears that the tension between "what it meant" and "what it means" is of a competitive nature, and that when the biblical theologian becomes primarily concerned with the present meaning, he implicitly (Barth) or explicitly (Bultmann) loses his enthusiasm or his ultimate respect for the descriptive task. And yet the history of the discipline indicates that all types of biblical theology depend on the progress of this descriptive biblical theology, to which the contribution of the theologically irrelevant representatives of the *religionsgeschichtliche Schule* is strikingly great.

From the very beginning of the use of the term "biblical theology" in the seventeenth century, there has been the tension between the contemporary (be it scholasticism, conservatism, liberalism, or existentialism) and the biblical, but it is in the light of historical criticism that this tension has become clarified as one between two centuries with drastically different modes of thought. Once this difference became great enough to place the Bible further away from us—to liberal theology the historical Jesus was closer to modern man than was the Christ confessed in the dogma of the church—the need for "translation" became a real one. Bultmann's plea for demythologizing, regardless of the way in which he carries it out, is certainly here to stay. But this makes it the more imperative to have the "original" spelled out with the highest degree of perception in its own terms. This is the nucleus of all biblical theology, and the way from this descriptive task to an answer about the meaning in the present cannot be given in the same breath on an ad hoc basis. It presupposes an extensive and intensive competence in the field of hermeneutics. With the original in hand, and after due clarification of the hermeneutic principles involved, we may proceed toward tentative answers to the question of the meaning here and now. But where these three stages become intermingled, there is little hope for the Bible to exert the maximum of influence on theology, church life, and culture. How much of the two last stages should belong to the discipline of biblical studies or to what extent they call for teamwork with the disciplines of theology and philosophy is a practical question, a question which in itself indicates the nature of the problem. If the three stages are carelessly intermingled, the theology as well as the preaching in our churches becomes a mixed, or even an inarticulate, language.

Is a Descriptive NT Theology Possible?

Many are those who express serious doubts about the possibility of the descriptive task as pictured above. Every historian is subjective in the selection of his material, and it is often said that he does more harm when he thinks himself to be objective—that is, when he does not recognize, not to say openly state, what his presuppositions and preconceived ideas are. We can smile when we see how an earlier generation of biblical scholars peddled Kantian, Hegelian, or Ritschlian ideas, all the time subjectively convinced that they were objective scholars who only stated "facts." All this naturally calls for caution; but the relativity of human objectivity does not give us an excuse to excel in bias, not even when we state our bias in an introductory chapter. What is more important, however, is that once we confine ourselves to the task of descriptive biblical theology as a field in its own right, the material itself gives us means to check whether our interpretation is correct or not. To be sure, the sources are not extensive enough to allow us certainty in all areas; and the right to use some comparative material, while disregarding other such material as irrelevant for our texts, gives further reason for uncertainty. However, from the point of view of method it is clear that our only concern is to find out what these words meant when uttered or written by the prophet, the priest, the evangelist, or the apostle—regardless of their meaning in later stages of religious history, our own included. Such a program is by and large a new feature in biblical studies, a mature fruit of the historical method. It does not necessarily disregard the intent of the biblical texts, but captures the implication of their kerygmatic nature when it lifts them out of the framework of "theological concepts" and places them back into their *Sitz im Leben* (the "life situation") of Israel or the church.

This descriptive task can be carried out by believer and agnostic alike. The believer has the advantage of automatic empathy with the believers in the text—but his faith constantly threatens to have him modernize the material, if he does not exercise the canons of descriptive scholarship rigorously. The agnostic has the advantage of feeling no such temptations, but his power of empathy must be considerable if he is to identify himself sufficiently with the believer of the first century. Yet both can work side by side, since no other tools are called for than those of description in the terms indicated by the texts themselves. The meaning for the present—in which the two interpreters are different—is not involved, and thus total cooperation is possible. Part of their mutual criticism is to watch whether concern for meaning or distaste for meaning colors the descriptions where it should not.

The Descriptive Approach and the OT

The tensions between the meanings becomes further complicated when we turn to the nature of OT theology, and this for two main reasons.

First, the OT contains material from many centuries of Israelite life.

22

This makes it obvious that there are different layers of meaning within the same account. The account of the sacrifice of Isaac may well once have functioned as God's own command of substituting an animal for human sacrifices, but in its present setting in Genesis 22 the meaning is clearly seen as a witness to Abraham's ultimate obedience. Jacob's dream at Bethel seems to be a tradition by which the validity of the cult of the Northern kingdom was upheld by reference to how the patriarch had found Yahweh at that place. Once the rivalry between the two kingdoms was a dead issue, the story took on—or returned to—the meaning of a more general epiphany. This problem of interpretation and hermeneutics is certainly not confined to the OT; it forms the crucial problem of gospel research when we try to push beyond the evangelists to the actual words and deeds of Jesus. But in the OT it is a more flagrant and paramount problem. Thus already the descriptive task is faced with the constant question of "layers of meaning" through the history and transmission of OT traditions. The history of interpretation is woven into the very fabric of the biblical texts themselves, and the canonization of Torah, Prophets, and Writings did not disrupt the ongoing reinterpretation in sectarian or normative Judaism, as we learn from the intertestamental and the rabbinic material. Thus any statement of a descriptive sort about what an OT passage meant has to be accompanied by an address: for whom and at what stage of Israelite or Jewish history? The track along which the biblical theologian pursues the meaning of the OT is thus that of the ongoing religious life of Israel as the chosen people of God and as responding to the events in its history which are interpreted as the acts of God.

Second, the church was born out of a dispute with Jewish interpreters of the OT regarding its meaning, and first-century Christian theology of the more verbalized sort, as that found in Paul, centers around the terms on which the church finds the OT meaningful—for example, as promise now fulfilled or as law binding on the members of the church. The Christian claim to the OT rested on the conviction that Jesus as the risen Christ was the Messiah to whom the OT witnessed. The church thereby sided with those interpreters of the OT who, like, for example, the Qumran community, saw the center of the OT in its prophecies and promises, including those found in the five books of the Law, while the Jewish exegesis which became normative more and more emphasized the law as the core of revelation and the precious sign of Israel's chosen status. Neither interpretation had any similarity with the one prevailing in the theologized form of the Wellhausen interpretation of Israelite history, where the significance of the OT was seen in the evolution of ethical monotheism. Here, again, it was the radicals of the *religionsgeschichtliche Schule* who caused the construction of this liberal interpretation to crumble, corrupted and weakened as it was by the apologetic interest in a meaning for the present.

Any writer in the field of OT theology must be aware of this double outcome of the ongoing interpretation of the OT material, each within the framework of a community of faith. For the descriptive task both outcomes appear as live options, and neither of them can claim to be the right one if judged by the potentialities of the OT material itself. The act of faith by which the interpretations parted ways does not add anything to the OT material as such. Thus a Christian and a Jewish OT theology differ only where the question of meaning is pursued beyond the material and the period of the OT texts themselves. Such a Christian OT theology may find its organizing principle in the NT understanding of the OT in first-century terms (another descriptive task being thus involved) or in any one principle of Christian hermeneutics from later centuries, our own included. Nobody could deny the validity, or even the necessity, for the church of such a task, especially since it is in the very tradition of the NT itself. Yet the same warning which emerged out of our study of the meanings in NT theology applies to such an enterprise. The distinction between the descriptive function as the core of all biblical theology on the one hand, and the hermeneutics and up-to-date translation on the other hand, must be upheld if there is to be any chance for the original to act creatively on the minds of theologians and believers of our time.

"Sacred History" and the Unity of the Bible

In OT theology even more than in its NT counterpart, history presents itself as the loom of the theological fabric. In spite of its intentions to be historical, the liberal interpretation of the OT overlooked this fact, substituting its evolutionistic interest in the development of ethics and monotheism for the sacred history in which Israel experienced its existence. In more recent times an anthropological approach to OT theology—not much different from Bultmann's approach, but unaware of its implicit demythologizing and dehistoricizing—has been tried with some success. Its success is partly due to its superior descriptive power if compared with that of the liberals.

In sharp contrast to what is called—with a gross generalization— "the Greek," we find the Semitic or Hebrew or biblical anthropology

24

spelled out, and sometimes this very anthropology is hailed as the essence of biblical theology. But in works like those of G. E. Wright and G. von Rad, OT theology seeks its center where the ongoing life of Israel—from a descriptive point of view—experienced it—that is, in its own history as a peculiar people, chosen by God. Especially in Wright this approach is coupled with arguments for the uniqueness of Israel as compared with surrounding people and cultures, a claim which seems to be a carry-over from another methodology. Israel's uniqueness was hardly based on its ideas about God or man but in its election consciousness, which in turn has given its thinking distinctive features which we may well call unique.

But the thrust of an OT theology, which finds the center in the acts of God (Wright) or in Yahweh's revelation through words and deeds in history (von Rad), is ultimately to establish how history is not only a stage upon which God displays his nature through his acts, but that the drama itself is one of history. The salvation that is promised is one within history, either in terms of return of the dispersed people from all the ends of the earth or as a New Jerusalem and a glorified Israel in a new age, which in spite of its otherworldly features comes in time and history at the end of this present age. This historical consciousness of Israel lives by the remembering of the past and the ever-new interpretation of it as a promise for the future. The cultic festivals, with their roots in Near Eastern ritual and their manifestations in the sacred kingship of the Davidic dynasty, become projected toward the eschatological future of bliss, righteousness, and peace. In all this the common denominator—from a descriptive point of view—is neither certain concepts of God as one or as acting, nor an anthropology peculiar to the Bible, but the ongoing life of a people cultivating the traditions of its history in the light of its self-understanding. It is guided therein by its priests, prophets, and teachers of wisdom, and thus this people moves toward a sure but ever-evasive *eschaton*, keeping the law, which is the mark of their chosenness.

Such a framework for OT theology is the only one that takes the descriptive task seriously, since it does not borrow its categories from the NT or later Jewish or Christian interpretation but finds the organizing principle in the very life situations out of which the OT material emerges as meaningful to the life of the people. From such a layer of meaning we may move back into the meaning of the different elements that were placed in this framework of sacred history. This may lead us to patterns of thought and blocks of tradition originally quite unrelated to the historical consciousness of Israel; but only with a full recognition of this framework can we adequately go behind it and analyze what the original elements of the tradition may have been and how they were modified by their setting in the religion of Israel. Only so can we know to what extent they retained their character as remnants—whether weak or vigorous and creative—of an earlier period within the total tradition. As such remnants they deserve the fullest descriptive treatment and should not be swallowed up by a generalizing sweep of sacred history as though that sweep constituted the entire content of the OT.

When the OT is treated in this fashion as the living and growing tradition of a people, it yields a theology which brings us up to the parting of the ways by Jews and Christians. The description thereof places us where the NT stands, and we face the issues of NT theology as once Jews and Christians faced them in the first century. It brings into the NT the dimension of time and history that is essential to our understanding of the NT in its own terms. The announcement by Jesus that the new age is impending, and the faith of the early church that the Messiah is enthroned in heaven since he is risen and since the Holy Spirit has been poured out, comes as a vigorous claim for fulfillment of the OT promises, not accepted by the majority of the Jews. Yet Paul is convinced that before the kingdom is established on earth as it is now in heaven, the Jews will accept Jesus as the Messiah (Romans 9—11, cf. below, p. 243). Thereby the drama of this age will come to its glorious end; the new age will be ushered in. Jewish exegesis in the Christian era went rather in another direction, and the eschatology that had reached its peak in Christianity as well as in parts of Judaism became more and more toned down. The emphasis shifted from the hopes for the future to the obedience in the present under the law. Rabbinic Judaism established itself as the normative interpretation of the OT, but the common denominator remained the same: the election consciousness that accepts the law as the gracious sign of God's special favor to his people.

The only question that is beyond reach for such a descriptive approach is: Who was right—the Jews or the Christians? Its answer remains what it always was, an act of faith. If we approached OT theology in terms of developing ethical monotheism, we could, at least theoretically, arrive at an answer. This is, at any rate, what the liberal theologians implied when they hailed Jesus as a teacher superior both to the best of the prophets and to the wisest of the rabbis. But once we have accepted history as the fabric of biblical theology, we are thrown

26

back to the same choice of faith that faced the first century. History does not answer such questions; it only poses them.

This highly simplified sketch of biblical theology in the encounter between the testaments suggests also in what sense there can be a biblical theology where the OT and the NT are held together as a unity. The significance of the OT for the NT is thus shown to be inescapable, just as it was in the early church before there was a NT in our sense. On the basis of the OT and its fulfillment in Christ rests the Christian claim to be the chosen ones of God, the true Israel in Christ, and—if gentile by birth—"honorary Jews," heirs to the promises given to Israel. The crucial question arises when we ask what impact the NT should have on the presentation of OT theology. When biblical theology allows for such impact, it goes beyond its descriptive task, unless what is being attempted is merely a description of how the early church understood the unity between the OT and its fulfillment in what came to be the NT. But if the biblical theologian should go on to say that this is consequently what the OT text meant, he would be making either a statement of his own faith or a statement about the faith of the NT. If he says that this is what the OT means for the present-day Christian, he has proceeded from description, via hermeneutics, to a contemporary interpretation.

Thus the treatment of the Bible as a unity in this sense is beyond the task of descriptive biblical theology. Indeed, such a biblical theology will tend to discourage and prevent too facile a unification. To cite one example: Paul's radical concentration on the OT promises and his view of the law as holy and yet obsolete, once Christ has come, led Marcion to do away with the OT. He was in a certain way faithful to Paul—far more so than some Jewish Christians—but since his conceptual framework did not allow for a God who dealt with humankind differently in different dispensations, he could not imagine God as the originator of a holy law which he later declared obsolete. In its defense against Marcion, the church by and large forgot Paul's dialectic of time, and leaned over backward placing the OT and the NT on an equal basis. A truly descriptive biblical theology would have prevented both extremes. Thus the historian, with his descriptive approach, may clarify the issue of the relation between the two testaments.

There is, however, one way in which descriptive biblical theology does consider the Bible as a unity. The "sacred history" continues into the NT. Israel's election consciousness is transferred and heightened by the Christians—Jews and gentiles alike. History is still the matrix of

27

theology. Jesus does not come with a new doctrine about forgiveness for sinners; when he comes, "it so happens" that sinners accept him and the righteous do not. The first shall be the last. He does not leave his disciples primarily as a group of pupils who have rehearsed the "teachings of Jesus" as a lesson to teach others, but he has promised them a place as princes in the New Israel and has urged them to watch for the signs of the times and the coming of the kingdom. They do so; and his resurrection and the Holy Spirit are indications to them that Jesus is now enthroned as the Christ on the right hand of God. The Parousia must be close at hand, and the Spirit is the efficient and sufficient down payment of their share in the age to come. As Israel lives through its history as a chosen people, so are the Christians now gathered together as the chosen ones, the church enjoying a higher degree of anticipation of God's redeeming grace and power than did even the messianic sect at Qumran. God is still the God of a people with an ongoing history, however short it may be: the NT develops its ecclesiology.

It is in such a framework that NT theology can be properly described, and this framework is basically the same as that of OT theology. Here is the common denominator from a descriptive point of view. Within this framework, which gives us the *Sitz im Leben* of NT thought as a message and a self-presentation, we may study different ideas and concepts. We may find out how they are related or how they conflict with one another. But none of these ideas exists as general and eternal truth apart from the self-understanding of the church as the chosen community.

Thus there is a unity of the Bible on a historical basis. And this is the basis on which the two testaments came together. If, however, we approach the unity of the Bible or one of the testaments from the point of view of concepts and ideas, we may still be able to discern a certain unity in its anthropology, in its concept of God, or in its attitude toward ethics. A descriptive study of, for example, Paul's concept of justification would find the roots in the Song of Deborah, perhaps the oldest piece of tradition in the whole Bible (Judg. 5:11; *ṣidqot* = "saving acts of God"). The Gospel of Mark could be seen in relation to the kerygma in Acts 10; 1 Corinthians 15, as we have learned from C. H. Dodd's *Apostolic Preaching and Its Developments*. But we would look for a *type* of unity that was different from the organic unity to which the testaments themselves witness. And we would be faced with a diversity of views without the means to understand how they fell into a meaningful pattern for the biblical writers themselves. Paul's dialectic atti-

28

tude toward the law, mentioned above in comparison with Marcion, is a case in point. We would be inclined to see a great—or merely contradictory—paradox in his statement about the holiness and the obsoleteness of the law, if we did not recognize that Paul thought in the pattern of dispensations. The tension between the teaching of Jesus and the early theology of the church would remain a total enigma were it not for the fact that the disciples interpreted what followed after his death as a drastic step forward in the timetable of God, leading toward the Parousia. Our description has to detect and clarify such a development. It could, however, hardly answer the question about whether the disciples were right or wrong in their interpretation. We can only describe what they did and why they thought they were right while others thought they were wrong.

What has now been presented as the first and crucial task of biblical theology—that is, its descriptive function—thus yields the original in its own terms, limiting the interpretation to what it meant in its own setting. An attempt has been made to show that such a task does not necessarily imply the disintegration of the biblical material into unrelated bits of antiquated information. It is quite capable of presenting the different elements as an organic unity *if that unity is the one which actually holds the material together in the Bible itself.* It has been indicated that any question of meaning beyond the one suggested by the sources themselves tends to lessen the challenge of the original to the present-day theologian and makes him unaware of the hermeneutic problem as a sine qua non for any such interpretation.

THE HERMENEUTIC QUESTION

As Raised by a Descriptive Biblical Theology

A more thorough familiarity with the net result of such a descriptive approach as the one outlined above raises the hermeneutic question in a somewhat new form. No period of Christian theology has been as radically exposed to a consistent attempt to relive the theology of its first adherents. The ideal of an empathetic understanding of the first century without borrowing categories from later times has never been an ideal before, nor have the comparative sources for such an adventure been as close at hand and as well analyzed. There have always been bits and pieces of an appeal to the original meaning over against different later dogmas and practices of the church. The School of Antioch fought the School of Alexandria by such means; the Reformers argued with the papal theologians, and the Anabaptists with the Reformers, on such a basis; the pietists criticized the orthodox scholastics in the same fashion, and the liberal theologians claimed the same type of arguments against the evangelicals, and so forth. But never before was there a frontal non-pragmatic, nonapologetic attempt to describe OT or NT faith and practice from within its original presuppositions, and with due attention to its own organizing principles, regardless of its possible ramifications for those who live by the Bible as the Word of God.

The descriptive approach has led us far beyond a conglomeration of diverse ideas, the development of which we may be able to trace. We are now ushered right into a world of biblical thought that deserves the name "theology" just as much as do the thoughts of Augustine, Thomas, Calvin, and Schleiermacher. The translation of its content cannot any more be made piecemeal. The relation to the historical record is not any more one where systematic theology takes the raw material of nonsystematic data of revelation and gives to it systematic structure and theological stature. The relation is not one between a witness of a theologically innocent faith and a mature and sophisticated systematic theology. It is a relation between two highly developed types of theology: on the one hand, theologies of history, from which all statements about God, Christ, man, righteousness, and salvation derive their meaning and connotations, in terms of their function within the plan and on the plane of history; and on the other hand, theologies of an ontological sort, where Christianity is understood in terms of the nature of God, Christ, man, and so forth.

Within this pattern of nature or essence Christian theology has always tried to do justice to the historical element in the biblical material. But under the pressure of the thought pattern inherent in the Western theological approach, biblical eschatology—that is, the matrix of NT thought—was taken care of in a "last chapter" of systematic theology dealing with the "last things." Thereby the very structure of biblical thought was transformed and its eschatology inactivated.

In more recent Protestant theology there have been serious attempts to do more justice to eschatology as the overarching category of systematic theology and the motif of the "two aeons," this age and the age to come, has been stressed—for example, by the Lundensian theologians. But once again the outcome is a radical transformation, in that the aeons become internalized as levels of existence and experience in the mind and life of every Christian according to the formula "At the same time justified and sinner." The life on the border between the two dispensations as Paul knew them is lifted out of its historical context and becomes a timeless description of an inner dialectic of the Christian existence.

The focal point for a theological preservation of the historical dimension in the biblical material was found quite naturally in the stern insistence on the incarnation in Jesus Christ. But in this process the incarnation was more and more intensively developed in terms of its ramifications for the nature of Jesus Christ, while its original connotations were far more centered in the chronological pattern of the Johannine Prologue: God had *now* come to men in Jesus Christ to tabernacle among them in a glory which outshone that of Moses and the law.

The situation could perhaps be best analyzed in the realm of NT Christology, where significant strands of tradition display what later on came to be branded and banned as adoptionism—that is, the concept of Jesus, who was made the Christ in his baptism, or in his resurrection, or by his ascension. In the light of later doctrinal development it is easy to see why such a Christology was deemed heretical. But there is no indication that there was any conscious tension or argument, within the NT and in its time, between an adoptionist position and one which spoke of Jesus Christ in terms of preexistence or virgin birth. This was apparently not a matter of conflict. It became so only when the biblical witness was forced to yield the answer to the question about the nature of Jesus Christ, and when this very question became the shibboleth of true doctrine. As long as the question remains within the theology of history, it does not ask *what* Jesus Christ is or how human and divine nature go together in him. It centers around the question: *Who* is he? Is he the Messiah or is he not? In such a context an adoptionist answer coincides for all practical purposes with that of the preexistence type. But once this framework is lost, the answers come miles apart from one another as contradictory, and the kerygmatic statements in Acts 2:32–37 are a sheer liability to the orthodox theologian when they hail Jesus as the one whom God has made both Lord and Christ after his crucifixion, placing him on his right side as the enthroned Messiah in heaven, whence he now could and did pour out the promised Holy Spirit as a sizable down payment of the age to come.

It is perhaps even more striking when Acts 3:18–21 urges repentance in order that times of refreshment might come from God and that he might send the aforetime-appointed Messiah, namely, Jesus, who is now retained in heaven. Here the Parousia is really not the second coming of later theology. There is only one coming of the Messiah, the one

31

at the end of time. We are used to considering the first coming—that is, the earthly ministry of Jesus, as a clear, uncomplicated "coming" of the Messiah, but recognize how many complications arose out of the interpretation of the second coming. To the theology manifested in Acts 3, the problem seems to have been the opposite one. The Parousia—what we call the second coming—was no "problem"; it was part of the Jewish expectations concerning the age to come. The problem was rather in the opposite direction: To what extent was the first coming, the earthly ministry of Jesus, a real coming? How much of an anticipation did it imply, and to what extent did Jesus exercise messianic power within it? Once he was hailed as the Messiah enthroned in heaven, it was clear to the gospel writers that Jesus was the Christ, but there are enough indications left in the synoptic gospels to show that he was so by inference from what had happened after Calvary, and by references about what he was to become.

Thus the pattern of history in this type of NT theology sheds new light on the discussion about the messianic consciousness of Jesus. Those who deny such a consciousness and credit the church with having made Jesus their Messiah overlook the nature of this theology of history, for which there needed to be no distortion of facts in the belief that Jesus was made the Messiah in his ascension and enthronement. Those who claim a straight messianic consciousness in Jesus overlook the evidence that the messiahship in Jesus' earthly ministry has a strong futuristic note. But from the vantage point of post–resurrection/ascension the church confesses: Jesus is the Messiah now, and consequently he was the Messiah then—but he had not really become so by then, nor is he yet the Messiah here on earth as he is to be at the Parousia. Such an attempt to catch the theological meaning as found in Acts 2—3 gives no sense to one who inquires into the nature of Jesus Christ, and it sounds strange to a "yes-or-no" approach to the problem of the messianic consciousness of Jesus. However, it was highly significant to those who were eager to understand where they were in the messianic timetable of Jewish and Christian eschatology. He who changes the question can only be misled or confused by using the biblical text as a direct answer to it.

Texts and problems have been chosen from some of the highly controversial areas of NT exegesis only as illustrations to clarify the problem before us. The exegesis involved may well require correction or refutation, but the thrust of the descriptive method would always be of the same nature. The hermeneutic problem of biblical theology therefore centers in the clash between two types of theology. Each type includes a wide variety of alternatives. On the biblical side there are the different types of OT theology, some contemporary with one another, some later developments of earlier strata. In the NT it is somewhat easier to discern a Matthean, Markan, Lukan, Johannine, or Pauline theology, and so forth. But they all live within the presupposition of their respective centuries, and they all answer questions which require a historical consciousness and an awareness of where in God's history they now stand.

On the systematic side there is perhaps an even greater diversity, but in our Western tradition we find the questions asked by the systematic theologian to be by their very nature above history and beyond change. Such a systematic approach has been considerably intensified by biblical criticism, with its conflicting answers to exegetical problems and its radical doubt or mild uncertainty about many events and data on which systematic theology would have to rest its case. Lessing's statement that eternal truth cannot be derived from historical data became the more pertinent to systematic theology once the biblical basis for orthodox Christianity was summoned to constant trial before the courts of historical criticism. But in a certain sense Christian theology had freed itself from its historical matrix already in the time of the apologists of the second century when the case for Christianity was spelled out in the terms of Hellenistic philosophy. It would be unwise to exclude some elements within the OT and the NT from a similar tendency; thus the need for and the possibility of a translation of biblical theology into new categories of thought is taken for granted from the very outset. Orthodoxy never had repristination as its program in the periods of its strength. The possibility of translation was given—as it is for Barth—in the reality of the subject matter, apart from its intellectual manifestation in the thought patterns of the original documents. God and Christ were not Semites in such a sense that the biblical pattern of thought was identified with revelation itself.

Consequently, theology through the centuries acted in great freedom and with good conscience and considerable creativity. The fathers and the Reformers alike had no idea of a biblical theology apart from other theological endeavors. They were convinced that they were biblical theologians in the only sense one could be a theologian; in this respect Barth is certainly right in claiming the authority of Calvin and Luther for his biblical approach. But once the concern for a biblical theology as distinguished from other types of systematic theology has made itself manifest, a new problem arises. By way of a wide variety of hybrids where systematic and biblical categories were hopelessly intermingled, this concern has now brought us to the point where we can make reasonably clear statements about the meanings of the original in its own terms. This is why we have the right to say that the result of descriptive biblical theology has raised the hermeneutic problem in a somewhat new form.

Alternative Answers to the Hermeneutic Question

In the light of descriptive biblical theology, it becomes possible to pass tentative and relative judgments on the alternative ways in which systematic theologians have stated the meaning for the present day—or for all times, if that is their conscious aim—of the biblical material. Such judgments can be made on the basis of the degree to which systematic theology succeeds in communicating the intention implied in the biblical texts, an intention which only a precise and uncompromised study of the original could detect. But such a judgment would always remain tentative, since the task of systematic theology is by its very nature one of translation from one pattern of thought into another, and every true and great translation is a creative effort, not just a painstaking and nearsighted exchange of the precise words of one language with its lexicographical equivalents in another language. Aquila's Greek text stands as the horrifying example of such a senseless approach. On the linguistic level we hold the view—at least Protestants do—that there is no language into which the Bible could not be translated well enough to communicate its message; and the student of the Greek gospels is already once removed from the Aramaic vernacular of Jesus' teaching. If this analogy were one of considerable precision, it would imply that there could be few philosophies, epistemologies, anthropologies, and the like, which could not furnish the framework for a systematic theology by which the meaning of the Christian Scripture could be stated. The history of Christian theology gives us reason to accept the analogy to a considerable extent. And the fact that the original is available gives us the right and the audacity to encourage such translation activity.

The attempt of the so-called liberal theology to detect the meaning for today in the evolution of an evermore-refined religious insight with a higher level of ethics could hardly be ruled out as one of the alternative answers to the quest for meaning. Its validity as a Christian theology would hinge upon its ability to live with a growing awareness that its categories of meaning are utterly alien to biblical thought. Such an awareness is harder for the liberals to take than for any other theologians, since they traditionally have rested their case on its historical truth, and claimed the historical Jesus as the first protagonist for their own views. In their attempt to grasp the intention of the biblical message, they were unusually handicapped.

In the wake of liberal theology in its academic form—in its popular form it is still very much with us—came the tendency to establish contact with the world of descriptive biblical theology by simply substituting its categories for those traditional to Western theology. Well aware of the peril of modernizing Jesus, one was less afraid of archaizing oneself. The achievements of the descriptive biblical theology were dumped right into the twentieth century. The fact that those results now displayed enough structure and religious intensity to give the impression of a real theology made it quite tempting to try such a return to the prelogical, the Semitic, the Hebraic, the first century. All these categories were now subsumed under the heading "biblical," and this in an evaluating fashion, so that the theological ideal became an ill-considered parallel to the well-considered descriptive ideal of divesting oneself of the twentieth century. The "biblical way of thinking" was spelled out over against "the Greek." Once more the descriptive and the contemporary became interwoven, this time on the terms of the result of the descriptive approach. From a theological point of view this meant that revelation was identified with patterns of thought and culture; the need or the possibility of creative translation—that is, the very glory of systematic theology through the ages—was undercut. No serious attempts at a conscious translation were made.

Such a criticism could certainly not be directed against what we may call the thoroughgoing translations, where the tendency is ahistorical or even antihistorical. Paul Tillich and Rudolf Bultmann are two pronounced representatives of such answers to the hermeneutic problem. Neither of them finds anything normative in a theology of history as presented by the descriptive approach. To both of them history is utterly mute as far as theological meaning is concerned. Second, historical data are to them too shaky a foundation for the theological enterprise. Tillich thus approaches theology from an analysis of being, and he is consistent enough to claim no, or little, biblical support for such a category. Bultmann, on the other hand, finds his point of departure as well as arrival in human self-understanding, and for this he claims considerable biblical authority, since, according to him, the very intention of

35

the kerygma is to challenge man's self-understanding. It appears, however, that Tillich, in spite of being perhaps the least "biblical"—in a conscious sense and by mode of language—of all contemporary theologians, is capable of communicating a wider range of biblical intention than does Bultmann with his highly anthropological concentration.

The most common response to the challenge of descriptive biblical theology is perhaps what may be called the semihistorical translation. Here the historical nature of revelation is taken seriously. The Bible is the record of the acts of God in history, and the kerygma is the powerful proclamation of these acts, a proclamation that shares in the creative power of the acts themselves. Thus the church is nurtured and renewed through the ages by this creative Word by which it rehearses the acts of God in sacred history. But somewhere along the line this sacred history has stopped, and there is only plain history left, with a more general providence at work. Thereby the God who acts becomes more and more the God who did act in biblical history. Consequently his acts appear as performed on the stage of history in order to demonstrate his nature. Theology reads his nature off the record of sacred history. The acts of God in history and the human response to them become calcified into a mold. This mold is then used by theology to make the true images or concepts of God as he who acts. The difficulty with such a translation into nonpropositional and nonphilosophical concepts is that it accepts the historical framework of biblical thought for biblical times, since it yields the illustrations for our grasp of God's nature and will; but once the canon of the NT has drawn the line, there is a change of categories. Sacred history has come to an end, and what remains is a history where these deepfrozen images of God's acts are constantly brought to life in the remembrance of the church. The tension between a historical understanding of the Bible and a theologically void history of the church raises grave problems of inconsistency.

Such a problem would lead us to suggest that the only consistent alternatives would be either a radical, ahistorical translation as mentioned above, or—if the historical framework of biblical thought were to be retained—a systematic theology where the bridge between the centuries of biblical events and our own time was found in the actual history of the church as still ongoing sacred history of God's people. The blueprint for such a theology could be found in that self-understanding of Israel, both new and old, which descriptive biblical theology has laid bare as the common denominator of biblical thought. Such a theology would conceive of the Christian existence as a life by the fruits of God's acts in Jesus Christ, rather than as a faith according to concepts deduced from the teaching of the prophets, Jesus, and Paul regarding God's acts. It would exercise some of the same freedom which Paul's and the other NT letters do when they refrain from any nostalgic attempts at playing Galilee in their theology. Rather, they transform the teaching of Jesus' earthly ministry into a system of theology and ethics. It would recognize that God is still the God who acts in history when he leads his church to new lands and new cultures and new areas of concern. A theology that retains history as a theologically charged category finds in its ecclesiology the overarching principles of interpretation and meaning. It does not permit its ecclesiology to be transferred to the second-to-the-last chapter in its systematic works, followed by that on an equally inactivated eschatology. A theological awareness of sacred history seems to imply by inner necessity a growing recognition of the church as something far beyond an organization for the promotion of evangelism and theology. Through the ongoing sacred history, which is commonly labeled "church history," the fruits of God's acts in covenant and in the Christ are handed down to the present time. Within this history the task of preaching and theology under the guidance of the Holy Spirit is part of an ongoing sacred history. The chasm between the centuries is theologically as well as historically bridged by history itself, not only by a timeless kerygma that reaches the individual in an ever-repeated punctiliar action. The church lives, not only by the aorist of the Holy Spirit, but by the perfect tense as the Greeks understood it: an action which is completed and the effects of which are still with us.

The Significance of "Canon" for
Biblical Theology

Such an approach would raise the question of the canon (i.e., the limitation of the Bible to—usually—sixty-six books, thirty-nine in the OT and twenty-seven in the NT) in its sharpest form. As far as the descriptive approach goes, the canon can have no crucial significance. The church has a "Bible," but the descriptive approach knows it only as the "Bible of the church." In order to grasp the meaning of an OT or NT text in its own time, the comparative material—for example, the intertestamental literature (Enoch, Testaments of the Twelve Patriarchs, Jubilees, etc.)—is of equal or even greater significance than some canonical material. The revival of biblical theology in our own generation depends greatly on the way in which such material was brought to bear on the original meaning of biblical texts. But when the descriptive task is addressing itself to the interplay between different parts of the Bible, as, for example, the NT understanding of the OT, it naturally takes cognizance of the limits of, as well as of the very idea of, canon. The descriptive approach also yields considerable insight into the nature and motivations for canonization itself and is capable of understanding the need as well as the rationalization connected with the long process of canonization. This in itself is one of the most puzzling and fascinating interplays of historical circumstances and theological concerns.

Once we go beyond the descriptive approach, the canon of Scripture becomes crucial. To many of the modern types of biblical theology, the phenomenon of canonical Scriptures seems to count little. To Barth it is inspiration rather than canon that matters, and the process of canonization is an external feature which neither adds to nor subtracts from the power of the inspired writings to allow the Word to authenticate itself ever anew to him who hears. This is actually consistent with an ahistorical theology, since canonization so obviously is a historical process. It strikes the historian, nevertheless, that the concept of inspiration was of little or no avail in the first centuries of church history, when the church moved toward a closed canon. Apostolic origin, a doctrine in agreement with the succession of teaching, and wide usage and recognition in the churches were the chief criteria when the early church dealt with a wide range of writings, many of which were recognized as equally inspired with those finally received among the twenty-seven. But once the canon was closed, the doctrine of inspiration served well as an answer to the question: Why are these books different from all other books? To Bultmann, canon seems to be of little significance. The Christian self-understanding, to which the Bible caters, is found within it, but there are also parts of it which do not display it. Furthermore, its meaning for the present rests on the same basis as that on which any historical document has "meaning" beyond its value as a source for historical information. Finally, the understanding of the intention of the Bible as kerygmatic is not deduced from its canonical nature; on the contrary, it is the kerygmatic nature that gives the Bible its claim to authority.

To the radically historical alternative, as outlined above, much depends on the understanding of canon as a crucial category of any theological enterprise. This is certainly what we would expect if the historical nature of revelation is retained in a theologically potent framework of the sacred history of God's people. It is quite significant that, for example, a biblical theologian like Cullmann, who has given such a strong impetus to the historical alternative, has also addressed himself extensively to the problem of tradition and canonization (see the chapters "The Plurality of the Gospels as a Theological Problem in Antiquity" and "The Tradition," in *The Early Church* [1956]), and that his discussion takes the form of a new attempt to clarify how Protestant and Roman Catholic theology differ in their understanding of the interplay between the continuous tradition and the line drawn around the Bible by canonization.

To the historical approach the question raised by Harnack's studies in the NT canon becomes theologically significant: why is there a NT, not only a fourth part added to the three units of the OT (Law, Prophets, Writings)? The descriptive approach suggests a theological answer: the NT—as well as the church itself—rests on the return of the Spirit. Judaism in the time of Jesus lived under the conviction that the Spirit had ceased, and when the question of valid scriptures was discussed, this cessation was related to the last of the prophets (i.e., Malachi). They recognized themselves as living in a period when Israel depended on the scriptural interpretations of scribes whose authority rested on faithful transmission, not on the Spirit in which one could say, as the prophets had done, "Thus saith the Lord." But they cherished the hope and the promise of the return of the Spirit. This would be one of the crucial manifestations of the coming of the new age. Thus it is quite natural that the conviction of the church that this new age had arrived and manifested itself in the Holy Spirit also gave the basis and theological rationale for what came to be the NT.

It is worth noting, however, that the closing of the NT canon is not based on any argument similar to that of Judaism regarding the OT—namely, that the Spirit ceased again. Such a view would have undercut the very faith and life of the church and was never considered in the argumentation regarding the NT canon in the first centuries. The development from diversified oral and written traditions to the twenty-seven books of the NT was of a more historical nature, guided by the necessity to protect the original from more and more undependable elaborations and distortions, some "heretical" but quite a few properly orthodox in their intentions. The gift of prophetic and inspired teaching was still a recognized phenomenon, an ever-repeated "aorist" of God's dealing with his church. But the significance of Jesus Christ and his apostles as ἐφάπαξ ("once for all"), and as the very basis on which the church was built—that is, the "perfect-tense" dimension of biblical thought, as referred to above—called for a distinction between this and what the church understood as original and as its magna charta. Thus Cullmann seems to be right when he suggests that early Christian tradition bore within it the element that served as a compelling cause for the process of canonization. This element may be defined as the "perfect-tense" element of Christian theology. As such it affirms the acts of God as unique in Christ and his apostles, but it also points toward an ongoing history of the theological existence of the church. God's acts are not punctiliar aorists, frozen and canned within the canon, nor do they belong to the timeless present tense of mysticism.

The question as to the meaning of the Bible in the present—as distinguished from the meaning in the past as stated by descriptive biblical theology—receives its theological answer from the canonical status of Scripture. In its most radical form, the question was: do these old writings have any meaning beyond their significance as sources for the past? On what basis could it be valid to translate them into new modes of thought? On what basis could such an original—and such a translation—have a normative function for the life of the church? Such questions can be answered only within the consciousness of the church. The answer rests on the act of faith by which Israel and its sister by adoption, the church, recognizes its history as sacred history, and finds in these writings the epitome of the acts of God. As such these writings are meaningful to the church in any age. It is as canon, and only as canon, that there is a Bible, an OT and a NT as well as the whole Bible of the church as a unity. The old question of whether the Bible rests on the church or the church on the Bible is a misleading question from the point of view of the historical alternative. To be sure, the church "chose" its canon. But it did so under the impact of the acts of God by which the church itself came into existence. The process of canonization is one of recognition, not one of creation *ex nihilo* or *ex theologia*.

One could perhaps see the Protestant Reformation as a reaffirmation of the line drawn protectively around the canon. In a situation when the growth of tradition threatened to submerge the "original"—as had the traditions rejected as noncanonical in the second and third centuries—Luther and Calvin reinforce the distinctiveness of the original and its superior authority in the life of the church. There are many things that we would like to know, historically as well as theologically, beyond what the Scriptures tell us. In the Roman Catholic tradition such quite legitimate and pious curiosity has centered around Mary, the mother of Jesus. Against such and other elaborating traditions the Reformers take a firm stand on *sola scriptura* as sufficient, yea, more than sufficient, unto salvation. The canon is enforced, and such a return to the "original"—given the circumstances of the time—engenders one of the most spectacular renewals of theology and church life that history has seen.

This is in its own way a suggestive illustration of how an exposure to the "original" plays into the life of the church. It gives us theology in a new key and breaks through many cherished presuppositions. It is perhaps not too much to suggest that the highly developed descriptive biblical theology of our own period in the long run may have a slightly similar effect. This is not to hail our age as capable of a new Reformation. But it does suggest that all theological renewal and creativity has as one of its components a strong exposure to the "original" beyond the presuppositions and the inherited frame of thought of our immediate predecessors in the theological task. Otherwise the history of theology would be an uninterrupted chain reaction of a philosophical nature, with Augustine correcting the earlier fathers, Thomas Aquinas correcting Augustine, Luther refuting Thomas, Schleiermacher touching up Luther and Barth, and Tillich carrying the traditional discussion up to our own time. The exposure to the "original," as it is made accessible by descriptive biblical theology, could give an alternative to such a development. This alternative is not new in principle; it has been at work through the ages. What is new is the radical concern for the original *in its own terms.*

If we were to take an extreme example of what this could imply, we could return to the area of Christology. We saw how in the NT "adoptionism" stands as an equal, side by side with other types of Christology, and how the reasons for its downfall were found, not in the NT, but in the framework of later philosophical presuppositions. If the ontology which caused its downfall in the theology of the church were not any more a live option to the philosophical structure of a systematic theology of our time, it would be quite possible to speak meaningfully and in a most orthodox manner about Christ in "adoptionist" terms when witnessing to his function and his reality. There may be many other reasons why this specific case should not be followed up; our only concern is to indicate in what way a descriptive biblical theology gives the systematic theologian a live option to attempt a direct translation of the biblical material, not a revision of a translation of a revision of a translation. It is easy to see the great need for such a possibility in the theology on the mission field and in the young churches, and there are

41

signs that Western Christianity could be well served by a similar approach, with its sharp distinction between past and present meaning.

The Preacher and Biblical Theology

A sharp distinction between what the texts meant in their original setting and what they mean in the present has considerable ramification for the work of the preacher, if he in any sense sees it as his task to communicate the message of the Bible to the congregation whose shepherd he is, and to the world which is his mission field. If we may use once more the analogy of the original and the translation—and this should not be considered more than an approximate analogy—the preacher is called upon to function as the bilingual translator. He should through his training and his ongoing studies attain the marks of a truly bilingual person—that is, one who is capable of thinking in two languages. (By "languages" we mean not the Greek and Hebrew of the Bible—although these would become more and more indispensable if the "bilingual" approach were taken seriously—but the modes and patterns of thought in the Bible.) The preacher's familiarity with the biblical world and patterns of thought should, through his work in descriptive biblical theology, have reached the point where he is capable of moving around in his Bible with idiomatic ease. His familiarity with the "language" of the contemporary world should reach a similar degree of perception and genuine understanding. Only so can he avoid the rhetorical truisms of much homiletic activity, where the message is expressed in a strange—sometimes even beautiful—mixed tongue, a homiletical Yiddish which cannot be really understood outside the walls of the Christian ghetto.

The demand for such a bilingual function of the preaching ministry may seem quite exacting, and indeed it is. It is also as it should be that the work of biblical as well as systematic theology finds its functional focus in the pulpit of the church. But it would be unreasonable to demand of the preacher—if now we may press our analogy once more—to become an academic grammarian of these two "languages" or a master of philosophical semantics. His task and his competence would remain by and large on the level of the vernacular, which he should have overheard long enough to be able to use it naturally and easily, as he would also use the Bible.

A mere repetition and affirmation of the biblical language, or even a translation which mechanically substitutes contemporary terms—often with a psychological slant—for those of the original, have little chance to communicate the true intention of the biblical text. To use an example from Bultmann's demand for demythologizing, the mere statement "Jesus is risen" directs the mind of most listeners toward a unique phenomenon, glorious or impossible as the case may be. On the basis of this phenomenon the believer is invited to base his hope for eternal life. A closer descriptive study of the resurrection passage suggests, however, that to the first listeners to the kerygma the phenomenon of the resurrection was not surprising in the same sense. All Jews—except the Sadducees—expected the resurrection as the climax of God's history; the phenomenon was nothing strange and new to them. The only new thing was that it had happened. The claim of the church that Jesus was risen thus meant to those who accepted it that the general resurrection, to which they looked forward, had started to happen; Paul consequently says that Christ has been raised as the "first fruits of those who have fallen asleep" (1 Cor. 15:20). In the same chapter the argument runs partly in the opposite direction to what we are used to think: "If there is no general resurrection, then Christ has not been raised" (v. 13; cf. v. 16). Those who first heard and believed the news about the resurrection were not absorbed in a consideration of the phenomenon as such, but received it as a message that the new age had started to manifest itself here and now. This certainly affirmed their hopes in sharing in Christ's resurrection in God's good time, but the center of the message was that the power of the new age was at work in their own world and their own time (cf. below, p. 198).

Bultmann suggests that the task of the preacher is to free this message from its biblical nucleus, the proclaimed fact of the resurrection as a historical event. But even for a preacher, who finds reason to object to such a demythologizing or dehistoricizing of the gospel, the problem which Bultmann points up remains a real one. Can the preacher say that he has communicated the message of Easter by stating and by underscoring the physical nature of the phenomenon of the resurrection as a stumbling block for unbelievers, but a rock of salvation for those who believe? His familiarity with the results of a descriptive biblical theology would urge him to place the emphasis where the texts themselves put it and to meditate, for example, along the lines of how the power of the new age manifested itself in Jesus Christ, not only as a token of our resurrection, but as the enthronement of Christ and as the possibility for man to live by the powers of the new age here and now. There would be many other lines like this which opened up from the gospel of Easter if the preacher did not become paralyzed—in faith or in doubts—by the phenomenon of the resurrection, deducing from it theological propositions, but let his familiarity with the biblical world guide him through the concrete and diversified way in which the early church recognized, and rejoiced, in the resurrection of Jesus Christ. His homiletic imagination would become enriched, and the message would have a chance to find its live and relevant translation.

If the task of the pulpit is—as suggested here—the true *Sitz im Leben,* "life situation," where the meaning of the original meets with the meaning for today, then it is once more clear that we cannot pursue the study of biblical theology adequately if the two tenses are not kept apart. For the descriptive biblical theologian this is a necessity implied in his own discipline; and whether he is a believer or an agnostic, he demands respect for the descriptive task as an enterprise valid in its own right and for its own sake. For the life of the church such a consistent descriptive approach is a great and promising asset that enables the church, its teaching and preaching ministry, to be exposed to the Bible in its original intention and intensity, as an ever-new challenge to thought, faith, and response.

3

Kerygma
and Kerygmatic

Introductory Note: It is with strange and nostalgic feelings that I include this article, the oldest one in the collection. It was written during my years as a graduate student in NT and as a young pastor trying to learn from his studies how to preach with precision. I am both shocked and encouraged when I now recognize how little I have changed over the years. This article could well be compared with the similar yet different perspective in "One Canon is Enough" (see below, 55–68).

Gustaf Wingren has been my actual and mental discussion partner over the years. He writes with drive and conviction. He is my Swedish Käsemann, with whom I debated in my book *Paul Among Jews and Gentiles* (pp. 129–33). Both are truly stimulating. Wingren has been well translated into English. My favorites are *Man and the Incarnation: A Study in the Biblical Theology of Irenaeus* (Philadelphia: Muhlenberg Press, 1959) and *Credo* (Minneapolis: Augsburg Publishing House, 1981). The book discussed in this article appeared in English under the title *The Living Word* (Philadelphia: Muhlenberg Press, 1960).

This article appeared in *Ny kyrklig tidskrift* (1951), and was published in German translation in *Theologische Literaturzeitung* 77 (1952), cols. 715–20.

Theology has its slogans. Eschatology is one of them, used with a full rainbow spectrum of meanings. In theology the same applies to the term "incarnation." Using such terms as one would use weapons in war, one defends and attacks theological positions. More recently the word "kerygma" has been added to the arsenal of slogans.

Preachers easily fall in love with the term "kerygma." Writing on *The Sermon and the Word of God*, Dean Olle Nystedt, one of the leading preachers of Sweden in the 1950s, made it his basic theme that the Bible is message and then explored the consequences of this view: "The fact that the Bible is a Message means that the Bible does not merely teach us what God has done and still does, but the Message—the very act of announcement—is an integral part of God's acting" (40). Nystedt notes that such a kerygmatic view fits well into the biblical understanding of Einar Billing—one of the greats of early twentieth-century Swedish theology and its Luther-renaissance. In particular, Billing's interpretation of the OT prophets—although Billing did not know of the catchword "kerygma"—strikes Nystedt as powerful and congenial.

It is, however, Gustaf Wingren who has compressed the intention and character of the Bible into the term "kerygma." In his *Predikan* (the Swedish word means both "sermon" and "the act of preaching"), he places the announcement of the kerygma in a grand perspective of salvation history from the resurrection to the coming of Christ.

Wingren's point of departure is the discovery by NT scholars of a basic message, the nucleus of the Creed: the proclamation of Christ's death and resurrection as the central fact for the faith, for the church, and hence for humanity. That proclamation is the kerygma in its true sense, exemplified most clearly in Paul's reference in 1 Cor. 15:3–5: "For I delivered to you as of first importance what I also received, that Christ died for our sins in accordance with the scriptures, that he was buried, that he was raised on the third day in accordance with the scriptures, and that he appeared to Cephas, then to the twelve." Paul refers to this tradition as "the gospel," but the Greek term "kerygma" (from *keryx*/herald) occurs in verse 14. While it has a broader meaning, scholars have seized on it as designating such summaries of the message centered in the death and resurrection of Christ. In Acts the missionary sermons have this "kerygma" as their nucleus.

In an inspired study, *The Apostolic Preaching and Its Development* (1936), C. H. Dodd had worked out and made popular this kerygma in the NT books—cutting across all diversity. But he was not alone. He rather expressed what has now become a consensus, and it is on this consensus—with Dodd as the principal framer—that Wingren builds.

At one point Wingren goes against Dodd. He has to do so in order to establish his thesis. Wingren writes:

> But this kerygma (in Acts) is obviously . . . *missionary* preaching. There is the possibility that such New Testament preaching tells us nothing at all about the preaching that took place in the churches. C. H. Dodd seems to make a clear distinction between *kerygma* and *didache*. The instruc-

tion/teaching (didache) builds on the kerygma and is given to the members of the churches, or to those who were about to become members. The kerygma, on the other hand, would be the very missionary message, "the public proclamation of Christianity to the non-Christian world." It is surprising that Dodd—who finds throughout the *whole* New Testament the imprint of one and the same ever repeated kerygma—can fall momentarily into making such a distinction. The epistles which preach the kerygma most clearly are such as 1 Peter etc., and other letters addressed to beleaguered churches. All the four gospels announce by their structure and disposition that the death and the resurrection are the center of the Christ act. No doubt, one can say that the New Testament as a whole is missionary writing, just as the Church is Mission. But then one cannot allow oneself making mechanical distinctions; then it is necessary to see both the beginning and the progressing life of the Christian as a life out of the Word, as a continuous return to the one gospel, the Word about Christ. It is false intellectualism to sever those incorporated into the church from the missionary kerygma. As a matter of fact, the message about Christ's death and resurrection has its ultimate aim in that, as we hear it, we die and rise. Since our self-will does not want to subject itself under this life process, the Word about Christ becomes ever new, unexpected, fresh until the day we die (Wingren, *Predikan*, 9; cf. English translation, 17f.).

Dodd's distinction is, however, not a "momentary lapse," as Wingren seems to think. It is clearly required by the evidence. For Dodd would never say that 1 Peter *preaches* the kerygma most clearly. On the contrary, about the NT epistles he says:

> It is difficult indeed to find the Apostolic Preaching in Paul's (or other) epistles. To begin with, and most importantly, by their very nature, the epistles are of course not kerygma. They are all addressed to readers who already are Christians. They treat theological and ethical problems which emerge when one tries to follow the Christian way of living and thinking in a non-Christian world. They constitute what the Early Church called teaching or admonishment. They presuppose the preaching rather than proclaiming the gospel. They expand and defend its meaning (Dodd, *Apostolic Preaching*, 9).

The kerygma is here seen as background, an observation that can be easily established. The kerygma is consistently introduced, or referred to, by verbs in the past tense as in the chief passage of 1 Cor. 15:3: "For I delivered . . ." This is important for any understanding of how early Christians thought of the function of the Word and the nature of the church. The very awareness of having been transferred from death to life, from darkness to light, places the kerygma with its saving proclamation at the initiation, that is, in baptism. The kerygma and its content are primarily woven into the act of baptism. Baptism is *the* locus of the kerygma—liturgically as well as theologically. Romans 6 is enlightening here. The act of baptism is patterned on the kerygma of Christ's death and resurrection. Paul's teaching—his speaking in present tense—is actually ethical admonishment, expressing the *consequences* of the already accepted kerygma/baptism. The ethical instruction takes place in the light of the kerygma referred to in past tense.

If we turn to 1 Peter, which Wingren refers to, we find that the stated intention of the author is not to preach the kerygma. Rather, "I have written briefly to you, exhorting and declaring that this is the true grace of God; stand fast in it" (5:12). The aim is exhortation and affirmation of the truth and validity of the already received kerygma.

True enough, Dodd finds parts of the kerygma in 1 Peter, but its use in the epistle can hardly be described as "preaching the kerygma" in the sense of *announcing* it as a herald who brings news. For example, when Isaiah 53 with its pregnant language of salvation through suffering is applied to Christ, it is not used as an invitation to salvation or even as a presentation of salvation. To the Christians it is a hallowed example of patience in suffering (2:21; cf. 3:18). Dodd's comment speaks of the atmosphere in 1 Peter as one most akin to "the one we can surmise behind the earlier chapters of Acts" (44), that is, one of persecution. In that setting 1 Peter gives its exhortation, shaped by kerygmatic elements but not proclaimed kerygmatically.

Thus there is no momentary lapse in Dodd at this point. But he and Wingren use the term "kerygma" in different senses. For Wingren kerygma defines the very nature of all preaching as a message, a proclamation (as by a *keryx*/herald); *and* as a definition of the content of the message (centered in death and resurrection). For him it seems self-evident that *all* preaching is—or ought to be—kerygma in the second sense, centered in the ever-ongoing process of dying and rising. For Wingren the whole Bible is kerygma in the first sense *and* the essential meaning of the Bible is concentrated in the kerygma in the second sense. Wingren uses the term "kerygma" for two different things. It could even be shown that those two senses, one of form and one of content, need not be related. Actually, they can stand in opposition to each other.

For Dodd the term "kerygma" is primarily a term for a certain content. For him it is a technical term for the summary of certain data in a history of salvation which can be identified as central and formative in the NT and as the creedal base of the church. The term "kerygma" is not loosened from the specific NT expressions of such summaries. Dodd speaks of what I would call the *actual* kerygma.

Thus we must retain and even sharpen the distinction between (1) what scholars refer to as the actual kerygma, and (2) the use of the term "kerygma" as a polemic and apologetic slogan in modern theological discussion. For this latter use I prefer the adjective "kerygmatic," since we are not dealing with a thing, a distinct entity, but with a mode of communication.

I call this second use polemic and apologetic. It grows out of a critique of psychologizing and anachronistic attempts at using the gospels as biographies of Jesus. With the aid of form criticism it could be argued that the intention of the gospels was not biographical but "kerygmatic," not one of just telling a story but one of proclaiming a message—from faith to faith. The apologetic use of this formal insight is often aimed at protecting the gospels from rationalism and historicism.

To say that preaching is or should be kerygmatic, that is, has the character of a proclaimed message, is a reasonable proposition. But that kerygmatic character is not tied to the actual kerygma. In addition, the teachings and exhortations of the Bible have been understood not just as information about God but as the Word of God. The material that is not part of the actual kerygma can function kerygmatically—as a creative Word of God. Hence it can hardly be correct to define the Bible as being on principle a proclamation of the acts of God (Nystedt, *Sermon*, 33ff.), even if that sounds beautiful and impressive. To claim that it is only the acts of God that constitute "the Word of God" in the Bible is a modern apologetic tour de force by which most of the pages of the Bible become suspect as inoperative.

In the NT the Greek words *keryssein* (to proclaim) and *parakalein* (to exhort) are not confined to the proclamation toward salvation on the one hand, and ethical exhortation on the other hand. In Acts 2:40 we read: ". . . and exhorted them, saying, 'Save yourselves from this crooked generation,'" by accepting the kerygma and being baptized (cf. 2 Cor. 5:20). Furthermore, *keryssein* and *didaskein* (to teach) are synonymous in Rom. 2:21 and both refer to ethical instruction: "You then who teach others, will you not teach yourself? While you preach against stealing, do you steal?" (It could hardly be argued that Paul here uses the terms to ridicule Jewish ignorance of the glories of Christian *keryssein*.)

The Norwegian scholar Ragnar Asting (*Norsk Teologisk Tidsskrift* 33, 1932) has addressed the subject of the sermon in the churches of the NT. He shows that its primary character was *paraklesis*, or exhortation. In so doing he takes his point of departure in the Jewish synagogue where the sermon followed the reading of the Scriptures and was an exhortation to faithfulness, patience, and various virtues. We can think of Acts 13:15: "After the reading of the law and the prophets, the rulers of the synagogue sent to them, saying, 'Brethren, if you have any word of exhortation for the people, say it.'"

The Epistle to the Hebrews describes itself as a *logos parakleseos*, a word of exhortation (13:22). The nonkerygmatic use of the kerygma in the church is well demonstrated in 12:13. The acts of the savior serve as encouraging examples of patience. Asting describes Hebrews as exhortations to hold fast to God's grace in Christ, and as admonitions toward virtues—in both cases buttressed by quotations from Scripture, just as in the synagogue sermons.

It is from such a state of affairs that one can best understand post-apostolic sermons (see, e.g., 1 and 2 Clement). Justin Martyr gives the best early description of sermons in the actual life of the church:

> The memoirs of the apostles or the writings of the prophets are read, as long as time permits; then, when the reader has finished, the one who presides speaks instructing and exhorting us to imitate these good things (1 *Apology* 67).

This nonkerygmatic style and form is pervasive in the church and in all evidence that we have. It has led to the common, especially Protestant, description of the second century as a dry period. Y. Brilioth (*Predikans historia*, 19; English trans., *A Brief History of Preaching* [Philadelphia: Fortress Press, 1965]) gives this view in a more careful form: "Prophecy is silenced and in its place stands instruction and a sober parenesis (ethical teaching) which strikes modern readers as rather anemic." But he sees clearly that "in any case, it is in this epoch that the Greek homily takes shape—and its equivalents in those churches that used Semitic tongues. The term *homilia* occurs for the first time in Ignatius's *Letter to Polycarp* (5:1) for the word spoken in the congregation, referring to exhortation" (17). Actually, the etymology of *homilia* suggests conversational style rather than proclamation, cf. Acts 20:11.

Such an evaluation needs considerable modifications, since the issue is not NT fervor versus second-century bleakness. The NT evidence shows that, as far as we know, speaking in the churches from the very beginning had this nonromantic, nonkerygmatic character, while the kerygma belonged to the mission speeches to outsiders. G. E. Philips makes the point well in his *The Transmission of the Faith* (London: Lutterworth Press, 1946), especially in a chapter with the telling title "Did the Church Sag Down After the Apostles?" Thus Brilioth's however-mild acceptance of the catechetical and parenetic elements as secondary is questionable (11).

Asting agrees with Harnack's description of preaching in the churches as being toward ethical strengthening. Yet he stresses that this does not imply a general moralism. He defines this moral preaching, especially within the NT, as "a demonstration of the consequences of the life in Christ" (89). Once the term "kerygma" has come into the common theological language, we could say " . . . the consequences of the kerygma."

It is characteristic of the word spoken in and to the congregations that the kerygma is not proclaimed as a creative, acting word. One does not live addressed ever anew by the kerygma. One lives out of its consequences. The kerygma is anchored in baptism, at the baptismal grave which one has passed through. The consequences of baptism mark the Christian life with newness of life and the gift of the Spirit. In Romans 6 the kerygma is not proclaimed. It is repeated and called to remembrance as an introduction and background to the ethical exhortation that constitutes the chapter. No news is heralded: "Once we know that . . . " (v. 6). This perspective is strengthened by the repeated stress on the once-for-all character of Christ's death—a motif which Paul brings in as important. Why? Apparently to make clear that the death and the initiated resurrection with Christ in baptism is also a once-for-all act in the life of the Christian (cf. Heb. 6:6).

When Christian preaching is defined as an ever-repeated proclamation of the kerygma, then the NT evidence and perception have been seriously skewed. And when this repeated proclamation of the kerygma is said to be a creative act of God aiming at our ever-repeated dying and rising with Christ, then Paul's stress on the once-for-all is turned upside down. Such a dynamic view may be appropriate to mission proclamation and is certainly present in the act of baptism. It is, however, blatantly absent from all that we know about all preaching in the worship of and by Christian congregations. The issue is not blurred by the open question of whether non-Christians could be present (e.g., 1 Cor. 14:22; see now glossolalia in my *Paul Among Jews and Gentiles*, 109–24).

What matters is whether the speaker consciously addresses Christians or outsiders. The distinction—upheld by Dodd and in an almost unanimous exegetical consensus—between mission preaching and congregational preaching is fundamental for any understanding of early Christianity in all its manifestations. The question may be raised: but what about Jesus? The answer is clear. While Jesus is presented as sometimes speaking to his disciples only, and sometimes in public (and often to both in undefined ways), the gospels as we have them are intra-Christian books for congregational use and edited for that purpose.

The Nonkerygmatic Kerygma. We could then sharpen our conclusion by saying that in congregational preaching the actual kerygma functions as nonkerygmatic. It was not proclaimed. It was referred to as what the believers had encountered that had had drastic creative effects. Now it was the background, or rather the ground for their new being, the foundation once laid. Both in ethical exhortation and in theological reflection the nonkerygmatic character of speech and thought is obvious.

The Kerygmatic Nonkerygma. But much that cannot be defined as actual kerygma (proclamation with its center in the death and resurrection of Christ) certainly has kerygmatic character in the sense of a message with power and authority: divine, prophetic, apostolic. Its character of Divine Word does not decrease automatically by its distance from the content of the actual kerygma. Even the most common-sense admonition can be kerygmatic in that sense. Its authenticity as a creative Word of God has no external criteria.

A contamination of the actual kerygma with the kerygmatic mode of communication, or vice versa, leads to much confusion. In any case, it blocks access to any realistic understanding of the NT evidence.

The distinction we have insisted on has considerable practical consequences for contemporary preaching. It may actually lead to a reversal of much that has become our unquestioned habits.

It often happens that we reserve the deeper mysteries of salvation for the initiated, the faithful, the mature Christians. When we address the relative or total outsiders, when we feel ourselves as missionaries, then we often stick to moral or psychological generalities. We say things that people usually know and accept, although they like to have them gilded by religious rhetoric. We speak of love and goodness and perhaps something beyond the grave. We moralize.

If we continue that division of our labors I guess that what will happen is what actually happens. The "outsider" will never come to understand what Christianity is about. The faithful will be lulled by a pervasive sense of guilt which feels strangely good since it proves that one is a true, humble Christian. For such people the specific moral exhortation—with the biblical conviction that a new life is possible—is the required Word of God, even, or just, because it is very far from the glories of the kerygma.

But what about an average worship service (esp. in a national and established church such as the Church of Sweden) where the sense of membership is vague or even frowned upon? Is that the place for missionary preaching, or for sermons to and for the faithful? The sermon in its congregational setting should contain teaching about the kerygma but should not be transposed into a mode and mood of ever-repeated proclamation. We may also gain inner and formal clarity if we know what we are doing, to whom we speak. Then each time it will be different. Preaching is many things. The lectionary and the liturgical year also give their hints. Especially if we make use of both the gospel and epistle and—not least—the OT. In established churches there will always be a place for both missionary preaching and the instruction and exhortation of the faithful. But there is a big and fateful step from such an awareness to the claim that "deep down" the two are one and the same. A theology that blurs the line between Christian mission and Christian nurture, between revival and worship, between *kerygma* and *didache/paraklesis* could emerge in an unbroken Christian culture where membership in the church is compulsory and unreflected. But such situations are becoming rare in Christendom.

4

One Canon is Enough

Introductory Note: This essay criticizes the attempts at finding a canon within the NT canon. It was prepared for an international study commission which met from 1967 to 1971. The commission was established by the Lutheran World Federation and the Vatican Secretariat for Christian Unity. The overall theme assigned to the commission was "The Gospel and the Church." The essay was published (together with other papers and the Final Report) under the title *Evangelium—Welt—Kirche*, edited by Harding Meyer (Frankfurt am Main: Verlag Otto Lembeck and Verlag Josef Knecht, 1975).

The topic was assigned to me in German as: *Mitte und Ganzheit* (Center and Totality). Hence the introductory musings. For this somewhat revised edition I have chosen the title "One Canon is Enough." As will be obvious to the reader, the text is based on a transcription of the tape from my oral presentation. The reader will also recognize that I am making use of ideas more fully stated in chapters 2 ("Biblical Theology") and 3 ("Kerygma and Kerygmatic") of this volume. It seems that I return to the question of canon again and again, as for example in "The Apocalypse of John and the Epistles of Paul in the Muratorian Fragment," in *Current Issues in New Testament Interpretation: Essays in Honor of Otto A. Piper,* ed. W. Klassen and G. T. Snyder (New York: Harper & Row, 1962), 239–45.

The translation "center" and "totality" is mine. Perhaps it should be "middle" and "fulness," or "center" and "fulness." But as I tried to figure out *was eigentlich gemeint war,* I entered on the problem with which I am here concerned—namely, whether the whole assessment of the content and the function of what we call the gospel is to be handled from a clear perception of its center, while the question of the periphery almost dissipates as uninteresting; or whether the question of the totality of witnesses within the Scriptures or within the tradition is rather what we should keep our eye on. And hence I translated highhandedly "center" and "totality." My presentation is in a theological—or should I say philosophical—key other than what is common in contemporary theological style. For I am highly suspicious of hypostases, like "the faith" which "does" and "thinks" and "accepts" and "acts" as a subject. In spite of—or for the very reason of—being a good Lutheran, I am suspicious even of the hypostasis "the Word," the fourth member of the Lutheran trinity, our worthy competitor with the Mary of the Roman Catholics. And I am highly suspicious of the hypostasis "the kerygma" as something that speaks and acts.

Such hypostatic uses of these terms are often buttressed by reference to the Hebrew word *dabar* which tends to transcend the distinction between "word" and "thing," and which does not only name but create that which it expresses. Johannes Pedersen (in *Israel: Its Life and Culture*) and others have given impetus to this view—but it is highly doubtful that such feelings were operative in, for example, NT times, or that it is a suitable basis for contemporary theological conceptualities. This leads me to be more careful than ever when using the word "Gospel" as if it were an almost personal power—doing, acting, walking around on its own—severed from God and Christ.

My commentary here is given in an ecumenical situation in which Roman Catholics and Protestants are in danger of passing one another in the night. Roman Catholics now have gotten on a "Bible kick"—as we say in American slang. They are now all for the Bible. You should have been with me when I spoke to five hundred Franciscan nuns in Buffalo, New York, and we had processions in which we enthroned the book. Being a Lutheran, I was given the honor of enthroning the book—although it is rather in the Calvinist tradition that the open Bible is a cult object on the Table of the Lord. We Lutherans think the Bible is rather for reading. But in a much deeper sense there was a real fascination and commitment to the Bible. However, I had the feeling that they should have invited Billy Graham rather than me, in view of the language they spoke and felt. As a Lutheran I had the feeling that I had a few things to tell them about some problems that we have had with the Bible. It is my hope that Roman Catholics can be warned in time, lest they repeat our mistakes. Let us at least pass one another in clear daylight.

The key in which I have chosen to speak may brand me as a theological and ecclesiological positivist: the data for me are the church as a community and the Bible as its Scriptures. There are many activities in this community, all of which are—one would hope—inspired, guided, judged, prompted, enlightened by the Scriptures, by the Word. And it is with such a simple model of the church and its Scriptures that I am approaching the question about the gospel as center and the gospel as totality. I speak as an *enfant terrible* and very tentatively. Since I am so tentative about this, my tone will be self-assured, as is often the case.

The way in which our topic has been stated is by no means without its coloring. It rests on a great many conclusions, hermeneutical as well as exegetical. There is a good deal of presuppositions (*Vorverständnis*). While German NT discussion has much to say about *das Vorverständnis*, it gives surprisingly little attention to its confessional, denominational *Vorverständnis*. Yet it is striking how Lutheran these Lutheran exegetes turn out to be in their exegetical work and their hermeneutical presuppositions. And this *Vorverständnis* has to be smoked out. It rests on a great many conclusions, hermeneutical as well as exegetical, as to the nature and function of the NT and its content. The NT is approached as a *witness*. That sounds good. And the term "gospel" is used in the sense that owes its predominance to the linguistic habits of one single writer, the apostle Paul. Yet, even in Paul the word is more amorphous and sometimes more colorless than we are given to believe.

This is hardly the place to sort out the development of the word "gospel/*euaggelion*" explaining its uses in Paul; or in the opening sentence of the Gospel of Mark, or in 1:14; or Matthew's standard phrase "the Gospel of/about the kingdom" (4:23, etc.); or the ominous and not-so-happy connotations of "to evangelize" in Luke 4:18; or the absence of the word in the Johannine writings (cf. Rev. 14:6); or the use of the term for what we have come to call the gospels. The question before us is rather whether the choice of the word "gospel" as the comprehensive term for the essence of Christianity is as obvious and self-evident as it seems to many. And, second, if such usage exactly prejudges the issues that should be considered in this essay.

The problem that our topic tries to place in focus could be stated in other terms. In order to bring the issues involved into view, I would suggest asking the following questions: What are the criteria by which the church interprets the Scriptures or assesses the will of God (or: interprets the Scriptures in order to assess the will of God)? Is there one overarching criterion (the gospel as center); or is there a wide variety of criteria, the sum total of which is decisive (the gospel as totality); or is the search for criteria a misguided activity?

It could appear to some as if such a formulation falls outside the province of the NT scholar proper, while, of course, the given formulation invites him to comment from his own field. If a NT scholar is someone who tells us what the NT meant, what Paul believed that he thought, and so forth, then the question with which we are here dealing is one of theological and contemporary interpretation. And I think it is very important for us biblical scholars in the church and in our faculties to recognize that much knowledge in philosophy, theology, and other nonbiblical disciplines is needed for making statements on these points. As a biblical scholar I have to warn myself—and also my Protestant and Catholic colleagues—against the implicit imperialism of biblical scholarship in contemporary theology. We have a tendency to appear closer to God by the very assignment of our task. We must, however, explode that illusion. To be sure, any discussion of how to live with the Bible presupposes a historically adequate understanding of the function of the actual texts in their original setting. But that does not solve the problem now at hand. I am not a biblical theologian of the kind who thinks that once one has described first-century theology, one has solved the theological problems of the twentieth century.

We should at least know what the actual function of these texts was. We cannot take for granted that terms like "gospel" and "witness" are adequate designations for the functions and the intentions of all the material found in the NT itself. By form-critical analysis we know for sure that the *verba domini*, the sayings of Jesus, were shaped by the needs of the church, and there is no good reason to believe that their primary or pristine function was as "a message" in the context of preaching. The earliest reference to words of the Lord can be found in Paul's first epistle to the Corinthians. I have always wondered about the fact that the two words of Jesus which Paul gives (in addition to the institution to the Lord's Supper) are first about divorce (1 Cor. 7:10) and second about pay to clergy (1 Cor. 9:14). Such words were used by the early church in order to settle specific issues. The parable about the lost sheep, which in Luke is one of Jesus' answers to the grumbling Pharisees (15:2), has become an introduction to rules on church discipline in the Gospel of Matthew (18:12–14). The words of the Lord certainly function to assess specific issues as early as in the 50s. And the way in which these words have come down to us can by form-critical analysis be assessed to have been shaped and formed in the same way by the needs of the church, a need which by no means is only that of kerygmatic proclamation. Only a Protestant, perhaps only a Lutheran, could have come up with a slogan like "In the beginning was the Sermon" (Martin Dibelius). One of the achievements of Bultmann's monumental "History of the Synoptic Tradition," as compared to Dibelius's "From Tradition to Gospel," is Bultmann's far-greater subtlety in the attention to different functions that shaped the forms of gospel material.

The gospel, in the sense of the message, is sometimes stylized in what we have come to call kerygmatic formulas, and constant reference is made to 1 Cor. 15:1ff. Such a kerygma is often said to be the missionary message of the early church. We do not really know, but we have become accustomed to saying so. It is the missionary message, the answer to the question: what is new that has happened in and with the Christ event? Whether it was a missionary message or not, it certainly is a striking and recurring central element in the teaching of certain biblical writers. And as such it forms a significant part of Christian teaching, reflection, and activity. Paul can refer to it as well known. He can use it as his basis, when he goes on to argue his case against his opponents. Often he refers to "my gospel" when he deduces from it his understanding of the issues at hand. Thus the message—once received in the missionary situation, if that was so—does not function as a message any longer, but as a creedal formula to be affirmed, interpreted, referred to. The gospel, in this sense, is not a message that hits the hearers again and again. It is rather a magna charta of the church, stating its freedom and its new bond in Christ. This observation is important for the total understanding of the function "the Word." Paul, for example, in 1 Corinthians 15, does not say, as if he were raising his voice or entering the pulpit: "Now listen to the Word which I pronounce as a herald, the word by which God creates . . . " Nor does it have any overt dimension of the famous *pro nobis* or *pro vobis* (for us, or, for you). Paul just says: "Now, you remember that the kind of main lines I gave you were such and such . . . " His words are not thought of as an event, not even a "word event." In my judgment, there is nothing kerygmatic or sacramental about it. It does not reenact in any sense whatsoever. There is nothing of that *dabar*-mystique of Johannes Pedersen to which we referred above.

The crucial problem is whether we interpret "Christianity" primarily as a message (gospel, kerygma, witness), or primarily as a community, a people, the church. The term "Christianity" is not found in the Bible. I am not enough of a biblicist to think that hence it should not be used.

But it seems to conjure up its own mental models. When we speak about Christianity what do we actually have in mind? Is it a message, or is it a people? We know that it is not an ideology; it is not a philosophy. But among the respectable alternatives I would suggest that we must make clear whether we really think of Christianity primarily in the terms of a message, a dogma, a teaching, a doctrine, or whether we should rather think in sociological terms and see that the primary data indicate that Christianity is a community, a people, the church.

Kerygmatic theology, especially in a Lutheran key, tends to speak as if the kerygma (the Word) did its work by an ever-repeated address to individuals through the ages. And thus the task of biblical scholarship within the church is to purify the sound of that creative message, by which somehow the saving events of old are repeated in the believer. This is a sophisticated theological way of "playing Bible-land." In Sunday school children often are asked to "play Bible-land," which is a sort of walking and talking with Jesus in Palestine. We may consider that terribly liberal and naive, but the kerygmatic "playing Bible-land" is highly respectable and considered deeply existential.

The kerygma bridges the chasm between then and now. We hear as they heard. That way of relating to the Scriptures is perhaps a possible way, but it is not the only possibility, and it has its liabilities. Whatever its merits, I would argue that it misrepresents early Christian piety. For according to the NT the Christian community lives on the basis of and by the consequences of what was wrought once for all in Christ. The members of the Christian community share in the Spirit that is one of the consequences of what was wrought in Christ. They are members of a people who are what they are in Christ and for Christ's sake. In other words, the primary datum is a church that depends in all respects on God's acts and words in Jesus Christ. And by that formulation one can account for those words of Jesus Christ that might very well have come through Christian prophets who spoke in the postresurrection situation in the name of Jesus and with his authority. It is in that church that it now makes sense to ask the question about the message, its center and its totality.

The practice of form criticism has its strange ambiguities when it comes to its hermeneutical ramification. It is a method where the *Sitz im Leben der Kirche* (place and function in the life of the church) by definition makes obsolete the time-honored distinction between Scripture and tradition. So definite is this insight that the Faith and Order meeting of the World Council of Churches in Montreal in the summer of 1963 pondered a draft that said that the church lives *sola traditione*, by tradition alone. It did not pass. But as a historically adequate statement, in the light of contemporary biblical studies it is an obvious statement, a platitude. It is obvious that on this analysis, Scripture *is* tradition, a special kind of tradition. Not even a special *kind* of tradition, but it is a special *amount* of tradition set apart in a special way. It is neither all the earliest tradition—to think that we have in the canon all the earliest tradition is of course wrong—nor am I sure that it contains the greatest spiritual achievements of the early tradition, because I feel a good deal more spirituality in some parts of the letters of Ignatius than I do in some parts of the NT. I do not think that to be a totally subjective judgment. To be sure, form-critical method has contributed substantially to a new era in the discussion between Roman Catholic and Lutheran theologians. The discussion of Scripture and tradition must be cast in drastically new forms.

At the same time, the form-critical method seems to heighten the hope of some as to the possibility of getting back to the pure message, unadulterated by the interpretive activities of the church, or at least to that pristine first activity of the church in its kerygmatic grasp. The well-grounded fear of ecclesiastical triumphalism, as well as the fear of the power of the church over the Word of God, leads to and strengthens attempts in this direction in order to find that pre-ecclesial message in its purity. The contemporary sophisticated equivalent to the outmoded dream of the simple teachings of Jesus is the pure kerygma. Both attempts are working the same way, that is, from a view of history where the beginning is pure and continuation is deterioration. I am often inclined to think that way myself, but as a historian and as a theologian I must question such a model. Why could it not be that they really finally got the point in A.D. 150, or at Trent, or at Augsburg, or at some other points in time and space? One may wonder whether we are caught in the genetic fallacy, whether the dream of the kerygma is not an anachronistic and just plain romantic operation by which the old dichotomy between Scripture and tradition, Bible and church, is perpetuated in the form of kerygma (gospel, message) versus church (later tradition, *Frühkatholizismus*).

It is my suggestion that the present state of NT studies and our understanding of Christian origins should lead us rather to define the problem in the following fashion: How does the church live with the Scriptures? How does the church practice openness, obedience, and

61

willingness to be judged and renewed by the Scriptures? How does the church live and interpret as a church bound by the Scriptures rather than binding the Word to its interests, its habits, its thoughts, and its sins?

It is striking to what extent we tend to discuss the Scriptures in terms of their value for security. The function of the Scriptures is not so much toward maximum perspective, freedom, imagination, sensitivity, prompting, and so forth, but basically in terms of assurance, either individually in terms of the assurance of the forgiveness of sins, or doctrinally in terms of the assurance of what is right teaching and doctrine. By the constant search for criteria we are, of course, back again to our urge for security. That should perhaps not be criticized, but it should be observed that we should watch ourselves, lest we treat the Scriptures as the main source of security as if that was their original and primary intention.

It is in such a setting that we want to give attention to the variety of theologies, the plurality of accents and emphases, in the NT. We would argue that neither a harmonization of the totality nor a promulgation (or, possibly, discovery) of a normative supermotif—either in the strict sense of motif in the style of Bishop Nygren's agape motif, or a normative supermotif in terms of death and resurrection honored by the term "kerygma"—would supply the optimal stance of freedom and creativity which our questions in the preceding point call for.

But first we note that the question of canon looks very different if one stresses "center" or "totality." To those who would stress the "center," the question about canon is of little interest. Or we should say perhaps that then the question about canon occurs in a noncanonical form by asking for the canon within the canon. Then one is bound to carry on the Lutheran tradition regarding the somewhat suspect status of the epistle of James. Once the center has been found and defined, it may well be that Ignatius may come closer to the canon within the canon, closer to the center, than do, for example, the pastoral epistles. So argues Rudolf Bultmann, and that in a very interesting way since Ignatius is full of so many things which really are not to Bultmann's liking. But in his treatment, the epistles of Ignatius somehow come out on the side of the angels.

For such an argument, it is only to be hoped that the canonical writings do comprise within them the material necessary to establish the right center. That question seems to bother few, although it should. What I have in mind here is, of course, Barth's and others' reference to the self-authentication of the Scriptures. Such a reference seems to short-circuit the fact that this Bible grew out of the trial and error of the church's experience over a period of three hundred years. I simply hope that this process left us with books capable of self-authenticating themselves at the present time. Had we had the gospel of Peter in the canon, or had we had Marcion's canon, or had we had the gospel of Thomas instead of the Gospel of Luke—then Christianity would look a little different, the center would look a little different, and the self-authentication would take place on somewhat different terms. But perhaps Barth would argue that in that case those books would not authenticate themselves. I have my doubts. For such an argument the only thing that is necessary is that somehow the net was providentially cast in the right way.

To those who argue from the "totality," the canon is theologically important. In one sense or another, it must then be affirmed that those boundaries of the canon, drawn over a period of three hundred years, indicate the limits within which variation is acceptable and even advantageous. The canon thus serves as a standard for diversity within unity and unity within diversity.

The plurality and variation within the NT are real. They cannot be overcome by harmonization. Or we could even say: when they are overcome by harmonization, the very points intended by the writers are dulled and distorted. The shifts in meaning and theology from Paul to the Deutero-Pauline texts are real changes and often imply the influence of new and "alien" thoughts and patterns, even when—or just because—they are the result of an intention to be faithful to the master in new situations.

The various eschatological and christological perspectives of the evangelists and of their sources make for real differences and cannot, or should not, be harmonized. The study and control of such variations in the gospels (and in other sources for Jesus material) could perhaps pave the way for tentative reconstructions of the "historical Jesus," and of his "very words." Joachim Jeremias has toned down such a claim by speaking about "the very voice of Jesus" which allows the method to remain intact, supplying a subtle difference. Then one notable candidate for the "center" of the NT is the life and teachings of Jesus, or perhaps, the actual intentions of Jesus. That is a real alternative, and we should perhaps have a little more respect for the good old liberals; Harnack's point was not a silly one, and if something like this is possible, it is a serious candidate for the "center" position.

63

Apart from the immense uncertainties implicit in such an approach, it is, however, commonly agreed that such a center would not be the center of any postresurrection Christianity, that is, of no Christianity known in the formative period of the Christian movement. For this reason, such a center would constitute perhaps a significant source when we seek criteria, but it could not be the only criterion. It would, however, bring up the well-known fact that, according to the synoptics, Jesus spoke not about himself but about the kingdom. But when we approach the questions from the point of the postresurrection kerygma then it seems that the kingdom of which Jesus spoke has been swallowed up into personalized Christology. The kingdom-language with its powerful theological potential has somehow been neutralized and emasculated. If it is true that Jesus really spoke about the kingdom, although the church itself became absorbed by the question of Christology, would it not be reasonable to see whether we should not find a new and fresh way to utilize this whole way of speaking about the kingdom, away from the personalized christological language? It should at least be seriously considered.

I have sometimes played with the idea that the Christians came to be called Christians because they concentrated on the personal term "Messiah," that is, a personal term and a very specific one. That was really what made them stand out, because the Judaism of the time used mainly nonpersonal terms in its "messianic" expectations. I have recently gone over intertestamental and Qumran material with a fine-toothed comb in order to collect occurrences of the word "Messiah" as a personal noun. There was a large amount of material to read—with a very small gain. At best we could say that Messiah is only one of some fifty ways to refer to the promised future, and not a common one. Once we start from a Christian perspective we read all references of this future as "messianic"; but this is a striking *interpretatio christiana*, one which in turn came to influence even Jewish scholarly terminology. The nonpersonal kingdom-language of Jesus may deserve a new hearing—one made difficult by the kerygmatic postresurrection approach.

But let us turn to a more specific example of intrabiblical diversity. Let us for the sake of a clear argument subscribe to the view that Paul in the Corinthian correspondence fights a type of theology very much like that represented by the bulk of the Johannine gospel. Paul argues against a piety that, according to him, overstates the power, joy, and achievement of the resurrection life. His opponents are people who consider themselves as having passed from death to life already, a quotation from the Gospel of John (5:24; cf. 11:26). In its "heretical" form this heresy is mentioned in 2 Tim. 2:18 as sponsored by Hymenaeus and Philetus, who claim that the resurrection has taken place already. In a very developed form we know the same type of theology from Justin's *Dialogue* (chap. 80), but the Gospel of John actually speaks that same language. To Paul that position is wrong, because it is a denial of the cross, a cross that certainly is not the place for Jesus to claim that "all is accomplished," as he seems to say according to the Gospel of John (19:30). To Paul this position is a denial of the very nature and essence of the cross, making believers haughty and spiritual snobs, unable to identify with the weak. In his argument against such a piety Paul uses eschatology not so much as a driving force but as a "brake," the "not yet," and stresses that faith is "hope" and not "having" or "seeing" (Rom. 8:24–25). If this is a correct analysis then we have in the NT not only two different accents in the interpretation of the faith, but two ways in which to interpret faith, one of which is severely judged by one biblical writer to be contrary to the gospel, and yet it occurs in a most honorable gospel, the fourth.

To harmonize these theologies is, of course, possible—is there anything that a theologian cannot do? Verses like John 5:25 may have been a not-so-subtle way to do just that. But to elevate Pauline sensitivity in this matter to the status of the true gospel and relegate Johannine theology to Proto-Gnosticism can, in my judgment, only be arbitrary. We do not at this point raise the questions about the criteria by which Paul or John would be judged true representatives, and that for reasons which will become clear. I would rather accept the diversity and consider the latitude an asset and a richness, rejoicing in the "totality." It should be noticed that the process of canonization that gave us our NT was not that of Marcion, who was a clean thinker, and hence attractive to many a clear-thinking theologian through the ages, for his message was uncluttered and uncontaminated. Nor does our NT come from a canonization process like that of Tatian's *Diatessaron* that achieved a catholic neatness by maximum harmonization. Thus our heritage is neither reductionism nor harmonization, but a canon that encircles genuine diversity.

To accept such variety without harmonization leads to a different question which grows out of the "incidental" character of the NT writings. It is, of course, easiest to demonstrate this point with the Pauline letters. Nobody would be more surprised than Paul to know that his letters made it into the Bible. Here we have certainly accidental writing. In many cases we can figure out—partly by "mirror-reading"—what the opponents and issues were. We must note how, for example, Paul's discussion about justification by faith in the proper Pauline style is confined to Galatians and Romans (and Philippians 3), while other motifs inform Paul's grappling with the problems in Thessalonica and Corinth. I belong to the group that believes that Paul's thinking about justification by faith addresses itself to the question of how Jews and gentiles could coexist and could think about one another in relation to the plan of God. From Augustine on, the Western introspective conscience took over, and we got the idea that Paul spoke about the problem of human sin and guilt in general—a Western problem, which reaches its theological explosion in Luther and its psychological explosion in Sigmund Freud.

Paul actually thought he was speaking about how Jews and gentiles fit together in the plan of God, which certainly is a drastically different problem. It is in Galatians and Romans that he discusses Jews and gentiles. That discussion plays no role whatsoever in 1 Corinthians, except as an analogy to other problems (e.g., 1 Corinthians 7, on marriage). First Thessalonians might have come into being before he had worked out his theological argument about justification. In a more general sense, all writings, and the traditions and sources used in them, operate and become colored and adapted to specific situations, conditions, and problems.

This being so, the question of interpretation and the question of "the message" of the Bible must lead away from general formulations of principles, or harmonized, emasculated, generalized biblical theology. They must lead toward the question: Is the situation to which the church speaks analogous to the situation to which a biblical passage is directed? Without such attention to analogous situations, even the most important biblical message—even the most "central" biblical message—may well be the wrong one to apply to a particular instance. I would like to handle this problem by serious attention to the question of application and analogy. My criticism of much contemporary "biblical theology" here is clear and sharp. I consider the attempt to create a biblical theology, a unified biblical theology, a futile and dangerous task. For a Lutheran it appears that if we could have that kind of biblical theology, why should we have anything else? We have the real thing—biblical theology. Of course, we can achieve such a theology by much anachronistic footwork or by doing things that are very alien to the biblical material. The only sense in which one can speak properly of biblical theology is in the sense of descriptive theology (what Paul thought that he thought), and then there must be various theologies. That is to say, the word "meaning"—and here my philosophical bias comes out—has no meaning whatsoever unless you ask: Meaning for whom? The idea is alien to me that some meaning hovers over or is embedded in the text or in the word, and that if we just had the right hermeneutical method, or system, then the text would open up and yield its "meaning." Meaning can only be assessed in terms of what is understood by a particular individual. What did Paul mean, or more humbly, what did Paul think that he meant? One could, of course, try to put Paul on the couch, as Erik Erikson did with Martin Luther in *Young Man Luther*. But as Erikson himself says, we know too little about Paul to be able to carry out such an operation. Luther's habit of speaking freely, after a glass or two, in his Table Talks, gives the psychoanalytical approach unusual advantages. And even so, we can only discuss in terms of specific meanings for individuals—be it Paul, or us, or many persons in between then and now. The relation between these meanings has to be tested by analogy of situations.

It is this "situation" principle, this attention to analogous situations, that makes the diversity within the NT an indispensable asset. It is such a proposition that makes the harmonization of the various theologies—into a homogenized biblical theology—an unnecessary and impoverishing activity. And with such a method of correlation the assertion of a center, a central message as the only thing that matters, appears to be just a way to choose one motif and pretend that it can be severed from its specific setting and its specific function. This applies to *all* candidates for the "center" position, be it justification by faith, or *theologia crucis* (theology of the cross), or forgiveness of sins, or the fatherhood of God, or the Word become flesh, or even the primitive kerygma. Of course, a very large part of basic Christian theology centered around the death and resurrection of Jesus. But in the specific case of 1 Cor. 15:1ff., which has become canonized as the canon of canons, it is very unclear to any reader what the relation between that kerygma and Paul's special argument might be. That makes me uneasy. The choice of this piece of kerygma is not only due to tradition but is somehow mixed in with the fact that Paul is arguing for his own authority—hence the importance of the witnesses. It becomes part of his argument about himself, and where that tradition ends and Paul's arguments begin is a moot exegetical question. Furthermore, the kerygma has many forms. First Peter 1:11–12 sounds quite different as it speaks about suffering and glory, but not about death and resurrection, and so forth. There are many "kerygmata." They all speak for and against specific alternatives in concrete situations. Only by functioning in analogous situations can they claim to be that Word of God which they are. It is an old fact that the right answer becomes wrong when applied to the wrong question. Now the church is clever in giving the right answers. But we are not always so sure, or I am not so sure, that we are relating them to the right questions or that we listen clearly to the questions at hand. This can be said in a very simple pastoral sense, and it can be said in a deep theological sense. Any reference to the kerygma as singular, or to a center which makes the totality less important and interesting, suggests that there is a master key which opens all the locks. But this is perhaps a hermeneutical mirage. I would rather use the whole set of keys supplied by the Scriptures. And the canon is the key ring.

RELEVANCE THROUGH STRESSING STRANGENESS AND DISTANCE

5

Quis et Unde— *Who and Whence?*
Matthew's Christmas Gospel

Introductory Note: The diversity of theologies and perspectives within the Bible is important, both in themselves and as they supply different options for theological work. The following essay, on Matthew's first two chapters about the "Who and Whence" (*Quis et Unde*) of Jesus Christ, could serve as a prime example of how drastically different one gospel is from the others. It was published in the *Festschrift* for one of the great exegetes, Professor Joachim Jeremias of Göttingen, *Judentum-Chrisentam-Kirche*, Beiheft 26, *Zeitschrift für die neutestamentliche Wissenschaft*, ed. W. Eltester (Berlin: Toepelmann, 1961), 94–105. Republished in German translation in Joachim Lange, ed., *Das Matthäus—evangelium*, Wege der Forschung, Bd. 525. (Darmstadt: Wissenschaftliche Buchgesellschaft, 1980), 296–311. My argument in simpler form and in the context of Matthew in general can be found in my commentary on Matthew in *Peake's Commentary on the Bible*, ed. M. Black and H. H. Rowley (Edinburgh: Thomas Nelson, 1962), 769–98.

For an up-to-date and overwhelmingly rich discussion of both Matthew and Luke, see Raymond E. Brown, S.S., *The Birth of the Messiah* (Garden City, N.Y.: Doubleday & Co., 1977). Brown accepts my idea of "Who and Whence" as the topics of Matthew 1 and 2 respectively (Brown, 52ff.). But when he goes on to expand it into "Who—How—Where—Whence," the force of my argument is considerably lessened. It is still my conviction that exactly and only the "Who and Whence," the *Quis et Unde* give the *structure* to Matthew 1—2. As to ideas, thoughts, and information, there are of course many *hows* and *wheres* and *whens* and *whithers* and *whys*.

The tendency to harmonize the material in the different gospels is deeply rooted in the Christian tradition and manifests itself especially in the treatment of what we usually call the infancy, or nativity, narratives in Matthew 1—2 and Luke 1—2. In spite of comments and observations to the contrary, the study of Matthew 1—2 labors under the conscious or unconscious presupposition that Matthew here recounts—in his own manner, to be sure—what Luke tells about in his first two chapters; that is, each gives an account of the birth of Jesus.[1] This presupposition is constantly reinforced by the *quaestio facti*. The differences between Matthew and Luke—or, as it mostly happens, between Luke and Matthew[2]—are properly discussed only within this presupposed framework of "birth narratives." These differences are well known and need only to be pointed out in their main features:

1. In Matthew the genealogy comes first, runs from Abraham to Jesus called Christ. It is revised—leaving out, for example, three of the kings mentioned in the OT (Ahaziah, Joash, and Amaziah), and with obviously too few generations in its third part—according to a pattern (3 × 14) and follows the ruling Davidic line. The genealogy's most distinctive feature is the mention of the four women: Tamar, Rahab, Ruth, and Bath-Sheba (ἡτοῦ Οὐρίου; RSV: "the wife of Uriah").

In Luke the genealogy has no relation to the birth narrative; it is connected with the υἱός μου of the Bath Qol at the baptism of Jesus (3:22). The genealogy runs in the opposite direction; from Ἰησοῦς . . . ὢν υἱός, ὡς ἐνομίζετο, Ἰωσήφ by a chain of simple genitives all the way back to τοῦ Ἀδάμ, τοῦ θεοῦ. Thereby it forms a corroboration of the message of the Bath Qol. The circle closes itself. The line to David goes via Nathan, that is, a nonruling line of the Davidic family. The Davidic element is not stressed; the point seems to be: υἱὸς θεοῦ.

2. In Matthew Joseph is the main person. It is he who receives the revelations and through him the action progresses. Dreams are the vehicles of revelation, a phenomenon peculiar to Matthew.[3] In Luke Mary is the recipient of revelation, and Joseph is described as he who stands by.

3. None of the events noted in Matthew 2 are mentioned, or alluded to, in Luke 1—2: the visit of the Magi, the flight into Egypt, the massacre in Bethlehem, the return to Judea, and the continued flight to Galilee and Nazareth. Furthermore, according to Matthew, Joseph and Mary live in Bethlehem,[4] and their settling in Nazareth is due to special guidance at a later time; according to Luke, Joseph and Mary live in Nazareth, they go to Bethlehem for the specific purpose of the census, and they return to their hometown (Luke 2:39; εἰς πόλιν ἑαυτῶν Ναζαρέθ). There is no evil Herod in the background, only shepherds

and pious Jews, Simeon, and Anna. And there is the elaborate parallelism between the Baptist and Jesus.[5]

4. In Matthew the text seems to rest on formula quotations, one for each point in Matthew's account.[6] There are no such formula quotations in Luke, where the relation to the OT expresses itself in allusions, and these are materially and formally concentrated in the canticles.[7]

Such differences are more drastic than anywhere in the canonical gospels—the synoptics versus the fourth gospel included. They should warn against treating Matthew 1—2 and Luke 1—2 as alternative birth narratives. The carefully organized structure of Matthew makes it unnatural to approach these divergencies by a direct discussion of the "source" or "sources" behind Matthew 1—2.[8] Whatever the sources, Matthew works here with a clarity of purpose, which should allow us to find out what *he* thinks that he is doing with his material. Such a first step is the most reasonable, since the organizing principles, and especially the formula quotations, are not confined to these two chapters, but are applied also to material of a synoptic nature.[9] But in chapters 1—2 this method has totally formed the material, a sign of the fact that at the time of the gospel this material had not yet frozen into a given form.

Matthew 2 is dominated by geographical names. This is the more striking in contrast to chapter 1, which has not a single one[10]—not even where we would expect them, that is, in 1:18f. The chapter begins with the mention of Bethlehem of Judea; it takes us to Egypt, describes the massacre at Bethlehem, takes us out of Egypt back to the land of Israel, bypasses Judea, takes us into Galilee, and settles us in Nazareth. For Matthew this itinerary is not a frame secondary to his intention. On the contrary, these geographical names constitute what is really important to him, as can be seen from his use of the formula quotations: the common denominator of the four formula quotations in chapter 2 is that they all contain geographical names, names which substantiate the point reached in the "itinerary." At two points it becomes obvious that the four Matthean quotations have the location rather than the "event" as their foci.[11]

1. The prophecy "Out of Egypt have I called my son" is placed by Matthew, not where the call out of Egypt takes place (v. 19), but where Egypt occurs for the first time (vv. 13–15). Hence it is obvious that Matthew wants to nail down "Egypt" in the itinerary.

2. LXX, Vulgate, Aquila, and the Targum[12]—all suppress the geographical name "Ramah"[13] in Jer. 31 (38):15, in a manner typical of the

73

LXX,[14] by translating it "in the highest." This may well be the prevailing interpretation in Judaism and hence Matthew's use of the geographical name is not self-evident, but stressed in order to serve a geographical quotation.

If the geographical information is the structure to Matthew 2, then this chapter gives the answer to a question similar to the two raised in John 7:41f.: "Is the Christ to come from Galilee? Has not the scripture said that the Christ is descended from David, and comes from Bethlehem, the village where David was?" (RSV). In the fourth gospel these questions are left open—a literary device or an actual witness to John's lack of knowledge or lack of interest in any Bethlehem tradition.[15] But the question must have been a real one: How was it that Jesus the Messiah came from a Galilean village?[16] Hence the *whole* second chapter of Matthew has its climax in its last verse: "that he should be called Ναζωραῖος."[17] The chapter shows how God himself, according to prophecies and through divine and angelic intervention, leads Joseph, and thereby Jesus, from Bethlehem to Nazareth. The cry in Ramah then forms a prophetic alibi: it is obvious that they had to get the boy out of Bethlehem. The title to be written over the chapter would be: "How It Came to Pass that the Messiah Came from Nazareth." It gives in a sense the opposite answer to that given in Luke, where Nazareth is the self-evident point of departure and "Bethlehem" comes into the picture through the census. In a similar fashion, in Luke Nazareth is the point of departure for the whole ministry of Jesus; it is the way in which his neighbors renounce Jesus that sends him out on his mission described in Luke 4:16–30. Also in Matthew the christological geography[18] is not confined to chapters 1—2. The thought expressed in 2:22f. is reinforced as the point of departure for the whole ministry of Jesus also in Matt. 4:12–17; but now it is not Nazareth[19] that counts, but Galilee, and in accordance with Mark 1:21, Matthew sees Capernaum as the center of Jesus' Galilean ministry. The transfer to Capernaum is substantiated in the phrase ὁδὸν θαλάσσης (4:15, RSV: "toward the sea"). Yet, in Matthew 2 the issue was of a more specific nature: Bethlehem-Nazareth.[20]

Granted that we have found the correct key to the composition of Matthew 2, however, there remains the far-more-complicated questions concerning the origin, form, and nature of the material that Matthew has made use of. It looks as if the story about the Magi, which has many striking features of its own, has already, prior to Matthew's use of the material, been an integral part of an account where *der Kampf des*

74

Königs gegen den Christus[21] is described in a language which draws on the similar motif in Exodus.[22] This assumption is strengthened by the mentioning of Herod's name nine times, and at all points of progress in the account, even after his death (v. 22). Nevertheless, in its Matthean form the chapter answers the question "Bethlehem-Nazareth," and it does so for apologetic purposes.

Such an understanding of Matthew 2 would also serve to elucidate two famous problems regarding Matt. 2:1–12: (1) It has remained a puzzling fact that this pericope has no explicit reference to the star-prophecy in Num. 24:17. This prophecy, of messianic significance both in Judaism and the early Christian testimonies,[23] seems to lie just under the surface in the Matthean account.[24] Now we can explain why it remains there, since the formula quotations here are organized only to serve the geographical account. (2) The unique way in which the Bethlehem quotation lacks the usual Matthean introductory formula is easier to understand if we see the apologetic tension between "Bethlehem as expected" and "Nazareth as revealed." This coincides with the situation of John 7, to which we have just referred.

Once it has been recognized how chapter 2 is totally focused in its *geographical* names, it appears that chapter 1 has not only a similarly apologetic purpose,[25] but also a similar structure, now centered around *personal* names. Already the way in which the two chapters end on a similar note and in a similar form points in this direction: ὅ τι Ναζω-ραῖος κληθήσεται / ἐκάλεσεν τὸ ὄνομα αὐτοῦ 'Ιησοῦν. We have mentioned the striking absence of any geographical names in chapter 1.[26] Of greater significance is the observation that from the point of view of literary form, Matt. 1:18–25 could be called a legend of divine name giving.[27] The revelation of the angel and Joseph's obedient answer are the nucleus of the pericope. Verses 18–19 give the background; note the ἰδού ("behold") in v. 20, preceded by the summarizing: "When he had come to such a decision . . . " The formula quotation from Isa. 7:14 should be understood as not belonging to the message of the angel. It is Matthew's interpretative comment, which is in agreement with all the other formula quotations in Matthew.[28] As a divine giving of the name, 1:18–25 has its genuine Matthean point of climax in its last words, as had chapter 2.

Most commentators give the disposition of Matthew 1—2 by drawing a decisive line of demarcation between the genealogy (1:1–17) and the Matthean birth narrative (1:18—2:25).[29] This is a striking example of Lucan influence upon Matthean exegeses. But it should be recognized that the whole of chapter 1 has its own integrity and that the line of demarcation really lies between the chapters. The genealogy in its Matthean form points to what follows in 1:18–25 by its accentuation of the Davidic line. This is clear from the way in which David is epitomized in verses 1 and 17, possibly also by the formula "three times fourteen," where David *(dwd)* equals $4+6+4=14;$[30] and in 1:6 the royal status of David, and only of David, is stressed.

The link between the genealogy and verses 18–25 is more specific because of the mention of the four women: Tamar, Rahab, Ruth, and Bath-Sheba. The common denominator for these four women is found in that they all represent an "irregularity" in the Davidic line. It is not only an irregularity that is overcome by God's recognition of them as mothers of Davidic descendants, but also an irregularity by which the action of God and his Spirit is made manifest.[31] However, as was the case in olden times, such divine interventions lead to slander from the contemporaries who do not understand the ways of the Lord. In this light Matthew presents his apologetic argument about how Jesus was engrafted into the Davidic pedigree.

This argument is introduced by the phrase: Τοῦ δὲ Ἰησοῦ Χριστοῦ ἡ γένεσις οὕτως ἦν. The unusual word order[32] indicates that Matthew consciously refers back to the constellation of the name Jesus and the title Christ in verse 16 (Ἰησοῦς ὁ λεγόμενος Χριστός). Matthew is now to explain the details of this last point of the genealogy, a point where the nature of the case has caused a rather complicated formulation.[33] He says: But as for this last link in the genealogy "Jesus[34] Christ," his origin[35] was on this wise. Thus already the syntactical form of verse 18a indicates that verses 18–25 are the enlarged footnote to the crucial point in the genealogy. The usual translation "Now the birth of Jesus Christ was on this wise"[36] is under Lucan influence as is definitely the title for example, in Huck's synopsis "The Birth of Jesus." As a matter of fact, the birth of Jesus is not described in Matthew, where the points are rather the angelic revelation to Joseph, and the naming of the child eight days after its birth?; cf. Luke 2:21. Schlatter has been more sensitive to the Matthean material in 1:18–25 when he calls the pericope *Die Einpflanzung Jesu in das Geschlecht Davids.*[37] This engrafting is described with considerable precision, in a way aimed at overcoming slanderous remarks by placing Joseph in that same attitude of suspicion, and by showing how Joseph's hesitation was overcome by the angelic revelation. Hence the suspicion is not that Joseph should have been the actual father of the child, but that Mary should have deceived him.[38] But even this rebuttal is secondary to Matthew's intention. The genuine point is that the child is a Davidic child. Thereby Jesus' place in the genealogy is explained. God has ordered this engrafting. Furthermore, the name Jesus is shown to be according to God's order. On both these points Joseph is explicitly reported to have obeyed: he takes Mary to his wife and gives her child the name "Jesus." The fact that the name "Jesus" is interpreted directly, without translation, has been used in favor of a Semitic source.[39] This is by no means necessary. That Jesus meant "Savior" could have been presupposed knowledge; gospels are not missionary material. The reason could also be of a more formal nature: an angelic message should not be loaded with interpretive comments of the sort which quite naturally could well be attached to Immanuel, since this verse is in itself a commentary added by the evangelist. The Spirit or an angel neither quotes nor exegizes.[40]

If we were to take our key from chapter 2 strictly, we could surmise that the salient point in the quotation from Isa. 7:14 was Immanuel, that is, the personal name; such an understanding would also make the explicit translation of Immanuel as "God with us" natural. Then the "a virgin shall conceive and bear a son" would be the *basis* for the application of the title "Immanuel," not the point itself.[41] That Immanuel is meant by Matthew as a title is clear from the plural καλέσουσιν, "They (=one) will call him . . . "—this against all known OT texts.[42] It should be noted that, while Isa. 7:14 was not—as far as we know—used as a messianic prophecy in Judaism, it stands within the Davidic line. And the title "Immanuel" underscores the messianic function of Jesus, who is to set his (!) people free from their sins. In short, the Immanuel prophecy substantiates the significance of the name "Jesus" as expressed in verse 21, an interesting and typically Matthean contrast to the easy conflation in Luke 1:31![43]

The two messianic/christological designations—Jesus and Immanuel—lead us to consider finally the relation of Matthew 1:18–25 to the biblical witness of the virgin birth. It is obvious that the supernatural birth of Jesus was known to Matthew, and the tradition was apparently known well enough to have given rise to slanderous remarks. But it is equally clear that Matthew is not announcing the birth story. Furthermore, in Matthew the virgin birth story is theologically mute: no christological argument or insight is deduced from this great divine intervention. There is little reason to read the Immanuel prophecy in the direction of "incarnation." The context suggests rather a Jewish, messianic understanding. In Jesus' messianic deeds God visits his people and sets them free from the hardships which their sins have justly caused. One could even raise the question whether Matthew has thought of this intervention of God through the Spirit as an absolutely "unique" event. Does he not see it as a glorious heightening of the divine interventions of old, by which God proved faithful to his covenant with Abraham and his promises to David? This last event causes everything to fall into the prophetical pattern of messianic fulfillment: born through divine intervention, recognized by Joseph, and thereby the Son of David, he is given the name "Jesus," that is, he comes with the bliss of the age to come—Immanuel.

These names are matters that count with Matthew. And they deserve attention and defense;[44] as did the tension between Bethlehem and Nazareth. Thus Matthew's first two chapters substantiate and defend the decisive names (chap. 1) and the locale (chap. 2) of the messianic event. It is only under such circumstances that we can understand Matthew's transition to the Markan material by the phrase: "In those days John the Baptist appeared . . . "[45] If Matthew had thought of what he had given in chapters 1—2 as an account of events, such a link would presuppose either a carelessness or a slavish and automatic combination of sources, which we do not find congenial to the Matthean procedure in general. If the point in chapters 1—2 is the one we have suggested, it makes good sense, since here in chapter 3 begins the "account," the "events." That account is prefaced by an apologetic and scriptural answer to the question: *Quis et Unde?* Strictly speaking there is nothing that could be called the Matthean "birth narrative" or *Vorgeschichte*, if we are to remain faithful to the Matthean intention in his gospel.

NOTES

1. This may or may not be what Luke is actually aiming at. In any case, he differs substantially from Matthew in the epic breadth; this is in accordance with his introductory remarks (1:1-4) and manifests itself already in chaps. 1—2. The descriptive element goes together with the explicit stress on the place of the event in Jewish history (1:5) and world history (2:1; cf. 3:1-2). See further M. Dibelius, "Jungfrauensohn und Krippenkind," *SHA Phil.—hist. Kl.* 22:4, 1932 (=M. Dibelius, *Botschaft und Geschichte I*, 1953, 1-78). The tendency to *describe* what originally was *believed* is one of the creative forces in the development of nativity gospels; see O. Cullmann, "Kindheitsevangelien," in E. Hennecke, *Neutestamentliche Apokryphen* (1959³), 272-74. It is significant that

Luke—not Matthew—shows the first signs of "filling in the gaps" in the historical continuum (Luke 2:40, the visit to Jerusalem at the age of twelve; and 2:52). It is also only in Luke that the virgin birth serves as an explicit reason for Jesus being Son of God: διὸ (1:35); see H. Conzelmann, *Die Mitte der Zeit* (*Beitr. z. hist. Theol.* 17, 1954[1]), 148f. Dibelius summarizes the aim of the Lucan account: "Die beiden Legenden vom Jungfrauensohn und vom Krippenkind verdeutlichen so die beiden Tendenzen christlicher Predigt: das Wunder der Erlösung zu beschreiben bald als übermenschliche Erscheinung, die das Gesetz menschlicher Lebensvorgänge ausser Kraft setzt, bald als Gabe Gottes in den engen Raum irdischen Daseins," in "Jungfrauensohn," 80 (78). For a more recent analysis of Luke 2:1–20 as a totality, see K. H. Rengstorf, "Die Weihnachtserzählung des Evangelisten Lukas," in *Stat crux dum volvitur orbis* (Festschr. H. Lilje, 1959), 5–30; cf. also R. McL. Wilson, "Some Recent Studies in the Lucan Infancy Narratives," in *TU* 73 (1959), 235–53, esp. its reference to R. Laurentin, "Traces d'allusions etymologiques en Luc 1–2," *Biblica* 37 (1956): 435–56; 38 (1957): 1–23; also *Structure et Théologie de Luc 1–2* (Paris, 1957).

2. The two major studies of the virgin birth both agree in taking their point of departure in Luke, treating Matthew as corroborating, or supplementary, material: V. Taylor, *The Historical Evidence for the Virgin Birth* (1920); J. G. Machen, *The Virgin Birth of Christ* (1930); cf. F. Kattenbusch's extensive review in *Theologische Studien und Kritiken* 102 (1930): 454–74. More sensitive attention is given to the Matthean material by K. Bornhäuser, *Die Geburts- und Kindheitsgeschichte Jesu* (Beitr. z. Förderung christl. Theol., R. 2:23, 1930) and, to some extent, G. Erdmann, *Die Vorgeschichten des Lukas- und Matthäusevangeliums und Vergils vierte Ekloge* (FRLANT, N.F. 30, 1932), but even so they seem to labor under Lucan "*Vorverständnis.*"

3. κατ' ὄναρ : 1:20; 2:12, 13, 19, 22; see also about Pilate's wife, 27:19. In Acts the term used is ὅραμα διὰ νυκτός or similar, 16:9, 18:9.

4. This does not follow with absolute necessity from Matt. 2:1, where a harmonizing exegesis could make a case for Nazareth *e silentio*; the line of demarcation to be drawn between chaps. 1 and 2 (see above, pp. 1–44) further minimizes the possibility of such an argument. But 2:22–23 remains the decisive stumbling block for such harmonization: to Matthew Galilee and Nazareth are new data, divinely revealed and prophetically announced.

5. See P. Benoit, "L'enfance de Jean-Baptiste selon Luc 1," *New Testament Studies* 3 (1956/57): 191–94. It may be of some significance for further study of the Lukan material that it thus deals with *two* messianic figures, one priestly and one royal. For the assessment of John-Jesus, see J. A. T. Robinson, "Elijah, John and Jesus: An Essay in Detection," *New Testament Studies* 4 (1957/58): 263–81.

6. The genealogy is, in its own way, of a similar nature, v. 17 forming virtually a statement of fulfillment.

7. Apart from the strong allusion to Isa. 7:14 in Luke 1:31; cf. Matt. 1:21, 23; there is no clear coincidence in quotations between Matthew and Luke. For an ingenious but hardly convincing relation between Matt. 2:23 and Luke, see B. Gärtner, *Die rätselhaften Termini Nazaräer und Iskariot* (Horae Soederblomianae 4, 1957), 8–18.

8. See B. W. Bacon, *Studies in Matthew* (1930), 154–64. A detailed argument for different sources and a minimum of Matthean activity has been given by W. L. Knox, *The Sources of the Synoptic Gospels* II (1957), 121–28. His argument forces him to split the formula quotations in Matthew between different sources and subsequent stages in the development of the gospel.

9. Bacon, *Studies in Matthew*, 155—following Streeter—stresses this "para-site-nature" of the Matthean material. There are also more internal reasons for ruling out the possibility that the quotations gave impetus to creating facts, events, or legends; see K. Stendahl, *The School of St. Matthew* (1954), 194–202.

10. Except in the phrase τῆς μετοικεσίας Βαβυλῶνος in 1:11, 12, 17, which serves as a temporal designation.

11. In the fourth quotation (2:13) there is no alternative; for the purely geographical meaning of Ναζωραῖος in Matthew, see below, note 17.

12. I.e., in the actual saying, but "Ramah" is retained in the fuller exposition of the verse.

13. On the identification of Ramah-Ephrath(a)-Bethlehem, see Joachim Jeremias, *Heiligengräber in Jesu Umwelt* (1958), 75.

14. On the treatment of geographical names in the LXX, see I. L. Seeligmann, *The Septuagint Version of Isaiah* (Mededeligen en Verhandeligen van het Vooraziatisch-Egyptisch Genootschap "Ex Orient Lux" 9, 1948), 76ff.

15. Cf. also 7:52. Bultmann, *Komm. Joh.*, 231^2, goes as far as to say: "Von der Bethlehemgeburt Jesu weiss also der Evangelist nichts, oder will er nichts wissen"; against this see C. K. Barrett, *Comm. John*. It seems reasonable to see the Johannine attitude as one where "Bethlehem" is an adiaphoron; the Johannine answer is rather to be found in John 1:46 where the question "Can anything good come out of Nazareth?" is met by the answer "Come and see."

16. G. K. Kilpatrick, *The Origins of the Gospel According to Matthew* (1946), 54, phrases the question: "If Jesus, commonly associated with Nazareth, really belonged to Bethlehem, how came he to spend by far the greatest part of his life at Nazareth?" But the length of residence is of no interest to Matthew (cf. above, note 1); only "Nazareth" and the Galilean point of departure, which is implied, are important.

17. For our argument at this point the discussion about Ναζωραῖος/Ναζαρηνός as sectarian or geographical designation is of no consequence. To Matthew the issue is purely geographical. For the latest discussion of this problem and of the source for the quotation, see B. Gärtner, *Die rätselhaften Termini*, and A. Medebielle, "Quoniam Nazaraenus vocabitur," *Studia Anselmiana* 27–28 (1956/57): 136–39. Ναζαρηνός could be considered a (Markan) Latinism, so Bacon, *Studies in Matthew*, 164; cf. the way in which the different writers use ἐσσηνοί/*esseni* (Josephus mostly, and Pliny) and ἐσσαῖοι (Philo), see W. Bauer, in Pauly-Wissowa, *RE*, Supp. 4 (1924), 419.

18. W. Schmauch, *Orte der Offenbarung und der Offenbarungsort im Neuen Testament* (1956), is of little help at this point, since his thesis is to show "dass die Orte der Offenbarung nur deswegen wie im wesenlosen Schein versinken, weil die Offenbarung auch ihren geographischen Ort so in sich einbezieht, dass sein Name nicht mehr und nicht einmal in erster Linie an dem irdischen Ort haftet,

sondern dem Träger der Offenbarung selbst unmittelbar verbunden wird" (26). Schmauch recognizes other elements in Matthew (15), but takes his refuge in the Johannine material to substantiate his thesis (16f.).

19. The reading Ναζαρά (B pc k) in Matt. 4:13, accepted by Tischendorf and Westcott-Hort, is doubtful, see A. Schlatter, *Der Evangelist Matthäus* (1959[5]). Influence from Luke 4:16?

20. Thus the structure of Matthew 2 lies even closer to the core of the discussion "Galiläa und Jerusalem" than its two independent protagonists suggested. E. Lohmeyer, *Galiläa und Jerusalem* (FRLANT, N.F. 34, 1936), and R. H. Lightfoot, *Locality and Doctrine* (1938), e.g., 115. The more recent contribution to this discussion, L. E. Elliott-Binns, *Galilean Christianity* (Studies in Biblical Theology 16, 1956) has hardly fostered the discussion since it moves from the specific into even more uncontrolled generalities.

21. See Schlatter, *Der Evangelist Matthäus*, 25.

22. The Exodus imprint is seen especially in the unexpected—hardly generalizing: Blass-Debrunner, *Grammatik* (1937[7]), §141—plural οἱ ζητοῦντες (v. 20; Exod. 4:19), and the more general suggestiveness of Moses/Jesus, and Egypt-Land of Israel, see J. Jeremias, *ThWBzNT*, IV, 874f. The Jewish background to the whole chapter is however of a broader nature since similar patterns of events have clustered around Abraham, see Strack-Billerbeck I, 77f.; cf. *Jewish Encyclopaedia* I, 86; and Laban-Jacob, see D. Daube, *The New Testament and Rabbinic Judaism* (1956), 189ff.; cf. L. Finkelstein, *Harvard Theological Review* 31 (1938): 299f.

23. See E. Burrows, *The Oracles of Jacob and Balaam* (1939), 71–100; and for Qumran and the Damascus Document, A. S. Van der Woude, *Die messianischen Vorstellungen der Gemeinde von Qumran* (Studia Semitica Neerlandica 3, 1957), e.g., 212ff., et index sub Numbers 24:24:17; cf. F. M. Cross, Jr., *The Ancient Library of Qumran* (1958), 169, on the star as the priestly Messiah at Qumran.

24. See Stendahl, *School of St. Mattahew*, 136.

25. This is generally recognized for 1:18–25; for 1:1–17 see below, concerning the reference to the four women.

26. See above, p. 73; cf. Klostermann, *Komm. Mt.* ad 1:18: "Ort und Zeit . . . bleibt im Dunkel."

27. Cf. Gen. 16:11, 15; 17:19; 21:3; and also Judg. 13:3; Strack-Billerbeck I, 63. This aspect is stressed by R. Bultmann, *Gesch. d. synopt. Trad.* (1931[2]), 317.

28. The sole example to the contrary would be in 2:6, a quotation placed on the lips of the scribes; see, however, the end of the preceding paragraph.

29. See, e.g., W. C. Allen, *Comm. Mt.*; A. H. McNeile, *Comm. Mt.*; and especially Lohmeyer, *Komm. Mt.* I earlier followed this common and, at first glance, obvious approach, see *Peake's Commentary* (1962), ed. H. H. Rowley and M. Black, 771. Schlatter, *Der Evangelist Matthäus*, comes closer to the truth, but does not capitalize on the distinction between Matthew 1 and 2, this partly due to his overall theme for these chapters: "Gottes Werk bei der Geburt Jesu," which gives a misleading emphasis to the "events."

30. On this and other aspects of the Matthean genealogy see J. Jeremias, *Jerusalem zur Zeit Jesu* II B (1937), 163ff. A fresh approach to the genealogies as means of historical writing has been made by O. Linton in a penetrating and

pioneering study, *Synopsis historiae universalis* (Copenhagen, 1957).

31. That this is the only possible interpretation has been demonstrated beyond doubt, with special attention to Tamar, by Renée Bloch, "Juda engendra Pharès et Zara, de Thamar," *Mélanges A. Robert* (1957), 381–89. This against G. Kittel in *ThWBzNT* III, 1f.

32. See Blass-Debrunner, *Grammatik* (1937[7]), Anh., 46 (ad §271), cf. Matt. 10:2. Yet in 1:18 the relation to the preceding is even stronger, since not only Ἰησοῦ Χριστοῦ but also ἡ γένεσις is taken from the preceding context, see note 35.

33. See F. C. Burkitt, *Evangelion Da-Mepharreshe* II (1904), 262.

34. Omitted by, e.g., Klostermann and Lohmeyer, mainly on the basis of syr[sin cur] (also 71 latt). The textual problems are here of a sort that cannot be solved apart from exegesis. Hence we would argue for the reading Ἰησοῦ Χριστοῦ on the basis of our interpretation, and we do so in fundamental agreement with Burkitt's penetrating textual analysis, *Evangelion Da-Mepharreshe*, 260–65.

35. I read γένεσις, and take it to retain its genealogical sense (cf. Matt. 1:1), Luke 1:14 notwithstanding; this is the natural sense in Matthew if we were not under the sway of Lukan and traditional "Christmas-pressure." On Βίβλος γενέσεως (Matt. 1:1), see also the extensive study by M. Lambertz in *Festschrift F. Dornseiff* (1953), 201–25, and J. Lindblom, "Matteusevangeliets överskrift," *Teologiska studier tillägnade E. Stave* (1922), 102–9. O. Eissfeldt, "Biblos geneseos," in *Gott und die Götter* (Festgabe E. Fascher, 1958), observes that the toledot-formula signifies "deutlich Punkte, an denen eine Verengung des Gesichtkreises eintritt" (34), and on the basis of Matt. 1:18 he understands Βίβλος γενέοεως as "Urkunde des Ursprungs" (36).

36. See the King James Version, which is representative of most translations including the RSV: cf. Klostermann: "Mit der Geburt des Messias verhält es sich aber so"; Lohmeyer: "Christi Geburt geschah also."

37. Schlatter, *Der Evangelist Matthäus*, 7.

38. X. Léon-Dufour, "L'annonce à Josèph," *Mélanges A. Robert* (1957), 390–97, follows the same line as Schlatter, *Der Evangelist Matthäus*, 15, in interpreting Joseph's attitude as one where awe and piety make him hesitate in taking Mary to his wife. But within this interpretation he makes significant observations about Joseph's role as the "namegiver" and the Davidic link.

39. On the complicated problem of Aramaic/Hebrew at this point, and for the general discussion see P. Nepper-Christensen, *Das Matthäusevangelium—Ein judenchristliches Evangelium?* (Acta Theologica Danica I, 1958), 84ff. Furthermore, Matt. 1:21, Luke 1:77 cannot be considered as a conscious allusion to Psalm 130 (129):8, as claimed by Kilpatrick, *Origins of the Gospel*, 54; see rather Knox, *Sources*, 126 n.1.

40. Stendahl, *School of St. Matthew*, 159; cf. Luke 1:31.

41. This "basis" is of course not insignificant in the total context. Note the additional ὅλον ("*all* this") in the introductory formula (cf. 26:56) which shows that the quotation sums up a whole chain of data. Nevertheless, it remains legitimate to ask where Matthew saw the point in this formula quotation.

42. Stendahl, *School of St. Matthew*, 97f. Luke 1:31: χαλέσεις (thou shalt call . . .) = LXX.

43. The observations made by W. C. van Unnik concerning "Jesus" and "Immanuel" would, on the whole, strengthen such an interpretation; see his article "Dominus vobiscum" in A. J. B. Higgins, ed., *New Testament Essays*, in memoriam T. W. Manson (1959), 287f., and notes 58 and 59.

44. Again it is in the fourth gospel that we find the closest affinity to this attitude; cf. above, p. 74 on the locale. John 1:19–51, and esp. vv. 35–51, could be best understood as a conscious syllabus on the names and the titles of Jesus: (Christ, Elijah, Prophet) Lamb of God, Rabbi (with Greek translation), Messiah (with Greek translation), "Him of whom Moses wrote in the Law, as did the prophets," Jesus from Nazareth (cf. above, note 15), Son of Joseph, Son of God, King of Israel, Son of man. Even the Prologue, and thus the whole first chapter, could be seen from this angel of names and titles; cf. W. Bauer, *Komm. Joh.* ad 1:41, and H. Windisch, *ZNW* 30 (1931): 218. For such affinities between the Johannine and Matthean structure and problematic, it is of significance that John comes by far closest to the formula quotations. Nepper-Christensen, *Das Matthäusevangelium*, 142f., 161f., has stressed this fact and used it to show that the Matthean formula quotations are relatively insignificant as decisive clues to the Matthean *Sitz im Leben*. He wants to see them rather as part of "Tatsachenberichte" (153). Our present study has driven us in the opposite direction by indicating that actually the "names," not the "events," are what matters. Consequently we must enforce our earlier suggestion that the common denominator between Matthew and John should be explained within the framework of the primitive Christian "schools," cf. Stendahl, *School of St. Matthew*, 163. Nor should it be forgotten that the primitive Christian claim was one about "names," Acts 4:12, *et passim*. The formulation in Acts 18:15, "but since it is a matter of questions about words and names" (περὶ λόγου καὶ ὀνομάτων) points in the same direction; so W. Bauer, *Wörterbuch* (1952⁴), ὄνομα III, col. 1042; cf. H. Bietenhard, *ThWBzNT* V, 270. Lake and Cadbury (*Beginnings of Christianity* I:IV, 228) take the opposite view: "talk and words," ὄνομα being the grammatical term for "noun"; cf. however, 18:5: "that the Messiah was Jesus," with Lake-Cadbury's comment.

45. "In those days . . . " without an antecedent is actually like the phrase "Once upon a time . . . " And some manuscripts (D it syr ^sin cur^) have no connecting δέ, thereby sharpening the discontinuity between chaps. 1—2 and what now begins in chap. 3.

6

Messianic License:
The Sermon on the Mount

Introductory Note: This essay was written in 1962 for a consultation under the auspices of the Fellowship of Reconciliation where people from traditional peace churches and from the mainline denominations together faced questions of war and peace and conscientious objection—a sharp issue indeed as the Vietnam War began to escalate. It was published in *Biblical Realism Confronts the Nation*, ed. Paul Peachy (New York: Fellowship of Reconciliation, 1963).

I think the points made here about the Sermon on the Mount constitute a level of meaning in the eschatological shape of Matthew's tradition. I have come to wonder, however, whether Matthew did not actually give this tradition a different and less eschatological setting by presenting the Sermon on the Mount rather as a demonstration of Christian ethics as superior and more penetrating than Jewish ethics (cf. the Preface to the second edition of my *The School of St. Matthew* [Philadelphia: Fortress Press, 1968]). A striking parallel to such a shift from a high eschatological pitch to a more pleasing ethical discourse is found in Josephus's account of the Essenes, see below, notes 2 and 16 in the essay on "Hate, Nonretaliation, and Love," pp. 137–50.

Matthew has an unusual gift of retaining the level of his tradition while at the same time making his own moves of style and meanings.

In his recent study of the Sermon on the Mount, Harvey K. McArthur[1] has rendered good service by giving us a clear classification of the different approaches toward the Sermon on the Mount through the ages; he has also furnished us with a fresh and rich collection of quotations, which actually amounts to a rather precise history of the interpretation of these bewilderingly significant chapters of Matthew's gospel.

He identifies not less than twelve main lines of interpretation of the Sermon as it applies to ethics. Hence anyone would hesitate, or even feel arrogant, if he were to add a thirteenth alternative. Yet I am encouraged to do so since I find McArthur's approach somewhat unsatisfactory on methodological grounds, when he in his last chapters attempts an eclectic solution.

When we thus begin with a critique of McArthur, we do so since his study at the same time registers the pulse of much contemporary Christian life and thought in these matters.[2] He divides the twelve approaches into two groups: six views of secondary value and six views of primary value. While this method may make immediate sense to our feelings and predilections as twentieth-century Westerners, it is worth noting that the views of "secondary value," on the one hand, are by and large the ones that are closest to rigorous descriptive and historical attempts to understand Jesus in his first-century setting. The views of "primary value," on the other hand, are mainly those that are less conscious of the distance between Jesus' situation and ours, but that consciously or unconsciously treat scriptural material as timeless truth, unconditioned by changes or developments within history or within the history of salvation.

This becomes especially clear when McArthur without much ado relegates "the modern dispensationalist view"—as, for example, in the Scofield Reference Bible—to the lowest place in the "secondary value" group: "I cannot regard [it] as shedding any light on the interpretation of the Sermon" (139). This view makes a distinction between the kingdom dispensation, to which the Sermon on the Mount has primary application, and the dispensation of grace (in which Christians now live), to which the Sermon has only secondary application. I would agree that in Scofield's form this is a misleading interpretation, but this should not eclipse the fact that this interpretation is the one which makes use of the most significant elements of the messianic and eschatological fabric of the NT.

The other "secondary value" views include Schweitzer's "interim ethic," which was a conscious approach to break through later Western developments in order to recapture the strange and shocking eschatological setting of Jesus' teaching. The "modification" approach may be evidenced already in the first century by Matthew's exception clause, not found in Mark's command about divorce (Matt. 5:32; 19:9; cf. Mark 10:11–12). The "double standard" approach with its distinction between "precepts," (which are binding upon all) and "evangelical counsel" (which are meant only for some) can be easily criticized when those "some" became identified with the clergy and the monasteries; but even McArthur has to admit that the distinction as such is well substantiated in the NT (e.g., 1 Corinthians 7; cf. also *Didache* 6:2f.). Luther's interpretations of the "two realms" are more attractive to McArthur. "With great reluctance I must place [it] in the list of interpretations of 'secondary value'" (133). His reluctance may be due to the fact that this view seems to be more removed from the first-century issues, as are all of his "primary value" views. But the "distinction between the two realms" is only a systematic and ahistorical theological translation, or transposition, of the original NT awareness of dispensations and personal differences, which also underlies dispensationalism, interim ethic, and precepts/counsels. Finally the use of analogy from Scripture in order to tone down the "difficult" passages in the Sermon on the Mount is the oldest and most obvious method in the history of religious interpretation. While it has—and should have—little attraction to modern interpreters with a sense for historical criticism, it is an approach that belongs to the very age in which the Sermon was written down.

Hence we find that McArthur—unconsciously, I am sure—has given secondary significance to those approaches that unearth, or express, the issues of the first century. Conversely he has listed as of primary significance those views that presuppose a more philosophical or theological or social or literary awareness: The Absolutist View (à la Tolstoy); Hyperbole; General Principles; Attitudes/Not Acts; Repentance; Unconditioned Divine Will. In this group the last alternative is that of Martin Dibelius. It is the one closest to the temper of contemporary theology with its dialectic stress of the unconditioned divine will on the one hand, and on the other hand the stress that this will, should not, and cannot be fulfilled as a law, since the "Christian Law does not demand of us that we *do something* but that we *be something.*"[3] When exposed to such an interpretation it is worth remembering that the dialectic mood may well be a useful contemporary technique to hold biblical teaching in balance, but that such a dialectic has its root not in Jesus' teaching but in the tension between statements, that in the actual ministry of Jesus were given in specific situations and to individuals, and in the problems that face the Christian consciousness of Western twentieth-century man.

The fact that Albert Schweitzer's insistence on an eschatological understanding of the Sermon on the Mount took the positive form of an "interim ethic" has had a somewhat unfortunate impact on the later discussion. The issue became "interim" *or* universal and timeless validity. This alternative, coupled with the constant Christian concern for proving the superiority of Jesus over against Judaism, has made it difficult to discuss the Sermon in the light of the Jewish question: What is to happen to the Law—the Torah—when the Messiah comes? In more recent times this question has received much attention. In 1952 W. D. Davies devoted a monograph to this subject,[4] and H. J. Schoeps has furthered Pauline studies by making this issue central to the understanding of Paul.[5] In this he followed up the intimations of Albert Schweitzer.[6] The Qumran texts have given us access to a new angle from which to view the Sermon, and H. Braun has made a thorough comparison between the "Sharpening of the Law" (*Toraverschärfung*) in the Qumran texts then available (the Manual of Discipline, the Habakkuk Commentary, and the Damascus Document) and the NT.[7] Hence there is a fair amount of material available for a discussion of the Sermon on the Mount in the light of a question that is authentic to the Jewish community in which Jesus lived and taught. We are not limited to arbitrary and atomistic quotations of isolated ethical statements of Judaism. We may be able to recapture the framework in which this kind of ethical issue had to be discussed in first-century Judaism.

It is a common view in Christian thought that the Pharisees constitute the epitome of strict legalism. Their attitude is often described in accordance with the principle *fiat justitia, pereat mundus,* let justice have its way, even if the world is destroyed in the process. But if one interprets the Pharisees along such lines, he overlooks the fact that one of the principles which guided the Pharisees in their interpretation of the Torah was actually driving them in the opposite direction. They were in fact the ones who argued, against, for example, the Sadducees, for the right of innovation and adaptation. They could justify such procedures by quoting Ps. 119:126—with a different twist from the Masoretic text—as saying "It is time to do something for the Lord."[8] Such new interpretations grew out of the conviction that the Torah was "livable," and hence it could not require anything which proved to be obviously impossible or detrimental to the life of the people. The classical example of such adaptations was the so-called *prosbul*, a legal fiction devised and argued by Hillel, by which the law of Deut. 15:1–3 (all loans should be cancelled at the beginning of every seventh year) was bypassed. As it read in the Torah it had become a serious threat to economic development.[9] In the Talmud this principle reaches the point where it is laid down by rabbinical authority that a decree is not to be imposed on the public unless the majority are able to abide by it.[10]

In the Qumran material, including the Damascus Document, we find the designation "seekers [or: interpreters] of smooth things" presumably with reference to the Pharisees (CD i, 18; 1 Q ii, 15, 32; 4 QpNah. 2; cf. Isa. 30:10). It is quite possible to relate this term to the tendency of which we have just spoken, since the Qumran texts give precise examples of a more strict interpretation than that of the Pharisees, for example, in the matter of rescuing animals on the Sabbath (CD xi, 14) and in marriage laws (no sexual intercourse in Jerusalem, CD xii, 1–2; no marriage with a niece, v. 8).

Such criticism of the Pharisees for an interpretation which tampers with the strict words of the Torah is not lacking in the clashes between Jesus and his opponents in the gospels. The best-known example is the discussion about divorce (Mark 10:2–9). Here a "sharpening of the law" is carried out in an even-more-drastic fashion by applying the principle of the supremacy of earlier decrees in the Torah as superior to later ones. The divorce decree in Deut. 24:1 is secondary and motivated by the hardness of men's hearts: it was a concession given through Moses; but the pure will of God which is from the beginning demands a union between man and wife, which cannot be dissolved.[11] It is significant to note that Paul uses the same type of argument when he establishes the unchangeable priority of the promise to Abraham over against the law given later through the mediator Moses on Sinai, a law which is conditioned by the sins of Israel ("it was added because of transgressions"), and which hence cannot claim to be the ultimate and unconditioned expression of God's true plan and nature (Gal. 3:15–20).

Thus even the law decreed through Moses can be seen as a concession, a step in the direction of pragmatic awareness of the possible and the livable. This is however unusual, and we are more familiar with the distinction between the Torah and the injunctions prescribed by the Pharisees. Such a distinction appears self-evident to us, but we should remember that the written Torah and the oral Torah were one entity in the minds of the Pharisees, and both had their roots in Moses' revelation. Nevertheless Jesus seems to have criticized the latter as "human tradition" (Mark 7:8), and his critique is striking since it is not motivated by saying: "you make it too hard for people," but by pointing out how such tradition leads to a cancellation of the actual commandments of the law: the giving toward Corban overrules the commandment to honor father and mother (Mark 7:9–13).

In Matthew 23—the discourse against the Pharisees—there is a more advanced and systematic handling of these issues. While the tone and the composition are peculiar to Matthew, it agrees at many points with the picture we can draw on the basis of the Markan material. Again, the shortcoming of the Pharisees is not in their demands, which are accepted on principle—"whatever they teach you, you should do and keep" (v. 3)—but the hypocritical element as, for example, in the matter of oaths. "The smooth interpreters" had recognized that there had to be some room for oaths. Hence they made distinctions that kept the most holy things out of the area of oaths (the Temple and the altar) while allowing oaths by matters related to these (the gold of the Temple and the gift on the altar). In language of irony the words of Jesus claim that such distinctions are ridiculous in the eyes of God and/or in the light of common sense (23:16–22).

Some of the above examples, but especially this last one, bring us close to material contained in the Sermon on the Mount. In Matt. 5:33–37, in one of the five antitheses, all swearing is dispensed with while Lev. 19:12 speaks only against *false* oaths. Apparently contemporary Judaism had moved in the same direction, in its ever-growing awe toward using God's name. Judging from this passage one had settled for "heaven" or "earth" or "Jerusalem," or "one's head," but again Jesus' words argue for these as tantamount to God himself. No clever, softening interpretations are allowed.

In the light of our observations the much-debated saying in Matt. 5:20 becomes as clear and as natural as one could desire: "If your righteousness does not go beyond that of the scribes and the Pharisees, you shall not enter into the kingdom of heaven" (au. trans.). Most difficulties in the interpretation of this programmatic sentence emanate from the presupposition that the "scribes and the Pharisees" were already the champions of an extreme rigor in the obedience of the law. But we have seen that their obedience, including "the fence around the law" (*M. Abot* i, 1), was built on a principle of accommodation. It is against such "smooth interpretations" that Jesus is reported to speak, and the five antitheses in Matthew 5, give ample support to such an understanding.

It is, however, too easy for many Christian interpreters to glorify Jesus' searching consistency over against the Pharisees at this point. The more one takes for granted that Jesus' ethic is superior *qua ethic*, the more he finds himself entangled in the discussions whether the Sermon on the Mount is "possible" or not, or whether it is meant to be "possible," or whether it has as its point the promulgation of the will of God as being by definition beyond humankind's capacity, and so forth. The often hopeless confusion of such discussions should open our eyes to the deep and serious level on which the Pharisaic ethic was elaborated. Once in a discussion about these matters with a rabbi who knew a good deal about the NT and the history of Christianity, I was much helped when he stated his views somewhat like this: the trouble and the glory of Christianity is that the church and the Christians for some reason think that the principles of the age to come can be applied already in this age. The Jews also know of a time in which the prophecy in Jer. 31:31ff. shall come true, when the law shall be within us, written upon our hearts, a time that will be characterized by that messianic fulfillment to which Jesus witnessed in the Sermon on the Mount. But that time has not come yet. Just as we find it wise and necessary to accept the law of gravity in our earthly existence, so we find it wise and necessary to live by Torah as long as we find ourselves in this world and this age.

While there can be different Jewish interpretations of how the age to come and/or the messianic age will affect the Torah, or affect man's relation to the Torah, there can be little doubt that this distinction between Judaism and Christianity is one of the most adequate, and most illuminating. The difference goes back to a question of eschatology. It all hinges on whether the new age, the age to come, has arrived for a full (or partial) manifestation here and now. The Christian would—and should—say yes, while the Jew would—and should—say no.

There can also be little doubt that the Jew would have the obvious facts of life on his side. This should help us to see that society as we know it, a society kept in order by law and justice, is built on principles identical with or similar to the concerns and practices which are criticized and invalidated in the Sermon on the Mount. The principle of retaliation is and remains an absolute necessity for any just society. The specific wording "an eye for an eye and a tooth for a tooth" was in its own time not a harsh decree but a step toward just limitation of oversized retaliation in the uncontrolled wrath of the vendetta: an eye—not a life! In NT times it was of course not applied literally, but as a principle of equitable justice. And a society without some machinery for a divorce is an impossibility, as can be seen from the complicated legal fictions of annulment, and the like, devised by churches that do not allow divorce.

Hence, the thrust of the Sermon on the Mount undercuts the order of society. It was this insight that forced Schweitzer to speak about the Interim Ethic of the Sermon on the Mount. But his interpretation was bound up with *his* interpretation of the NT eschatology, and it grows out of his despair as a theologian to relate the stark words of the Sermon to the world in which the church finds itself. And yet, exactly this despair set him free from domesticating the Sermon, and hence his interpretation of the actual text is more valid than most other attempts. But I wonder if there is not another possibility. That possibility could be called "messianic license." The key to this interpretation may be found in Matt. 19:10–12.[12]

Here it is obvious that Jesus' interpretation of marriage and divorce appears to the disciples—just as we have said it should—totally impossible. At that point Matthew gives a logion in which, again, one of the commandments of the law is cancelled, and this time one found even in the creation. On the basis of Gen. 1:28 every Jew was under obligation to marry and procreate. Not even the most ardent rabbi could say that he forsook marriage for the study of the Torah. When one of them is quoted as saying so, he is repudiated.[13] Only two types of excuse from marriage were recognized: those who were born "eunuchs," and those who had been made "eunuchs." To these the logion in the gospel adds a third category: those who make themselves eunuchs for the sake of the kingdom of heaven. This is truly messianic license, promulgated by Jesus, and running counter to the law. By his arrangement Matthew interestingly enough gives this "ruling" as an ancillary to the impossibility of Jesus' "ruling" on divorce. We should note that also at that point the issue was that a marriage *had* to go to divorce under certain circumstances; the more modern question Is divorce permissible? turns the problem upside down.[14]

We know that the issue about "celibacy" was a genuine one in the primitive church, since Paul argues in favor of it in 1 Corinthians 7; yet, we note that Paul has no knowledge of a "command from the Lord" in this matter (v. 25). While his argumentation is similar to that of Jesus, the issue is whether it is permissible to forgo marriage, also in the case where a man already has promised to marry a woman (v. 36ff.); Paul holds that even in such a case it is better and more blessed to refrain from marriage. His motivation is eschatological: the form (*schema*) of this world is about to pass away (v. 31), and the birth pangs of the new age are upon the church (v. 26). Hence he also argues from the point of view of the coming of the kingdom, and he does it on his apostolic authority, as one who has the Spirit of God (v. 40). The fact that he does not refer to a Word of the Lord (as in v. 10), indicates that the logion in Matt. 19:10–12 may well be a later development, or at least one known only in some quarters as, for example, in the Matthean church.[15] Since Matthew and Paul are the best examples of early Christian teachers with more advanced Jewish education, we can feel confident that such an argumentation is well in accordance with the Jewish setting of the teachings of the early church and of Jesus himself. And we note that also the Sermon on the Mount has to be understood primarily on exactly this Matthean level, not by uncontrolled attempts to reach directly back to Jesus himself. Especially in the five antitheses of Matthew 5, which constitute the key passages of the Sermon for our purposes, the material is to a large extent peculiar to Matthew, and the arrangement is totally his.

The messianic license would then mean that Jesus gives his disciples the permission, the license to act in a way which undercuts the very structure on which society is built; his sharpening of the law reaches an intensity where the law is fulfilled at the expense of its function as the law of this age, or as the law of Moses given to men in order to counteract sin, that is, at the expense of that law which was tainted by its accommodation to the hardness of men's hearts.

The authority for such teaching can be found in Jesus' consciousness of being a messianic figure. Or one can equally well stress the high eschatological intensity in his teaching. The messianic license is possible since the power of the new kingdom is at hand. Since God is about to judge the world, man can be allowed to refrain from meting out his judgments. By complete trust in God's impending judgment man is *allowed* to turn the other cheek and leave the ultimate judgment to God (cf. Rom. 12:17–20; and 1 QS x, 17–20). Man can even afford to love his (and God's) enemies, just as God in his knowledge of the final judgment can afford to treat the good and the evil equally in this world (Matt. 5:43–48). Whether we like it or not, there can be little doubt that the ethical teachings of the Sermon on the Mount, and vast areas of the NT, have their ground in the strong conviction of God's impending judgment of the world.[16] While much of its beautiful specifics cannot be deduced from this ground—many other and less attractive alternatives were possible, alternatives which would breathe hatred and arrogance—it is nevertheless true that they could not exist without such a firm ground. The specifics are to a large extent peculiar to Jesus, but the structure of thought is part and parcel of Jewish eschatology, and the Qumran texts have corroborated this state of affairs.[17]

93

Against such a background Jesus tells his disciples that they are allowed to turn the other cheek, thereby disregarding the dangers which such behavior would constitute to a society built on justice. Such an understanding of the Sermon on the Mount comes strikingly close to what seems to be at the heart of the discussion about pacifism. For many a Christian—and for many who arrive at pacifist leanings without conscious reference to Christianity—the problem is this: Is it right to enjoy the clean thinking and feeling of pacifism in a world and in a country where chances are that the pacifists will remain a minority and where they hence "profit" from the protection of the Armed Forces? Or one could ask in a more general way: Do I have the right to decide for others in this matter? Granted that I would be willing to take the consequences of my convictions as a disciple of Christ, but what about those who do not share my faith? (Such a discussion of pacifism is of course not suited for the cases where passive resistance, etc., is thought of as a superior means to political or social goals, but it is highly relevant to pacifism as a nonpragmatic, religious conviction.)

The understanding of the Sermon on the Mount as messianic license speaks directly to this type of qualm and question. It does so precisely since the answer given has the form "you are allowed to," not "you must" or "you can." The Sermon on the Mount is actually a rebellious manifesto which gives to disciples of Christ the right to break the law in the name of Christ. But it is important to remember that it *is* subversive, and that the disciple must be prepared to pay the price for such action. So it was then and so it may be now. The license cannot be easily translated into a higher ethic. It can only be appropriated in faith and will always threaten the equilibrium of God's created world, which after all is God's world under law, sometimes even under God's law.

One question remains, and that question throws us back into the very confusion of the many ways in which Christians have tried to come to grips with this powerful piece of biblical legacy. How do I know when or if I have the right to claim such messianic license for my actions? Many of the interpretations through the ages show awareness of this momentous question. But if this license is, as the Jewish rabbi pointed out, related to the bold and strange claim that the kingdom has come, although it does not look that way, then our next question must be: In what sense does the church claim that the kingdom has come? To me the answer is—theoretically—simple. The kingdom manifests itself in the Holy Spirit, which is the down payment and the first fruits of our inheritance (2 Cor. 1:22; 5:5; Eph. 1:14; and Rom. 8:23). And I would argue that this answer is relevant to our inquiry. As far as man is driven by the Holy Spirit he can claim the messianic license when he finds himself faced by the question—be it from the inside or from the outside—whether he has the right to act as a partaker of the new age.

Much can be said against such a view. I would like to distinguish between validity of the interpretation of the Sermon on the Mount as messianic license—which I would like to defend as a possible historical interpretation—and this attempt to answer the question of actual application to our present-day situation—which I would offer in a more tentative mood. Such an application hinges upon most complex hermeneutical considerations and requires scrutiny by both systematic theologians and ethicists.

There is much power in the Sermon on the Mount. The church is responsible for the right handling of it. It is responsible for the right use of this divine atomic energy; it is also responsible for avoiding undesirable fallout. Paul shows himself to be aware of both, for example, in his letters to the Thessalonians concerning work. By and large, the church has at this point been more successful in this later, protective function. Perhaps the time has come when we dare to speak more openly about the messianic license.

Many would say that if what matters is the Holy Spirit, then this license should be for everyone, since every Christian has the right to know himself as sharing in the Spirit. Yet it should be noted that the gifts and the promptings of the Spirit differ. There is much wisdom in the Roman Catholic distinction between the commandments for the majority and the counsels for those in orders, since the messianic license should not be transformed into a command for everyone. It may well be that such a distinction in itself is a valid one, and that without it the Sermon on the Mount and many other words of the NT lose their serious specificity and become hopelessly watered down to general principles or maxims, which are seldom taken seriously. We may fall into a dishonest romanticism, in which we read and sing about the costly discipleship, but little happens, and the structures of the world quench the Spirit. It may well be that what was wrong with the distinction between "commandments" and "counsels"—the latter understood as messianic license—was not the distinction itself, but the way in which it became institutionalized and identified with the ecclesiastical structures of the Roman tradition. In any case, it should not be forgotten that there is the diversity of the gifts of the one Holy Spirit, and that Jesus told some people to go home (Mark 5:18–19) while others were ordered to leave their homes and follow him (Mark 10:29–31).

Many questions remain, and new questions are raised by an awareness of the messianic license. Such a reading of the Sermon on the Mount—or the parts thereof immediately relevant to our discussion[18] —seems to have little direct significance outside the church. From the point of view of historical exegesis, this fact could be used to defend our interpretation as being well in keeping with the original setting and intention of the gospels.[19]

We are also faced more acutely with the "testing of the spirits." The tension between the individual and communal reality of the Spirit can hardly be resolved by any formula. But without the church's recognition of diversity in the promptings of the Spirit it would be hard to set the Sermon on the Mount free to work creatively and productively in the church in ways which could be more in accordance with its intention.

NOTES

1. *Understanding the Sermon on the Mount* (1960).

2. Cf. I. W. Batdorf, "How Shall We Interpret the Sermon the Mount?" *Journal of Bible and Religion* 27 (1959): 211–17.

3. M. Dibelius, *The Sermon on the Mount* (1940), p. 136; McArthur, *Understanding the Sermon*, 127.

4. *Torah in the Messianic Age and/or the Age to Come* (Journal of Biblical Literature, Monograph Series 8; 1952); see also H. J. Schoeps, "*Restitutio principii* as the Basis for the *nova lex Jesu*," *Journal of Biblical Literature* 66 (1947): 453–64. For the development in the early church, see now P. G. Verweijs, *Evangelium und neues Gesetz in der ältesten Christenheit bis auf Marcion* (Studia Theologica Rheno-Traiectina 5; 1960).

5. *Paul: The Theology of the Apostle in the Light of Jewish Religious History* (1959; Eng. trans., 1961), 168–218.

6. A. Schweitzer, *The Mysticism of Paul the Apostle* (1930; Eng. trans., 1931), 176–204.

7. *Spätjüdisch-häretischer und frühchristlicher Radikalismus. Jesus von Nazareth und die essenische Qumransekte, I-II* (Beiträge zur historischen Theologie 24:1–2; 1957).

8. See G. F. Moore, *Judaism* I, 259.

9. For further discussion and examples, see ibid., 260ff.

10. Ibid., 262, n. 4. Cf. also D. Daube, "Concessions to Sinfulness in Jewish Law," *Journal of Jewish Studies* 10 (1959):1ff.

11. Cf. D. Daube, *The New Testament and Rabbinic Judaism* (1956), 71ff.

12. For the exegesis of this passage about the "eunuchs," see now J. Blinzler, *Zeitschrift f. d. neutestamentliche Wissenschaft* 48 (1957), 254–70. Blinzler does not accept "eunuch" as a term for celibacy; cf. however W. Bauer, in Festschrift für G. Heinrici (1914), 235–44.

13. He diminishes the image of God, which is man (Tosephta Yebamoth 8:4); see Strack-Billerbeck, *Kommentar zum N. T. aus Talmud und Midrasch*, vol. I, 807. See 805–7 for other rabbinic material relevant to the discussion of Matt. 19:10–12.

14. Cf. Joseph's attitude when aware of Mary's pregnancy (Matt. 1:19): on the one hand, he was *dikaios*, righteous, and hence he *had* to divorce her, on the other hand he was kind, and hence he wanted to do it without unnecessary publicity. For this interpretation, see A. Descamps, *Les Justes et la Justice dans les évangiles et la christianisme primitif hormis la doctrine proprement paulinienne* (Universitas Catholica Lovaniensis, Diss. Theol. II:43; 1950), 34–37.

15. It is of course possible that the pre-Matthean setting of this logion referred to the fact that Jesus himself was unmarried.

16. See K. Stendahl, "Hate, Nonretaliation, and Love," *Harvard Theological Review* 55 (1962): 343–55. On the basis of Qumran and intertestamental material it appears that nonretaliation is not to be too easily identified with love; it is often, but not in Matt. 5:43–48, more closely related to the eschatological "hatred" toward evil and toward the enemies of God, of his Messiah, and of the messianic community. (Essay 10 in this volume.)

17. Cf. K. Stendahl, *The Scrolls and the New Testament* (1957), 16f.

18. It is important to remember that what we have come to call "The Sermon on the Mount" is not more of a unit than any of the other four "discourses" in Matthew (10:1—11:1; 13:1–53; 18:1—19:1; 24:1—26:1), although the Lukan "Sermon on the Plain" (6:20–49; cf. 6:12) may indicate that there was a similar composition prior to our gospels. Many difficulties in the overall interpretation of the Sermon on the Mount would be avoided if the interpretation of the parts and the interpretation of the total "Sermon" were clearly kept apart.

19. Cf. however, A. N. Wilder, *Eschatology and Ethics in the Teaching of Jesus* (1950[2]), esp. 133–41, for a penetrating and balanced analysis of the wisdom element in Jesus' teaching in its relation to the eschatological sanction.

7

The Sermon on the Mount and Third Nephi in the Book of Mormon

Introductory Note: This essay was presented to a symposium in 1978 at Brigham Young University in Provo, Utah. Jewish and Christian scholars of religion were invited to reflect on Mormonism from the perspective of Jewish and Christian parallels. For me it became a stimulating task, not only an opportunity to read the Book of Mormon and other Mormon writings. Beyond the specific attention to the Latter-day Saints, it struck me how cavalier we biblical scholars have been in our attitude toward the biblical "after-history." Every scrap of evidence for elucidating the origins of Christianity and its first formative periods receives minute attention and is treated with great seriousness, however marginal. But, as this essay makes clear, the laws of creative interpretation by which we analyze material from the first and second Christian centuries operate and are significantly elucidated by works like the Book of Mormon or by other writings of revelatory character: Swedenborgian, Christian Science, Jehovah's Witnesses, or the Divine Principles of the Unification Church. All such authentic writings should not be confused with spurious gospel forgeries, many of which are discussed by Per Beskow in *Strange Tales about Jesus* (Philadelphia: Fortress Press, 1983).

My essay was published in *Reflections on Mormonism: Judaeo-Christian Parallels*, ed. Truman G. Madsen (Provo, Utah: Religious Studies Center, Brigham Young University, 1978), 139–54.

This is the first attempt on my part toward an exegesis of the Book of Mormon. I consider it as an opportunity in many ways. I hope you do not feel offended if I say that for a biblical scholar it is an absolutely unique privilege to be right here in one of the laboratories of God's guinea pigs. What I mean is this: here is a community of faith centered in a specific revelation in the 1830s. That is like visiting with the Christian church, ca. A.D. 150—a fascinating opportunity indeed for a NT scholar. Here amongst you are people who remember by family traditions those who surrounded the bearer of the revelation that you honor in Joseph Smith. It is an exciting prospect, and I thank you for the opportunity.

In thinking about the Sermon on the Mount and 3 Nephi, especially chapters 12–14, I would like to apply also to 3 Nephi methods, types of reflections, that come naturally to me as a biblical scholar. It would be awkward if I did not apply the same methods to both records.

Third Nephi is the part of the Book of Mormon which covers, in thirty chapters, the period of A.D. 1–35. It is the one which deals in its own way with the ministry of Christ. Here are the revelations of Christ to the Nephites.

There is the reference to A.D. 34: there was "darkness for the space of three days over the face of the land. . . . if there was no mistake made by this man [i.e., "the just man who did keep the record"] in the reckoning of our time" (3 Nephi 8:1–3). I take this humble note in the Book of Mormon as a general awareness of the well-known problem concerning the absolute and the relative calculation of the years for the ministry and the death of Jesus. As a biblical scholar I find it intriguing to be in a community whose sacred book states on its title page, "And now, if there are faults they are the mistakes of men"—or "humans," as we say nowadays, or should say. Could it perhaps be agreed that such admissions strengthen the respect for true revelation rather than weaken that respect?

The section of 3 Nephi which we will deal with here (chaps. 7–8) transposes the ministry of Jesus into a ministry of Nephi, a man of miracles in the name of Jesus. Thus the power of Jesus' miracles shines through those chapters. Then comes a section that deals with the three days of darkness; with the thunder and the splitting of the rocks, a transposition of Good Friday and Easter into a cosmic dimension of the events at the death of Jesus Christ. And then in 10:19 it says about Jesus Christ:

> Showing his body unto them, and ministering unto them; and an account of his ministry shall be given hereafter. Therefore for this time I make an end of my sayings.

And then in italics, as an insertion, it says:

100

> Jesus Christ did show himself unto the people of Nephi, as the multitude were gathered together in the land Bountiful, and did minister unto them; and on this wise did he show himself unto them.

This refers especially to chapters 11 through 26.

It seems important to me that in various ways these chapters are a conscious edition not only of the teaching but of the ministry of Jesus. This revelation, which is, so to speak, the NT part in the Book of Mormon, places much emphasis on the commission to the Twelve, and a very strong emphasis indeed on baptism and the function of baptism in the community. It begins with a revelation of the risen Lord, wherein the Thomas-text from the Bible, "put your finger here, and see my hands, and put your hand and place it in my side," is extended—as is often the case in apocryphal and pseudepigraphic material—into a text for which a larger group, in this case the multitude, are invited to participate.

The Twelve receive the admonition that there should from now on be no disputations (as there so often have been in Christendom). With chapter 12 there begins the equivalent of the Sermon on the Mount. Part of that section is addressed to "the Twelve," and Jesus is seen calling and sending the Twelve. Once more the baptismal emphasis dominates. Baptism is a central phenomenon.

The other distinct emphasis is on "believing in Jesus and his words," a note absent in the Matthean Sermon on the Mount. "More blessed are they who shall believe in your words" (12:2) is one of the most striking differences perhaps between the Sermon on the Mount and its equivalent in Nephi. In 3 Nephi several times there is the emphasis upon believing, "coming unto Jesus" (12:3). This is one of the persistent differences. Here are saints who are clearly and totally centered around the importance of coming unto Jesus and believing in him. To be sure, Matthew says that Jesus, "seeing the crowds, he went up on the mountain, and when he sat down his disciples came to him, . . . and [he] taught them" (Matt. 5:1). But after that there is no reference in the Sermon on the Mount to the importance of coming to Jesus. In Matthew's sermon Jesus is a teacher giving no attention to himself, be it as a Messiah, or the forerunner of the Messiah, or an announcer of secrets. In 3 Nephi the simple scene has been expanded into the theme of coming to him and believing.

Another significant addition (if you call it an addition) is this: while Luke says, "Blessed are those who hunger, for they shall be filled," and Matthew says, "Blessed are those who hunger and thirst for righteousness, for they shall be filled," both in the Inspired Verson of Joseph Smith and in 3 Nephi they are to be "filled with the Holy Spirit." From my perspective this is a typical expansion of a text (as was Matthew's expansion on Mark—"the targumizing," the Christianizing of a text). But it is also an interesting model, for I see this as an example that the form in which the biblical material has shaped the mind of Joseph Smith (be it consciously, unconsciously, or subconsciously) is that of the King James Version. The Greek word behind "filled" is *chortazo*, which means "fill the stomach," as one fills the stomach of animals, not "fill up" in the sense *pleroo*, which is the biblical term for being filled with the Holy Spirit. It is rather unnatural to use the Greek *chortazo* for making the addition "with the Holy Spirit," but it could easily be done on the basis of the King James Version, which does not distinguish between the two Greek words.

Far more important is the preoccupation of the Nephi tradition with the right understanding of the relation between the Mosaic law and the prophecies and what Jesus might have meant when he said that he had not come in order to destroy the law but to fulfill it. "Think not that I am come to destroy the law or the prophets. I am not come to destroy but to fulfill." This is identical in Matt. 5:17 and 3 Nephi 12:17. Then 3 Nephi reads "but *in me* it hath all been fulfilled" (italics added), whereas Matthew speaks in future terms, "till all be fulfilled."

A most striking difference is found in what follows. In Matt. 5:20:

> For I say unto you, That except your righteousness shall exceed the righteousness of the scribes and Pharisees, ye shall in no case enter into the kingdom of heaven.

And in 3 Nephi 12:20:

> *Therefore come unto me and be ye saved;* for *verily* I say unto you, that except *ye shall keep my commandments, which I have commanded you at this time,* ye shall in no case enter into the kingdom of heaven (italics added).

(I give the New Testament text as in the King James Version, since the Book of Mormon uses that style of language, and I believe that it can be best understood in its details and as a total phenomenon on the basis of the King James Version.)

These passages prompt some observations that I find to be significant keys to a comparison of the Book of Mormon with the NT:

1. the absence of the reference to scribes and Pharisees, to which I shall return;
2. the "come unto me and be saved." We have already spoken about "come unto me." Here the word *saved* is also important;

3. the "verily," used sparingly in Matthew and abundantly in Johannine speech;
4. the reference to "my commandments," another Johannine feature (cf. however Matt. 28:20);
5. the admonishment "to keep" these commandments of Jesus;
6. the reference to "this time."

All these features by which 3 Nephi differs from Matthew point in the direction toward that which we shall call a Johannine Jesus, the revealed revealer who points to himself and to faith in and obedience to him as the message. In the Matthean Sermon on the Mount, Jesus is pictured rather as a teacher of righteousness, basing his teaching on the Law and the Prophets, scolding the superficiality and foibles of the religionists of his time, proclaiming the will of God and not the glories of himself. Nor does the Sermon on the Mount specifically speak of "being saved."

The saying about the salt of the earth has preceded the passage just discussed. It shows some difference from the Matthean version whereby the parabolic nature of the saying is broken. We are told in 3 Nephi, "I give unto you to be the salt of the earth; but if the salt shall lose its savor wherewith shall the earth be salted?" (v. 13). The emphasis on the sending of the disciples is strengthened, but the clear parabolic style is ruined by the odd idea that it would be good for the earth to "be salted." What farmer would like that?

We could also note that the tendency is toward the interpretative and clarifying expansion. As twentieth-century Bible readers, we are quite familiar with this tendency because of the New English Bible. This, like many of the other contemporary translations, is anxious to be clear, anxious to function well for the individual reader in his isolation. It leaves few sayings ambiguous or requiring interpretation. "In the beginning was the Word" (King James Version and Revised Standard Version) becomes "When all things began, the Word already was" (New English Bible). I call this tendency "targumic," referring to the beautiful, clarifying, and updated Aramaic translations of the Hebrew Bible. The relation between Matthew and 3 Nephi looks to me like one of "targumizing."

One more example, Matt. 5:23–24, reads:

Therefore if thou bring thy gift to the *altar*, and there rememberest that thy brother hath aught against thee;

Leave there thy gift before the *altar*, and go thy way; first be reconciled to thy brother, and then come and offer thy gift (italics added).

And in 3 Nephi 12:23–24 we read:

> Therefore, if *ye shall come unto me, or shall desire to come unto me,* and re-memberest that thy brother hath aught against thee—

> Go thy way unto thy brother, and first be reconciled to thy brother, and then *come unto me with full purpose of heart, and I will receive you* (italics added).

In 3 Nephi the altar is gone, replaced by Jesus (me), and since the issue is "to come unto me," and that "with full purpose of heart," and since the concrete example in Jesus' words is gone, it is only natural to expand the admonition to those who desire to come—a gracious expansion toward the future. Thus the simple teaching of Jesus about reconciliation in the community, which has no christological note, has now become absorbed in the pervasively Christ-centered pattern of 3 Nephi: "Come unto me—with full purpose of heart—and I will receive you."

As I try to cover a few more of the distinct differences, let me point to another feature that must strike us all. It is one of style. I refer to the abundance of the introductory words "verily" and "verily, verily," the Greek and Hebrew "amen." There are nineteen instances of "verily" and twenty-five of "verily, verily" in 3 Nephi 11–27 (there are very few in the rest of the Book of Mormon). By this stylistic device the teaching of Jesus is actually changed from moral and religious teaching into proclamation and explicit revelation of divine truth. The whole speech has thereby changed its character.

There are also the typical targumic and expansive phenomena. I am not speaking so much of how the accounts in Samuel and Kings look when retold in Chronicles, although that is a kind of parallel to what is going on in the Book of Mormon. I am more interested in the implicit rationalism of the expansions. You remember the saying, "Verily I say unto thee, Thou shalt by no means come out thence [from that prison], till thou has paid the uttermost farthing" (Matt. 5:26). Now, the rationalizing expansion is this: " . . . and while ye are in prison can ye pay even one senine?" (3 Nephi 12:26). On reflection, it is clear that it is awfully hard to come up with cash while you are in prison. But that reflection breaks the structure and blurs the point of the parabolic saying.

Third Nephi has a drastic recasting of what in Matt. 5:27–30 is the harsh sharpening of the commandment of adultery—the looking at a woman in lust and the plucking out of the offending eye and cutting off the offending right hand. In 3 Nephi no specific offense is mentioned; and the graphic and suggestive teaching is replaced by reference to a commandment and is recast in generalized and Christianized form:

> Behold, I give unto you a commandment, that ye suffer none of these things to enter into your heart; for it is better that ye should deny yourselves of these things, wherein ye will take up your cross, than that ye should be cast into hell (3 Nephi 12:29–30).

We also note the absence of Jerusalem (Matt. 5:35) in the saying about oaths. I think this is consistent with another element in the Book of Mormon, and one of importance to us if we want to understand its place and function in the continuum of holy Scriptures.

For that purpose it is instructive to think of the Septuagint (LXX), that is, the Jewish translation of the OT into Greek. In that translation geographical names were often transformed into words with conceptual meaning (e.g., Ramah became "on high") or replaced by updating equivalents. Thus geography was often suppressed or transformed. As W. D. Davies points out in his essay in this volume (*Reflections on Mormonism*), the Book of Mormon has a great fascination with geography. At this point and elsewhere in the material now under consideration, however, the tendency is in the opposite direction: geographical and historical and concrete elements are suppressed or flattened out. Specifics like "altar" and "temple" and "Jerusalem" are gone. The revealer and his commandments are dehistoricized, and the address to his Christian followers is made more clear.

The majestic final sections in Matthew 5 and 3 Nephi 12 show some significant differences. For some reasons the reference to him "who lets his rain fall over both just and unjust" is not there. I combine that absence with the fact that, while the Book of Mormon excels in biblical style, in it one of the most delightful and striking stylistic features is missing, or at least is less prominent. I refer to the *parallelismus membrorum*, that is, saying one thing by two analogous expressions: "he maketh his sun to rise on the evil and on the good, and sendeth rain on the just and on the unjust" (Matt. 5:45). That style of parallelism is not to the same extent part of the biblical daughter, the Book of Mormon. It may be of interest to ask why that is so.

In any case, in the instance under discussion the doubleness is not contained. Instead, what we have is a more doctrinal and christological touch as to "those things which were of old time, which were under the law" (3 Nephi 12:46). Those things are now all fulfilled "in me." And: "Old things are done away, and all things have become new" (12:47).

Thus 3 Nephi once again makes sure that the theme from 12:18 shall be the focus of the whole; and we know how important that is, since the whole of chapter 15 will expand at length on this matter.

The chapter ends by giving the mighty word of Jesus a christological accent. While Matthew has, "Be ye therefore perfect, even as your Father which is in heaven is perfect," 3 Nephi's christologized text reads, "Therefore I would that ye should be perfect even as I, or your Father who is in heaven is perfect" (12:48).

In the thirteenth chapter of 3 Nephi (Matthew 6), the clarification and especially the commandment-clarification is at work. In the Sermon on the Mount the statement begins, "Take heed that ye do not your alms before men, to be seen of them: otherwise ye have no reward of your Father which is in heaven" (Matt. 6:1). That is, do not carry out your almsgiving in order to receive praise. It is interesting that Nephi does not see Jesus as a teacher in his community who takes the ongoing requirements of the Torah for granted and then makes comments on it. In 3 Nephi 13:1 we read: "Verily, verily, I say that I would that ye should do alms unto the poor." To Jesus (and Matthew) the commandment and practice were given in the Torah. It was not his commandment. Only the warning against hypocrisy was his. But in 3 Nephi it becomes Jesus' commandment—like the "new commandment" in John. It is as if one were not satisfied unless it came from Jesus; one is not quite satisfied with just a comment of Jesus on the practice of alms. And that very much sets the tone of the chapter.

I come now to the most important and interesting difference that I have found in looking at these texts: in the Lord's Prayer (Matt. 6:9–15; 3 Nephi 13:9–13), the prayer about the coming of the kingdom and the prayer about the bread are not found in 3 Nephi. There the Lord's Prayer reads: "Our Father who art in heaven, hallowed be thy name. Thy will be done on earth as it is in heaven. And forgive us our debts . . ." and so forth. I understand that this raises questions that are well known among Mormon scholars.

Those verses about the daily bread and the coming of the kingdom are contained in the Inspired Version by Joseph Smith. So the question is why they are not in 3 Nephi. As to the reference to the kingdom, I would suspect that the setting given here in 3 Nephi, with the revelation of Jesus Christ to the Nephites, and perhaps the self-understanding of the church as that of Latter-day Saints, suggests that it is somehow improper to pray for the coming of the kingdom. By a preliminary study of the concordance to the Book of Mormon I can find no single passage where the terms "kingdom of God," "kingdom of heaven," or "kingdom" are used in the typical synoptic way of "the coming of the kingdom." It seems that the kingdom-language is used in other, also biblical, ways in the Book of Mormon: "Entering into the kingdom," "dwell in the kingdom," "received into the kingdom," "inherit the kingdom," "sit down in the kingdom," and also the less biblical usage, "saved in the kingdom." "The kingdom of heaven is soon at hand," we are told in, for example, Alma 5:28, but the idea of its coming is not found, so far as I can see, in the Book of Mormon.

But so rich is the Latter-day Saints' community that there is another book, or more than one, that you honor as scripture; and in section 65 of the Doctrine and Covenants there is a revelation to Joseph Smith (1831) which is very much in the style of the Lord's Prayer. Its context is of interest, as it includes "Yea, a voice crying—Prepare ye the way of the Lord, prepare ye the supper of the Lamb, make ready for the Bridegroom" (v. 3). In that eschatological setting come the words: "Call upon the Lord, that his kingdom may go forth upon the earth, that the inhabitants thereof may receive it, and be prepared for the days to come, in which the Son of Man shall come down from heaven, clothed in the brightness of his glory, to meet the kingdom of God which is set up on the earth" (v. 5). Thus, here the Son of man comes down to the kingdom of God which is already established on earth. And hence it would not be natural to pray for the coming of the kingdom. The revelation continues: "Wherefore, may the kingdom of God go forth, that the kingdom of heaven may come" (v. 6). This distinction between the kingdom of God and the kingdom of heaven seems to be important. The kingdom of God is the mission that is "going forth upon the earth." The kingdom of heaven is the consummation and is to come.

It could, of course, be argued on the basis of these observations that the Lord's Prayer in 3 Nephi could have read: "Let the kingdom of heaven come," and that such a usage would be the more appropriate since Matthew uses this term almost exclusively—rather than kingdom of God. But I tend to think that this distinction between the kingdom of God as present and the kingdom of heaven as future does not significantly inform the kingdom-language of the Book of Mormon. Or the prayer could have read, "Let thy kingdom go forth." But as the text stands, it is perhaps more reasonable to assume that neither of those uses of the kingdom-language fits into the basic perspective of the language of the Book of Mormon when it comes to a prayer of Jesus.

Why the prayer for bread is missing in the 3 Nephi version is not easy to explain, except that there is a marked tendency away from material things. In 3 Nephi 18 and 20 we have substantial elements of two whole chapters that deal with questions of the bread (and wine) in miraculous and sacramental terms.

It could, of course, be argued that the original meaning of the Greek *arton ton epiousion* and its Aramaic base, which the KJV renders by "daily bread," actually refers to the "day of the future," that is, the messianic banquet, and this is miraculous, sacramental, and eschatological. But that is another question, since the biblical material behind the Book of Mormon strikes me as being in the form of the KJV.

That concludes my passage-by-passage comparison, although points similar to the ones I have made could be demonstrated again and again throughout the three chapters of the Sermon on the Mount. Suffice it to add that the Matthean ending, which refers to how Jesus "taught them as one having authority, and not as the scribes," is missing in 3 Nephi, or rather is expanded into a whole chapter (3 Nephi 15), a revelatory speech about how the law of Moses is superseded and the giver of the law fulfills the law. We shall return later to the significance of the absence of the scribes and Pharisees in the Nephi edition of the Sermon on the Mount. Furthermore, 3 Nephi 15 also relates this speech to "the sheep of another fold," and that in a language reminiscent of John 10.

Allow me to reflect with you also on the main points in the chapters of 3 Nephi which follow those already discussed, for I see them as a significant summary of the ministry and teaching of Jesus. The reflection on shepherd and sheep continues and leads to extensive quotations from Isaiah, especially Isaiah 52. In chapter 17 we find many things that remind the Bible reader of John 14—17, that is, the farewell speeches: "I go unto the Father"; the delay and the tarrying, "a little while, and ye shall not see me: and again, a little while, and ye shall see me."

In chapter 17 we find also "a marvelous and touching scene," as the chapter heading so rightly describes it. It is marvelous partly because of the very dominant role of children. And as you analyze textually that passage where the children figure so prominently, it is very clear that it is related to "Suffer the little children to come unto me." There is a very conscious children-dimension to this event.

Then in chapter 18 you have the sacramental bread and wine. You have it with an introduction in the style of John 4, the disciples having gone for food while Jesus is sitting there. You have the church disciplinary injunction of not eating unworthily (cf. 1 Corinthians 11). And in chapter 19, you have a Pentecost where the whole tone of the chapter comes from the style and terms of John 17, the high-priestly prayer of Jesus. This leads into prophecies, mainly from Isaiah and Malachi.

Now, I want to ask myself and you: what is the picture of Jesus and his ministry that emerges out of all this—out of the Sermon on the Mount particularly, but also out of this whole section in 3 Nephi, and out of the whole of 3 Nephi?

There can be no doubt about some of the answers. The most striking feature that I discern when I compare 3 Nephi with Matthew or with the three synoptic gospels is the transposition into Johannine style. The Gospel of John, as you know, is famous for the fact that to a large extent it consists of revelatory speeches or revelatory discourses. Most analysts of the Gospel of John see in it two distinct types of material or sources. The signs, the seven signs, are often more miraculous than they are in the synoptics, so that the blind are born blind; the rescue of the disciples who were in the boat in a storm is heightened by that strange saying, "they were glad to take him into the boat, and immediately the boat was at the land . . . " (John 6:21). Everything gets a little more miraculous. Another example is the healing of the centurion's son. In the Gospel of John we are told that the healing occurred exactly at the time when Jesus said, "Your son will live" (John 4:53). It may be of interest to compare the synoptics and 3 Nephi on this point also. Perhaps also here 3 Nephi is akin to John. "When God is at work you can never understate the case" seems to be the theological principle at work to the greater glory of God.

Be that as it may, the real analogy between the Johannine Jesus and the Jesus of 3 Nephi is found in the style of discourse. The message in both is that he is the Redeemer, the Savior, "I Am . . . ": "I am the life, I am the way, I am the seed that falls into the ground. Come unto me. Believe in me." In the synoptic tradition, however, —of which the Sermon on the Mount is a part—Jesus does not speak about himself. He speaks about the kingdom. But in the Gospel of John every symbol, every image, that occurs about the kingdom is transposed into an image for Jesus. Jesus tells stories about the shepherd and the sheep. But in John, Jesus *is* the Good Shepherd. Jesus tells stories about the seed of the kingdom. But in John, Jesus *is* the seed. And as I have shown, the tendency toward the centering around faith in Jesus is perhaps the most striking tendency we find when comparing Matthew and 3 Nephi. That is also the dominant note in John.

Another feature we isolated was the transposition into revelatory speech style, which also is that of John, including the "verily, verily" and "behold, behold"—all part of the revelatory speech style. The emphasis on faith in Jesus is not a theme in the synoptics and especially not in the Sermon on the Mount. In the synoptic gospels one believes in God and trusts in the coming of the kingdom.

This transposition is in keeping with the whole image of Jesus' ministry in 3 Nephi. It is not only a matter of the genre of revelatory speech. It is the very absorbing of Jesus into the image of a Redeemer and lifting him out of history into a more timeless space as the "Revealed Revealer."

Thus let me summarize my observations by saying that the image of Jesus in the whole of 3 Nephi, and even more in the portion giving the Sermon on the Mount, is that of a revealer, stressing faith "in me" rather than in what is right according to God's will for his people and his creation.

Jesus is not any longer a teacher in the ongoing community of God's people, correcting the foibles and the misconceptions of religious people. Let me exemplify that in a very precise manner. During this symposium W. D. Davies stated that there is no other Christian community or community out of the Judeo-Christian tradition which has as positive and non-anti-Semitic ways of speaking about the Jews as have the Mormons. I found this case convincing. In my own observations I have noticed that the word "Pharisee" does not occur in the Book of Mormon. The Christian habit of using the term "Pharisees" as the symbol for the wrong attitude toward God is not part of the Mormon tradition. That is truly refreshing and welcome and unique.

Also in our comparison of the Sermon on the Mount and 3 Nephi we have seen this disappearance of the scribes and Pharisees (e.g., Matt. 5:20//3 Nephi 12:20; Matt. 7:28–29//3 Nephi 15:1–2). It is worth noting, however, how this gain has been bought at a very high price; for this disappearance of the Pharisees and scribes leads to the obliteration of one of the most significant elements in the synoptic image of Jesus. I refer to Jesus' persistent critique of the foibles of religious people. This intrareligious critique strikes me as indispensable in the picture of Jesus. It is actually an integral element in the very tradition of the Pharisees themselves, a precious confirmation of the prophetic tradition.

The interesting thing is that once this critique of the foibles and pitfalls of pious and devoted people is gone, and once Jesus is made into a revealer demanding "faith in me," the internal criticism in the religious community has disappeared from the image of Jesus, and perhaps from the community itself. Jesus has become the revealer demanding "faith in me." He is not anymore the wise teacher as to what might be morally or religiously right in the sight of God.

Jesus' scathing and promising words about "the first becoming the last and the last becoming the first" and about the foibles and pitfalls of prayers, alms, and fasting have been transformed into commandments, moral and otherwise. In becoming a revealer image, the image of Jesus has also become the founder of a church and the promulgator of its ordinances.

Let me then summarize my observations. I have spoken out of the kind of perspective with which biblical scholars look at biblical texts. I have applied standard methods of historical criticism, redaction criticism, and genre criticism. From such perspectives it seems very clear that the Book of Mormon belongs to and shows many of the typical signs of the Targums and the pseudepigraphic recasting of biblical material. The targumic tendencies are those of clarifying and actualizing translations, usually by expansion and more specific application to the need and situation of the community. The pseudepigraphic, both apocalyptic and didactic, tend to fill out the gaps in our knowledge about sacred events, truths, and predictions. They may be overtly revelatory or under the authority of the ancient greats: Enoch, the patriarchs, the apostles, or, in the case of the Essenes, under the authority of the Teacher of Righteousness in a community which referred to its members as Latter-day Saints. These are in the style and thematic vocabulary of the biblical writings. It is obvious to me that the Book of Mormon stands within both of these traditions if considered as a phenomenon of religious texts.

I would further see the Book of Mormon as an exponent of one of the striking tendencies in pseudepigraphic literature. I refer to the hunger for further revelation, the insatiable hunger of knowing more than has been revealed so far.

That can be a beautiful thing, but it has its risks and its theological costs. You may have heard about the preacher who preached about the gnashing of teeth in hell. And one of the parishioners said, "But what about us who have lost our teeth?" And the preacher answered, "Teeth will be provided." Preachers think they have to have an answer, otherwise they are letting the Bible, Jesus, and God down. The apocryphal and pseudepigraphic writings, when looked at from the outside, are driven by this *horror vacui*. The gaps of knowledge have to be filled in somehow. Take, for example, all the various apocryphal gospels about

111

the birth of Jesus. There is no end to the information given about all the gynecological details of the conception and the birth of Jesus. The hunger for knowledge is enormous. Actually, the Gospel of Luke takes the first step in that direction. And we are all familiar with how, out of the prophecies of Daniel and the book of Revelation, there are so many open questions, and the hunger to know more engenders interpretations and new revelations.

One can, of course, think differently about these matters. One can see it all as an authentic need, authentically filled by revelations and by religious geniuses who by the grace of God have had visions and the capacity of interpreting them—as the gospels of Luke and of Matthew began to fill in the gaps about the birth of Jesus. For neither Paul nor Mark nor John nor any of the other NT writers seem to have known or cared about those things. But the hunger is to know more, and more precisely, to lead either to the collection of traditions or to revelations so as to fill out the picture. For this is a powerful law of religious and human existence. There is Emanuel Swedenborg, and there is Ellen Gould White, and there is Mary Baker Eddy, and there is the Reverend Moon who gives to Christianity not a United States transplanting, as does the Book of Mormon, but a Korean transplanting. The public relations by which the Moon movement is seeking respectability is of the twentieth-century variety, and perhaps not wholly of the Spirit. But this should not blind us to the phenomenological similarities between all these movements. It is of great importance to reflect phenomenologically on such new outpourings of revelation, and in the case of Mormons and Moonies the transplantation from continent to continent is of special interest in an expanding and shrinking world.

Let me then finally reflect on how we more canonical Christians live with our more-limited knowledge. For I guess that I personally am a minimalist. When I am asked about further data on resurrection, preexistence, and so forth, I like Paul's answer. "But some one will ask: How are the dead raised? With what kind of body do they come?" His answer is not an answer, but he says, "You fools," and he just refers to God's power to do a new thing about which such speculations are futile (1 Cor. 15:35ff.). One of the humbly glorious things in the Bible is Jesus' own limits in these matters—there are things that nobody knows, "not even the Son" (Mark 13:32). Here we have an ascetic attitude instead of the insatiable hunger to know more. Perhaps such a comment is irrelevant to those who are gratefully convinced of additional revelation in and through Joseph Smith or otherwise. But as I look at the whole spectrum of God's menagerie of humankind and its history, including its religious history, I think it is important to reflect on the limits as well as the glories of the hunger for and joy in additional information.

Sometimes I feel the weight of a famous quote from the prophet Micah which speaks deeply to me. That quote came to my mind when I studied the Sermon on the Mount. There Luke reads, "Blessed are you that hunger . . . " (Luke 6:21). Matthew reads, "Blessed are those who hunger and thirst *for righteousness* . . . " (Matt. 5:6). In the Book of Mormon the saying has moved away from both the hunger of the stomach and the thirst for justice to the religious realm of the Spirit (3 Nephi 12:6). And there is nothing wrong in that; it is our common Christian tradition and experience to widen and deepen the meaning of holy words. But let us never forget that quotation from Micah which reads, "For what else does the Lord require of you but to do justice, to love kindness, and to walk humbly before your God" (Micah 6:8). For there is sometimes too much glitter in the Christmas tree.

8

Prayer and Forgiveness:
The Lord's Prayer

Introductory Note: During my study years in Sweden we had two brilliant NT professors. My teacher was Anton Fridrichsen to whom I owe my love for the Bible as a challenge to critique what one would like it to mean (see my Foreword to his *The Problem of Miracle in Primitive Christianity*. [Minneapolis: Augsburg Publishing House, 1972]; and my critique of my teacher in *The Bible and the Role of Women*. [Philadelphia: Fortress Press, 1966]).

The other great teacher was Hugo Odeberg at Lund University. Immensely learned, with a touch of the Kabbalah, he opened my eyes to a type of Christian midrash, both in a Jewish and a mystical key, an odd mixture of the rational and the irrational. He also corrected my views of the Pharisees—although his book on the subject is flawed by its final sections where the very insights he has presented are negated by his lifting up the Johannine perspective on the Jews as the normative one for Christianity (*Pharisaism and Christianity*. [St. Louis: Concordia Publishing House, 1964]).

This essay on the Lord's Prayer was written for a collection in his honor (*Svensk Exegetisk Årsbok* 22/23 [1957–58]: 75–86). I have returned from time to time to the study of the Lord's Prayer. When the Coptic text to the Gospel of Thomas was published (A. Guillaumont, et al., *The Gospel According to Thomas*. [Leiden: E. J. Brill; London: Collins, 1959. See now The Nag Hammadi Library in English. New York: Harper & Row, 1977]), I was struck by Saying No. 48: "If two make peace with each other in the same house, they shall say to the mountain, Be removed! and it will be moved" (cf. also No. 106 with a more typical Gnostic sense of the same thought). This saying seems to lend additional weight to one of the main points of my original essay, that is, the interplay between the power of prayer and the mutual forgiven-ness.

115

For an interpretive paraphrase of the Lord's Prayer and for some further reflections in relation to missions, see "Your Kingdom Come," *Cross Currents* 32 (1982): 257–66.

In the Gospel of Matthew, the Lord's Prayer has a concluding remark which is an elaborate expansion of the "law of mutuality" regarding forgiveness as found in the fifth petition " . . . and forgive us our debts as we also have forgiven[1] those upon whom we have a just claim."[2] This is done by the following statement:

> For if you forgive men [others] their trespasses, your heavenly Father also will forgive you; but if you do not forgive men [others] their trespasses, neither will your Father forgive your trespasses (Matt. 6:14–15).

This underscoring of mutual forgiveness is not exactly what could be expected at this point in Matthew's gospel. He has dealt with the urgency of reconciliation in its proper context in chapter 5, and his present preoccupation is with prayer as one of the three basic religious duties: almsgiving, prayer, and fasting. Furthermore, the Matthean form of the Lord's Prayer does not suggest such an emphasis on forgiveness. Compared with the Lukan form of the prayer, it is wholly centered around the eschatological manifestation of the kingdom, while Luke gives more room for the ethical incentive.[3]

Thus we have the right to ask for some reason why Matthew came to sum up the Lord's Prayer exactly in this fashion. The logion about conditional forgiveness in Matt. 6:14–15 is found also in Mark 11:25. This later reference is in a context that deals with prayer. Following the application similar to the logion about the withered fig tree, there is the logion about the power of prayer in faith; then follows: "and when you stand praying, forgive, if you have anything against any one; so that your Father also who is in heaven may forgive you your trespasses."[4] This verse (Mark 11:25) is under strong suspicion of being a gloss, influenced by Matt. 6:14,[5] and the problem is certainly more complicated than V. Taylor makes us believe when he says, without recognizing any difficulties, that "the Markan form is important because it suggests that the Lord's Prayer was already known in Rome before A.D. 60."[6] This presupposes the prayer in its Matthean form, with ὁ ἐν τοῖς οὐρανοῖς, a terminology which is a distinctive Matthean feature in the whole of his gospel, but is found only here in Mark. To this can be added: that Matthew (21:20–22) follows Mark in this pericope but only through Mark 11:24; that Mark 11:26 is a clear case of a transfer from

Matthew, which did not take place in the best manuscripts; and that, while ὁ πατὴε ὑμῶν ὁ ἐν τοῖς οὐρανοῖς sounds more like Matt. 6:9 (6:14; οὐράνιος),[7] παράπτωμα, which is found only in Matt. 6:14–15 and Mark 11:25–26 in the gospels, points to the saying in Matt. 6:14.

This adds up to a rather solid argument against Mark 11:25. Nevertheless, there may be reasons for suspending such a judgment for a while. None of the reasons are decisive, taken one by one,[8] and Mark 11:25 differs a good deal more from Matt. 6:14 than is usual in the case of regular intersynoptic harmonizations of the type which we can study in a broken manuscript tradition. If we found a good reason for a close relation between the power of prayer and the condition of forgiveness, it would be less strange to find this logion at this point.

What causes special consideration is that the *Stichwort* προσεύχεσθε-προσευχόμενοι (Mark 11:24, 25) would not exist if verse 25 were not a logion in its own right, known to Mark. If it is considered a gloss, we must presuppose that a scribe saw some reason to bring in the word about forgiveness where he found Mark speaking about the power of prayer, and that he did so because the Lord's Prayer—which does not seem to refer to the power of prayer—ended on the note of forgiveness. But a study of the relation between prayer and forgiveness as found in Matthew 6 will show that the awareness of that relation was soon lost in the consciousness of the church. It is only in the earliest strata of the gospel tradition that it can be found, and consequently we find it harder at this late date to explain a synoptic transfer than to see Mark 11:20–25 as a genuine pericope, where Mark has a good reason to combine the logia on the power of faith and on prayer with a logion on forgiveness.

If we return to Matthew, we find forgiveness and prayer closely linked together in Matthew's section on how to handle a lapsed brother (18:10–35). The parable about the lost sheep in Luke answers the question: How can Jesus associate with sinners? In Matthew it is an example of the right concern for a brother who has gone astray (v. 12: πλανηθῇ; v. 14: τοῖς μὴ πεπλανημένοις: not found in Luke). The description of the procedure to be followed in such a case places the emphasis on his forgiveness, but there is also a clear reference to his excommunication. The church has to be a true ἐκκλησία; when all attempts to talk the backslider into repentance have been in vain, he is excommunicated by the "power of the keys."[9] As in 1 Cor. 5:4, this power is administered by prayer,[10] and the logion in Matt. 19–20, as used by Matthew, refers to this procedure. The two who pray together and the two or three who come together in Jesus' name are in Matthew's mind the two or three witnesses mentioned in verse 16. The procedure is parallel to that in 1 Cor. 5:4. Thus their action is as valid and powerful as that of Jesus himself. Matthew brings his logion about powerful prayer right into his section on disciplinary procedure. The logion itself must have had a broader scope. It refers to the omnipotent[11] prayer, περὶ παντὸς πράγ-ματος, as it is uttered here on earth (ἐπὶ τῆς γῆς; cf. the pattern of v. 18 and the third petition of the Lord's Prayer). In such an activity, Christ is present. But to Matthew the promise of omnipotent prayer is used as a support for the valid procedure when the ἐκκλησία acts in matters of discipline. Therefore the saying in verse 19 is introduced by πάλιν.

The procedure of private admonition and warnings prior to bringing a complaint against a brother before the assembly of the community has been found also at Qumran (1QS vi, 1; CD ix, 2ff.). Before we return to the Lord's Prayer, this parallel is worth further attention. The disciplinary activities at Qumran were not primarily of an educational nature. They were not a means to train the members in the attitudes of obedience for its own sake. They were primarily the device by which those who were not qualified were "excluded from the Purity" (1QS vi, 25), that is, from the meal and the purifications that surrounded its celebration. This had to be so, since the Qumran community did not understand itself as a party within Judaism or as a fellowship for study and obedience, but as the new covenant (CD viii, 21). They were not a party but a sect.[12] As an eschatological community, they were the ones who had already now a part in the age to come. The statement in 1QS vi, 1, parallel to Matthew 18, stresses the good relation between the brethren, and the more precise regulations in vi, 24–vii, 25 are mainly concerned with relations between the members. The eschatological community is by necessity one of unbroken, well-ordered fraternal relations. He who upsets the balance of this communal harmony has thereby proved himself not to belong to it. If he does not listen to the admonition of his fellow brother and the witnesses, he cannot any longer touch the purity.

If this communal climate is brought to bear on a self-expression of the early church as that in Matthew 18, what follows? In Matthew 18 there is more emphasis on the urgent necessity to go out of one's way to forgive a brother. And he who "listens to the church" (v. 16) is apparently forgiven without any specified measure of punishment, as those listed in 1QS.[13] But once these attempts have proved futile, he has to go. He is transferred back into the sinful world, he becomes like a gentile and a tax collector. The church that takes this action against him does so because it acts on earth as the omnipotent representative of Christ. As the true messianic community it can reinstate or excommunicate a brother; it has the power of omnipotent prayer περὶ παντὸς πράγματος—and consequently it also has power in this matter.

When Matthew brings in the parable of the unmerciful servant (18:23–35) at this point and lets his section on intercommunal relations end on the note "So also my heavenly Father will do to every one of you, if you do not forgive your brother from your heart," he definitely gives to this parable a significance for the unbroken fraternal relations in the community, without which the church cannot be the church.

Thus we have found in Matthew 18 a complex of sayings that has been so composed by Matthew that they apply the teaching of Jesus to the needs of the church when it faces intercommunal problems. While the emphasis is on forgiveness, the provision for excommunication adds precision to the picture. In this context, Matthew finds it natural to bring in a saying on omnipotent prayer. It is the community of forgiveness that administers the very action by which forgiveness is granted, or by which the unbroken relationship between the brethren is protected when threatened by one who does not ask for forgiveness. Thus a pattern begins to emerge, within which prayer–forgiveness–omnipotent prayer are closely related to one another.

The few Lukan sayings pertaining to this matter point in the same direction. The logia about forgiveness in Matt. 18:15 and 18:21–22 have their parallel in Luke 17:3–4, immediately followed by a logion about the faith which can uproot trees (i.e., the closest Lukan parallel to Mark 11:20–23). The admonition to fraternal forgiveness is once more connected with the omnipotence of the prayer of the disciples. It is significant, however, that Luke apparently just follows "Q"; it is not a conscious arrangement of his, and we find no indication that Luke has recognized any relation between prayer and forgiveness as a meaningful pattern in the traditions he handles.[14]

It may be that we now have the pieces of a pattern that can help to explain the way in which Matthew combines the Lord's Prayer with a saying about forgiveness. To Matthew the Lord's Prayer is a prayer for the coming of the kingdom. In the light of the Qumran material, it becomes more plausible that this applies to the *whole* of the prayer, not only to its first three petitions.[15] As for the enigmatic ἐπιούσιος, Jerome's report on *maḥar* ("of tomorrow") in the Gospel of the He-

119

brews[16] takes on new significance, especially since the two or three earlier occurrences claimed for ἐπιούσιος have proven nonexistent or of
no significance.[17] The clear reference in 1QSa to the meals at Qumran as
anticipations of the messianic banquet, as well as the futuristic note[18] in
all forms of the words of institution to the Eucharist, suggests that ὁ
ἄρτος ὁ ἐπιούσιος is the bread that is about to be given, just as the
kingdom is about to come.[19] Such an interpretation does not necessarily make the Lord's Prayer liturgically bound to the celebration of the
meal; the meal was significant enough to have a central place in their
prayer apart from the actual celebration, if it was understood in relation
to the messianic banquet.

Just as we saw the Qumran meal to be well in focus when matters of
interfraternal relations were strained or restored, so the thought of the
Lord's Prayer goes immediately from the participation in the heavenly
banquet, and its anticipatory counterpart on earth, to the need of
forgiveness and forgiven-ness. Both ὀφειλήματα and οἱ ὀφειλέται then refer to interfraternal sins,[20] that is, that which makes it
impossible to be partakers in the messianic meal; and the καί which
connects the fourth and the fifth petitions strengthens such an interpretation. The prayer continues by looking toward the future: may the
messianic birth pangs of the community not be beyond our strength![21]

Such a consistent eschatological interpretation of the Lord's Prayer
makes it not only a prayer *for* the kingdom, but a prayer *of* those who
now have a part in the kingdom. Since their part in it, as a community,
presupposes true fraternal relations, the very right to utter such a prayer
depends upon a status of mutual forgiven-ness. This is not a condition
in the sense of *do ut des*. The condition is grounded in the nature of the
messianic community. This seems to be why Matthew finds it quite
natural to end the Lord's Prayer as the prayer of the messianic community on the note of forgiveness. He does so not because he liked the
fifth prayer more or because he felt that prayer to be the crucial one. He
does it because the right to utter this prayer presupposed a mutually
reconciled community. Their own status of forgiven-ness is jeopardized
if they do not forgive, and thus remain a true messianic community.

There are similar and yet different sayings where prayer and
forgiveness go together. In Matt. 5:23 he who comes with a gift for the
altar is admonished first to reconcile himself with the one who has
something against him.[22] The similarity to the sayings we have considered so far is obvious, but the difference is also clear. Here the act of
worship serves as an additional incentive to seek reconciliation before it

is too late; the accent falls on the urgency of reconciliation as such, not on its necessity for omnipotent prayer. We are within a more general prophetic framework.

In James 5:15ff. we receive a few glimpses of the actual life in a congregation. While the confession as well as the prayer is "for one another," the prayer is that of him who has "faith" in the sense of trust in God. It is prayed with power by the righteous, as Elijah did. Then follows an admonition to go after a brother who has gone astray, and the language reminds us of Matt. 18:10–15. But the mutual forgiveness is not described as conditional for the power of prayer; what matters are the faith of the individual and his character—not status—of being just. In spite of the obvious communal aspect of the procedure, the sectarian or messianic note is missing. We are within a more general Jewish framework, as we would expect in the Epistle of James.

Thus the pattern of prayer–forgiveness–omnipotent prayer is not a paramount feature in our material. It had its time, as well as its place, as a creative and helpful way of thinking, only in certain segments of the early church. It may well be that once the Christian life was described and characterized by the endowment with the Holy Spirit, as in the Lukan writings and in Paul, the activities both of discipline and of prayer in the church were understood in terms of the Spirit.[23] Both the reference to the prayer for the Spirit in Luke 11:13 and the proceedings with Ananias and Sapphira point in that direction (Acts 5). Paul links prayer and Spirit together (Rom. 8:15; Gal. 4:5), and he finds in the Spirit the principle for fraternal equilibrium in the church (1 Corinthians 12). In the light of the interpretation of the sayings about interfraternal forgiveness given above, the Johannine writings, and especially 1 John, are found to be closer to Matthew in understanding agape as the sine qua non for intercommunal relations. But we have also discerned a pattern of thought in which the prayer of the community with a promise of omnipotence was grounded in a communal forgiveness, without which the claim and joy of messianic bliss could not exist. And so a logion, which in itself had a broader meaning,[24] was taken by Matthew to serve as an appropriate reminder to the church whenever they prayed for the coming of the kingdom. He did not, as did the Epistle of James, refer to the intensity of trust in God or of righteousness. He did not, as did Luke, use this context for encouraging insistent prayers. He did not, as did Paul, recognize the Spirit as the prerequisite for the true prayer Abba-Father. Matthew just wanted to make sure that those who said the Lord's Prayer should be able to pray it with force, as the com-

121

munity where the kingdom already had manifested itself among brethren who knew that they had nothing against one another—ἀψήκαμεν
τοῖς ὀφειλέταις ἡμῶν.[25] Their favor with God depended as much
on his forgiveness as on their own willingness to forgive. Therefore
"whenever you stand praying, [especially if you expect your prayer to
share in the power of the messianic age] forgive, if you have anything
against any one; so that your Father also who is in heaven may forgive
you your trespasses."[26]

NOTES

1. See below, note 25.

2. See below, note 20.

3. The use of the iterative present tense ἀφίομεν and the παντὶ
ὀφείλοντι (πᾶς being a device for generalizing catechetical style). The petitions which Matthew has in addition to Luke foster the eschatological understanding of the prayer in his gospel.

4. The similarity between Mark 11:25 and Matt. 6:14 led to intersynoptic parallelism, which accounts for Mark 11:26 in the majority of MSS = Matt.
6:15.

5. So, e.g., Klostermann, ad loc., and F. C. Grant in *Interpreter's Bible*, ad loc.
Grant sees the text of Syr[sin], which is rich in intersynoptic harmonics, as the
"bridge."

6. *Comm. Mk.* (1955), 467.

7. In the case of a later transfer it would be quite natural for the wording of
the well-known prayer to break through.

8. (1) παράπτωμα is a *hapax legomenon* in Matthew as well as in Mark. (2) The
fact that v. 26 is a clear harmonization in part of the MSS, following Matthew
more closely than v. 25, makes it possible to see v. 25 as original in Mark. (3)
Matthew deviates considerably from Mark already in v. 22 (Mark 11:24) and
may well have preferred to have the saying on prayer and forgiveness in the
context of his teaching about prayer. (4) While Matthew makes ample use of
the term "Father in heaven," it is hardly probable that he added it to the Lord's
Prayer, because he liked it, but he found it in the prayer, and he lived himself in
a milieu where this way of speaking was the natural one (so K. G. Kuhn,
Achtzehngebet und Vaterunser und der Reim [1950], 34). Its unique occurrence in
Mark could suggest a liturgical language known to Mark but not quite natural
for his own style.

9. This refers here clearly to the practice of excommunication, while the same
saying in 16:19 is the basis for Peter's authority to promulgate Halakha. See for
this and the following, K. Stendahl, *The School of St. Matthew* (1954), 28.

10. Stendahl, *School of St. Matthew*, and C. H. Dodd, *New Testament Studies*
(1953), 58ff.

11. I have chosen the word "omnipotent" on purpose, well recognizing that
it could be considered a misleading overstatement. As I hope to show in the

following, the point is the "sharing in the powers of the messianic age." Words like "irresistible" or "compelling" would suggest a different attitude and direction where man is seen over against God, while the omnipotent prayer is "on the inside" of the divine power.

12. For this distinction in relation to discipline, see K. Stendahl, *The Scrolls and the New Testament* (1957), 7f. The Pharisees were a party, i.e., they did not claim an identity between the membership in their fraternities and the partaking in the age to come.

13. This is the positive aspect of the "higher degree of anticipation" in the church compared with Qumran. The negative aspect of the same is seen in the case of Ananias and Sapphira (Acts 5:1–11) where none of Qumran's gracious casuistry applies to "one who lies in the matter of wealth" (1QS vi, 25); see Stendahl, *The Scrolls*, 8.

14. See above, p. 121.

15. Kuhn, *Achtzehngebet*, 33 (following Dalman) suggests that the Aramaic basis for τὸ θέλημα should be *rě'uta'* (the Hebrew *rāṣôn*); θέλημα for *rāṣôn* is found in LXX, Psalm 39:9 (Heb. 40:9). "May your good pleasure ["regarding the elect" = εὐδοκία] be manifest"; cf. Phil. 2:13. (This would bring the third petition well in line with Luke 2:14, the song of the angels, with its bipartite form: Glory be to God on high—on earth peace to men of [His] choosing; see E. Vogt in Stendahl, *The Scrolls*, 114–17.) The third petition would then have no ethical implication but be only a third and—as expected according to stylistic patterns—somewhat longer form of the one prayer for the manifestation of the kingdom on earth. Such an interpretation would fit better to the verb γενηθήτω which is usually taken for a passive to ποιεῖν ("thy will be done"; Dalman and Kuhn: *titā'bed*) instead of as a form of γίνεσθαι in its proper meaning of "becoming manifest" (Aram. *tĕhe'*; so Burney, *The Poetry of Our Lord* [1925], 113). This interpretation could be argued against on the basis of Matt. 26:39, where the third petition is woven into the Gethsemane story. This could, however, be a development on the basis of the ambiguous Greek usage of the prayer.

16. *Comm. in Matt.* ad 6:11. Origen, in his extensive discussion on ἐπιούσιος in *de Oratione* 27:7–13 (English trans. J. E. L. Oulton, in *The Library of Christian Classics*, vol. 2 [1954], 298–303), recognizes the word as an ad hoc creation by the evangelists and argues for the derivation ἐπί + οὐσία, using περιούσιος (Exod. 19:6) as a linguistic parallel. Toward the end of his discussion he says: "But someone will say that ἐπιούσιος is formed from ἐπ-ιέναι so that we are bidden to ask for the bread appropriate to the coming age, in order that God by anticipation (προλαβών) may give us it now, with the result that what is to be given tomorrow, so to speak, should be given us 'today,' 'today' signifying the present age, and 'tomorrow' the coming age. But the former interpretation being in my judgment the better, let us . . . " (27:13; Eng. trans. J. E. L. Oulton, 302). His choice is apparently based on theological or homiletical preference. See below, note 19.

17. See B. M. Metzger, *Expository Times* 69 (1957/58): 52–54, on the disappearance of the papyrus with the text for No. 5224 in F. Preisigke, *Sammelbuch griech. Urk. in Ägypten*, vol. 1 (1915), and the corrections concerning the Lindos

inscription, published by C. Blinkenberg, *Lindos*, vol. II:2 (1941), col. 777, 18. Dr. Dikran Hadidan, librarian at Pittsburgh Theological Seminary, has succeeded in tracking down the obscure references to a use of ἐπιούσιος in the margin of Holmes-Parsons edition of the LXX to 2 Macc. 1:8 (cf. *Th.W.B.* II, 587). The "Codices Sergii" were found to be a list of variants which Priest Sarkis Malian compiled in Jerusalem in 1773. (Armenian MSS No. 4 of Die Österreichische Nationalbibliothek in Vienna.) Among these variants is an Armenian *hapax legomenon*, found three times in 2 Macc. 1:8, meaning "of continuity." The term is different from the usual terms used for the shewbread, one of which is also used for ἐπιούσιος (or rather for *'amina'* of syr^[c,s], cf. Num. 4:7) in the Armenian translation. There was no Greek translation made by Sarkis Malian. Dr. Hadidan suggests to me that Parsons or one of his associates made the guess that this should be ἐπιούσιος, but a study of the Armenian text apparently does not substantiate such a guess.

18. I.e., the references to the Parousia. The "banquet" in the context of the Eucharist, see Luke 22:30.

19. The understanding of ἐπιούσιος must be considered as basically a Greek problem. What caused the creation of a *novum* like this one? The Aramaic idiom, *"habh lana lahma yoma den weyomahra"*—even misread, *den deyomahra*—suggested by M. Black, *An Aramaic Approach* (1954), 152f., does not give a good ground for τὸν ἄρτον ἡμῶν τὸν ἐπιούσιον as the unit it actually forms in the Greek. The derivation from ἐπ-ιέναι remains the superior on many counts: Already the elision points in that direction; no form of ἐπεῖναι without elision is known, and (apart from ἐπιόψομαι) all cases of nonelided ἐπί-contraction are those of sigma and digamma stems. The current participle [τῇ] ἐπιούσῃ [ἡμέρα‚] is the natural basis for the adjective. Furthermore, the creation of a new word would demand a distinct term which one tried to coin in a distinct way. One may guess that the idea of "daily bread" (Vulgate's *quotidianum* in Luke) has been strongly suggested by Matt. 6:25–34. Neither the earlier translations nor Origen had managed to arrive at so plain—or even flat—a translation or interpretation.

20. οἱ ὀφειλέται are those upon whom one has a just claim. The nature of the community makes it necessary to forgive them, or to have them excommunicated. Matthew's ὀφειλήματα (over against Luke's ἁμαρτίαι) may point in the direction of communal sins: that which I owe (my brethren), being under obligation; the word is so used in the only other place where it occurs in the NT (Rom. 4:4), and the stem ὀφειλ- has always this connotation in the NT; see, e.g., Matt. 18:28–34; Rom. 15:27. It is not used in the NT or in the LXX about "sins" as such (Bauer's *Wörterbuch* lists only the passages in the Lord's Prayer for this meaning; cf. however, Aram. *ḥôbā'* which combines the meaning of "debt" and "sin").

21. "And if those days were not shortened, no flesh would be saved"; but they will be so for the sake of the elect, Matt. 24:22.

22. Cf. Mark 11:24, where the case is in the reverse: εἴ τι ἔχετε κατά τινος.

23. Cf. the broken textual tradition in the first petitions in Luke's form of the Lord's Prayer, with remnants of what seems to have been Marcion's text for the

first petition (ἐλάτω τὸ ἅγιον πνεῦμα σου ἐφ' ἡμᾶς καὶ καθαρισάτω ἡμᾶς; A. von Harnack, *Marcion* [1921], 189) retained in the place of the second. E. Lohmeyer, *Das Vater-Unser* (1946), 182–92, sees here the expression of an "Urchristentum, das eng an alttestamentliche Hoffnungen gebunden ist und in Johannes und Jesus die Wegbereiter des Herrn oder seines eschatologischen Werkes erblickt" (191), and he quotes K. Lake's commentary to Acts 19:2, "that to Paul and to Luke, Christianity was essentially a means of obtaining 'Holy Spirit.'" While it is true that the prayer for the Spirit—esp. with the addition, ". . . and cleanse us"—cannot claim originality in Luke, it remains a puzzling fact that it fits so well into Luke's own frame of thought, and it sounds as a reference to Pentecost as Acts describes it.

24. This is clear already from the use of τοῖς ἀνθρώποις. The same applied to the logion about omnipotent prayer in Matthew 18.

25. The aorist ἀφήκαμεν is well attested, and over against Luke's present ἀφίομεν it describes this act of forgiveness as a matter of fact: we *are* those who have forgiven; Luke's present tense refers to the repeated action, as does his καθ' ἡμέραν. We would think that the stern conviction of belonging to those mutually forgiven should make any prayer for forgiveness superfluous. The texts from Qumran with their penitential hymns and with their yearly rite of rededication indicate that it is not necessarily so. There, as well as in, e.g., the Psalms of Solomon, the distinction between "sinners" and "righteous" does not exclude concern and contrition for the "sins of the righteous."

26. It is obvious that this saying from Mark 11:25 fits well into the pattern with which we have been dealing. In the final analysis it remains naturally a possibility that its occurrence in Mark, *in accordance with a pattern which was soon forgotten*, is a coincidence. The fact that both of our main passages are Matthean (chaps. 6 and 18) may even lend further support to the theory of its Matthean origin. On the other hand, there is enough reason to leave the question open.

9

Sin, Guilt, and Forgiveness in the New Testament

Introductory Note: The reader will no doubt notice a somewhat different style in this piece. While I made some adjustments as I translated my original German text, the substance is that of two entries in the standard encyclopedia *Die Religion in Geschichte und Gegenwart*, 3d ed., vol. IV (Tübingen: J. C. B. Mohr [Paul Siebeck], 1962), cols. 484–89 and 511–13. The German original had extensive bibliographies which I have not reproduced here.

Since I have preoccupied myself so extensively with the questions of sin, guilt, and forgiveness in my *Paul Among Jews and Gentiles* (Philadelphia: Fortress Press, 1976), it seemed reasonable to make place for a somewhat broader and diversified study of the early Christian evidence.

SIN AND GUILT

In Western Christianity sin and guilt are closely related terms and realities, and in doctrines of salvation that relationship is a conscious presupposition. It is therefore surprising that the NT has no firm and clear terminology for "guilt" and that the words for "being guilty" are sparse. The strongest evidence for sin understood as guilt is found in Luke (e.g., 15:18; 18:13). The idea of debt (*opheilema*, etc.) in Luke 7:41f. uses the metaphor of commerce as does the Matthean story about the unforgiving servant (Matt. 18:23–35), and it has the overtones of community ethics as in the Matthean Lord's Prayer: Forgive us what we owe our brothers and sisters as we have forgiven our debtors (5:12; cf. Luke 11:4 with "our sins").

Enochos (Matt. 5:21f.; Mark 3:29; 14:64; 1 Cor. 11:27; Heb. 2:15; James 2:10) and *hypodikos* (Rom. 3:19) mean "guilty" in the sense of liable to punishment, a usage rooted in the language of legal procedures. There is no use of the corresponding nouns.

127

The NT scarcity of specific terms for guilt does not mean that sin is not seen as guilt. In Romans 1—3 Paul surveys the sins of humanity for the very purpose of demonstrating human responsibility as he wants to demonstrate how the whole world is held accountable (*hypodikos*) to God for its sins (3:19—20). But it is important to note the absence of any attempt at distinguishing sin from guilt for the purpose of theological reflection on the phenomenon of guilt as such.

THE PEOPLE AND THEIR SIN

In the perceptions of the NT writings, the coming of Jesus, his teaching, and his activity are closely tied to the problem of sin. This very problem is seen as finding its eschatological solution in Jesus Christ. He comes to the people of Israel, a people aware of its sinfulness. The zeal for the law that characterized the Pharisees had as its deepest intention to prepare the people for the messianic era and to speed its coming: the Messiah will come on the day when the whole of Israel keeps the law. Thus it is not surprising that Jewish thought and discussion about sin often operate within the framework of theodicy, that is, the question about the power of evil and God's ultimate victory (e.g., the Psalms of Solomon; 4 Ezra; 2 Macc. 6:12–17).

Thus Jesus comes to "this adulterous and sinful generation" (Mark 8:38), and when Matthew interprets the name "Jesus," "for he will save his people from their sins" (1:21), then that is thought of in collective and eschatological terms: he will redeem and establish the people of Israel (cf. Luke 1:77; Ps. 130:8). One is reminded of Jer. 31:34, where the new era comes: "for I will forgive their iniquity, and I will remember their sin no more."

JESUS AND SINNERS

Jesus proclaims the coming of the kingdom of God. As with John the Baptist, this proclamation is a call to repentance. For John the Baptist forgiveness of sin is bound to his baptism. For Jesus it is the mark of his whole mission. He has authority to forgive sins (already) on earth (Mark 2:10, parr.). His declaration of liberation from sin is so decisive that in the synoptic gospels and Acts the noun "sin" (*hamartia*) occurs only in sayings about forgiveness.

The impression that Jesus had been a friend of publicans and sinners was strong and lasting. This image presupposes the distinction between two groups—righteous and sinners—that was essential for contemporary piety. Jesus sought and invited the very people whom the right-eous—the Pharisees and the sages—saw as least concerned about Isra-el's deliverance since they did not take seriously their religion and their obedience to the law. Most of the synoptic sayings about sin and sin-ners are found in passages where this relation between Jesus and sinners is defended. Such words of Jesus are often introduced by a sentence about how Pharisees grumbled about the company Jesus kept. This is an especially strong motif in Luke (e.g., 15:2; 7:36ff.; 18:9). Famous is the irony in Mark 2:17, parr.: "Those who are well have no need of a physician . . . I came not to call the righteous, but sinners." In the syn-optic gospels Jesus never tries to convert the righteous, and Nicodemus is treated harshly when he seeks out Jesus (John 3). Bypassing the right-eous, Jesus goes to the sinners.

This persistent trait in the gospels should not be understood as if Je-sus had planned it that way. Rather, it is something that happened as he brought his messianic message to Israel. He was turned down by the persons who considered themselves best prepared, and he was accepted by folk with shaky religious and moral credentials.

The Beatitudes (Matt. 5:3–12) are addressed to people who humbly long for God to bring their oppression to a glorious end. Such a stance was the right one according to Pharisees. The so-called Anawim piety of a Simeon or a Hannah (Luke 2:25–38) was not alien to the Pharisees. What is new in the gospels is that this attitude is applied to sinners. This transformation "happens" when it is the sinners who show themselves ready to welcome the message and claim of Jesus. At the crucial messi-anic moment they do become the privileged, the first, the children of God. This reversal is already in the gospels extended to representative gentile individuals (Matt. 8:11; 15:21–28, parr.). From Paul we are familiar with the term "sinners" as a generic term for gentiles, even where there is no reference to special sins (e.g., Gal. 2:15).

It is in this event within the ministry of Jesus that early Christian the-ology of grace and forgiveness has its origin. The memory of the sin-ners' response to Jesus becomes a radical change in the socioreligious structure of the community: the first become last and the last first (Mark 10:31, etc.).

PAUL AND SIN

Paul's understanding of sin must also be seen as part of his reading of God's history. What he says about sin is tied to the pillars of sacred history: Adam, Abraham, Moses, and Christ. Sin enters the world with Adam's disobedience, and with sin comes death. The crucial passage is Rom. 5:12, a verse with far-reaching consequences in the history of theology and culture. Augustine's use of the Vulgate's *in quo* = "in whom," that is, "in Adam all sinned," greatly influenced the development of the doctrine of original sin. But the Greek word *eph'ho* ("because . . . " in the RSV, or "in as much as all sinned" in the NEB) cannot sustain that fateful doctrinal edifice. (For the detailed arguments, see the excellent discussion in C. E. B. Cranfield, I.C.C. Commentary, 1975 ad loc.) Paul here takes for granted common Jewish understandings of the fall of Adam (cf. his midrash on Genesis 3 in Rom. 7:7–12). In Romans 5 his specific interest is rather to demonstrate the relative insignificance of the law of Moses: people died just as much before Moses as after Moses, even those who had not transgressed a specific commandment as did Eve and Adam (5:14; cf. 2:12). Hence sin is a pervasive human condition and the law does not help —it rather escalates not only the awareness of sin but sin itself (7:14; Gal. 3:19). In a sharpened statement (1 Cor. 15:56) Paul combines his inherited view of Adam with his peculiar view of the law and Moses: "The sting of death is sin, and the power of sin is the law."

As a Jew, Paul had learned that the law was God's gift which gave Israel the possibility of life and righteousness and acted as the corrective of sin. Now he argues that the law does not have that power since it is "weakened by the flesh" (Rom. 8:3). Thus it seemed to him that the purpose of the law was not "productive of life" (although it could have been, had God wanted it so; Gal. 3:21).

Thus Moses and the law become ineffective; or, when effective, the effect is negative. Paul finds the positive factor in Abraham, his theological hero. For he received the promise four hundred thirty years prior to the law (Gal. 3:17), and it was prior to circumcision that Abraham believed, and it was reckoned him unto righteousness by the one who justifies the ungodly, that is, the gentiles (Rom. 4:3–5).

Paul's thoughts and arguments in these matters and his drastic reversal of Jewish teaching add up to a powerful tour de force. In my book *Paul Among Jews and Gentiles* I have tried to show that this Pauline pattern of thought is triggered by Paul's desire to defend and substantiate his calling, his mission to the gentiles. It is in the drama of God's new act of grace to the gentiles that Paul's theological reflections on sin and law have their center. Hence he rarely uses the word "sin" in plural, nor does he speak of specific sins. He never uses the expression "forgiveness of sins." In Rom. 4:7 he quotes Ps. 32:1 (LXX, "Blessed are those whose iniquities are forgiven . . . "), but does not pick up the forgiveness-language in his application of the quotation.

There is no basis for the common belief that Paul's theology was born out of his struggle with his own conscience trying to live up to the commandments. On the contrary, he speaks of himself as quite successful in that respect (Phil. 3:6). The only sin of his to which he refers is that he had "persecuted the church of God" (1 Cor. 15:9).

Paul often speaks about his weakness. But never (except *perhaps* in Rom. 5:6 and 8) does he see weakness as sin, or as a sign of sinful nature, nor does it cause him guilt feelings. The weakness comes from without; it tests him and sobers him; it teaches him a style of ministry. Having the treasure in clay pots makes it easier for him to show that the power and glory is God's and not his own (2 Cor. 4:7).

As imaginative and unique as Paul's reflections on the drama of sin, law, and justification are, just as standard and commonplace are his ethical instructions about virtues and vices. Here he seems to draw happily on the catechisms of Hellenistic Judaism. It seems that Paul was not too interested in such things. His moral instructions take on more life and character when he deals with communal problems. In 1 Corinthians he applies to great advantage the political metaphor of the body and its members. And in counseling coexistence and mutual respect between Christians of conflicting life styles he coins the marvelous principle: for whatever is not done out of individual conviction is sin (Rom. 14:23; cf. v. 5).

SIN IN THE JOHANNINE WRITINGS

In the Johannine gospel we find again that what is said about sin is part of a messianic perspective. When the Jews and "the world"—the stylized term for unbelief in John—do not accept Jesus the Revealer, then that is the sin (8:24), and the Spirit will convince/convict the world of sin "because they do not believe in me" (16:9). Only the Son can free from sin (8:34–37); his sonship means that no one can convict him of sin (8:46; cf. 1 John 3:5). The sin of the "blind" Jews is the greater since they think they see (9:41; cf. 19:11). Sin reaches its climax with the coming of the Son (15:22; cf. 3:19). Jesus is greeted by John the Baptist as "the Lamb of God, who takes away the sin of the world" (1:29; cf. 1 John 3:5). The understanding of illness as punishment for sin is presupposed (5:14), but it is overshadowed by the unique importance of the

131

Revealer having come: illness gives Jesus the opportunity of revealing God's acts (9:1–4).

The First Epistle of John does not differ from the gospel's view of sin. In both, sin is related to darkness, lies, and that liar Satan (cf. Revelation). In 1 John we find the famous "paradox" which states that it is impossible for the children of God to sin (3:9; cf. John 15:3; 13:10), and the rebuke of those who say they have no sin (1:8). But it is reasonable to think that this becomes a paradox only in retrospect, when the feel for the context is lost in favor of a one-dimensional use of Scripture as timeless doctrinal statements. So in spite of theological and even manuscript manipulations, it seems that each statement is quite clear in its own literary context.

SPECIFIC SINS

Specific ethical instruction in the NT is usually expressed in catechetical lists of virtues and vices. From the *Didache* we know such material in the form of the two ways (1–3; cf. the Epistle of Barnabas 18–20). Mark 7:21f. parr. offers similar material. The virtues and vices listed are hardly specific for Christianity but commonplace in Hellenistic Judaism and in the teaching of popular Greco-Roman philosophers. In such lists there is no attempt to place a Christian ethic over against that of the surrounding culture.

The image of gentile sins that Paul uses for his specific purposes in Rom. 1:18ff. is the commonplace Jewish perception of the gentiles, and his specific critique of the Jews (Romans 2) echoes what the sages did in criticizing the superficiality of their contemporaries, including the shaming of the people at home by the achievements of the gentiles (2:12–16; cf. Matt. 5:47 with the Lukan parallel using the designation "sinners" for "gentiles," Luke 6:33). The teachings about Sabbath, kosher laws, and divorce have, however, a special accent. The sayings of Jesus in passages, such as Mark 2:27f. parr.; 7:18–23 parr.; 10:1–12 parr., are not without their rabbinic parallels, but their thrust goes beyond the confines of Jewish teaching by becoming programmatic. Here, as also in the Sermon on the Mount, we see a radical sharpening and transcending of the commands, a move grounded in the intensity of the eschatological situation. With the kingdom at hand it is allowed and possible to practice radical ethics. For Luke the "exibit A" of such sharpening of the demand is Jesus' objection to divorce. In Luke 16:16–18 it is the prohibition against divorce that demonstrates how not a dot of the law becomes void. Matthew rather demonstrates this same principle by the antithesis of the Sermon on the Mount where the messianic license (see above, p. 85ff.) leads to a superior ethical perception.

The Christians live in a world where the devil prowls around, seeking someone to devour (1 Pet. 5:8). Apostasy is and remains *the* sin to guard against. Even so, the NT writings are less preoccupied with that grim risk. The predominant tone is rather one of grateful awareness to God who "called you out of darkness into his marvelous light" (1 Pet. 2:9). It is certainly not a mood of constant self-incrimination, or even self-examination. On the whole the NT writers think of sin as something past; they are not preoccupied with present consciousness of sin. To be sure, there are admonitions, but they are commonplace. And when Paul carries out his church disciplinary excommunication in an extreme case in Corinth (1 Corinthians 5), it seems that he has no doubt that it is a step toward the salvation of the grave sinner's spirit. When the RSV translates "you are to deliver this man to Satan for the destruction of the flesh, that his spirit *may* be saved in the day of our Lord Jesus," then we must remember that the subjunctive "may be saved" (5:5), is governed by the syntax, not by any doubt in Paul's mind about the happy outcome. So we should read this as "in order to save his spirit." So powerful is God's calling that it is hard for Paul to think that it will not lead to salvation, even for a rascal like that.

TERMS FOR FORGIVENESS

The various NT writings divide significantly in their use of the term "forgiveness of sins." In the synoptic gospels and in Acts it serves as the summary term for what Jesus or the baptism in his name (and in an anticipating manner also John the Baptist) requires and brings. Actually the word "sin" hardly occurs in these writings except in the expression "forgiveness of sins," or when the verb "forgive" appears with "sins" as the object. It is significant that here the word is "sins" always in plural, designating a state rather than a specific sin or set of sins (cf. Matt. 1:21 where the name "Jesus"—from the Hebrew stem "to save"—is interpreted as the one who shall save his people from their sins: the forgiveness of sins removes the blockage for the restoration of God's people).

The rest of the NT almost totally lacks this formulaic expression. The only exception is an apposition in Col. 1:14 (cf. Eph. 1:7; on Rom. 4:7, see above, p. 131). The "passing over" of former sins (Rom. 3:25) does not refer to forgiveness, but to the way in which God in his restraint waited to settle the accounts. (The best understanding of this web of ideas is found in Sam K. Williams, *Jesus' Death as Saving Event: The Background and Origin of a Concept* [1975]; cf. also his article, "The Righteousness of God in Romans," *Journal of Biblical Literature* 99 [1980], 241–90.) Twice in Hebrews "forgiveness" is used in the discussion of the true sacrifice (9:22 and 10:18). In John 20:23 (cf. 1 John 5:16ff. and James 5:15) the forgiveness of sins has as its frame of reference the church's disciplinary practice of confession and absolution.

For contemporary Christians who often summarize the gospel in the message of God's forgiveness these data are somewhat surprising. Most particularly surprising is the absence of forgiveness-language in Paul, the patron saint of Lutheranism, with its stress on sin and forgiveness. How then are we to account for these data? An attempt may look like this: Jesus had spoken of forgiveness of sins, and that terminology became part of the gospel tradition. But in one's own language one wanted to give more specific answers to the question: *How* is this forgiveness to be found in Jesus Christ? Hence the "heavier" expressions of salvation, redemption, reconciliation, justification, and so forth. In Matthew we can see that process at work when, on reflection, the forgiveness of sins is tied to "my blood of the covenant" (in the words of institution, 26:28), and not to the message and baptism of John (Matt. 3:2) where Mark and Luke contain passages about forgiveness (Mark 1:4 parr.).

THE ESCHATOLOGICAL PERSPECTIVE

The synoptic gospels see the healing of the paralytic and Jesus' words on that occasion as a programmatic statement about Jesus' authority to forgive sins (Mark 2:1–12 parr., esp. Matthew). Here Jesus is the Son of man to whom the authority was given to be the eschatological judge (cf. John 5:27). This authority he exercises already now, "on earth" (2:10). As the appointed judge (cf. Acts 17:31) he acts in an anticipatory manner, declaring a sinner free. It is significant for the earthly mission of Jesus that the negative side of his authority, that is, the condemnation, is never spoken with finality to any person or situation. The curses of Jesus always have a conditional and future form, with a margin of repentance. Only the fig tree is cursed—the symbol and the symbolic act serving as a cushion between the curse and the people (Mark 11:12–14 parr.).

THE HOW AND THE WHY

Forgiveness of sins was a self-evident part of the coming of God's restoration (Jer. 31:31–34: " . . . and I will remember their sin no more"). The coming of the Messiah becomes a sign of that forgiveness. The specifics of Jesus' life, death, and resurrection are all interpreted as bringing about that forgiveness. He gives his life as a ransom for many (Mark 10:45); he is the Lamb of God (John 1:36); the image of his healing ministry (Matt. 8:17) and his death merge with that of the suffering servant in Isaiah 53 (most elaborately in 1 Pet. 2:21–25). In Hebrews, Christ is the ultimate sacrifice, priest, and sacrifice together and once and for all, and in 1 John 2:2 the redemption is "for our sins, and not for ours only but also for the sins of the whole world." The vocabulary of the church intensifies and grows in reflections for which the forgiveness of sins becomes only one of the many ways to reap the fruits of a cosmic and eternal salvation.

LIMITS TO FORGIVENESS

For Luke the story about the lost sheep (15:4–7) is in defense of the company that Jesus keeps with sinners. But for Matthew it serves as introductory sayings about church discipline, and hence the sheep is not lost but has strayed (18:10–14). For in matters of lapsed and delinquent members, everything must be done to lead them back to the community—unless in the end there must be excommunication. The thrust of the passage is toward reconciliation, forgiving seventy times seven times (Luke has typically "seven times a day") and remembering that we all are forgiven plenty (18:15–35). It is in carrying out these church disciplinary procedures that Matthew sees the meaning of the saying, "Where two or three are gathered together in my name, there I am in their midst," hence lending authority to the procedure, which is strikingly similar to what Paul practices in 1 Cor. 5:1–5 (cf. John 20:23). Other church disciplinary actions can be described with gruesome finality as in the story of Ananias and Sapphira, where Peter performs a healing miracle in reverse (Acts 5:1–11) in the case of dishonest dealings with the community; and Hebrews teaches, in times of persecution, that there is no return or repentance for the apostate (6:4; 10:26f.). First John 5:16f. speaks of "deadly sins." For such there can be no intercessions.

Such limits to forgiveness grow out of a stark and realistic awareness

135

of the drastic finality of *the* great forgiveness offered in the first repentance and in baptism. For one did not understand the forgiveness of sins
as an idea that could or should be applied everywhere in the world or in
the church. Rather the forgiveness of sins was a mighty act of God that
created a new community of "saints." The Matthean form of the fateful
saying about the unforgivable sin (Matt. 12:30ff.) may actually shed
light on this self-understanding of the church: to speak against "the Son
of man" (the Jesus of his earthly ministry) is still allowed for a period of
repentance; but once the Holy Spirit operates in the new community,
then there is no longer a margin for repentance.

10

Hate, Nonretaliation, and Love: Coals of Fire

Introductory Note: This essay deals primarily with one of the "hard sayings" in the NT: Rom. 12:19–21, and the coals of fire heaped on the heads of enemies. In a way, it is a test case for a hermeneutical model that glories in unearthing the original intention of Paul, for the passage cries out for softening interpretations. As has been shown by Sam K. Williams, the motif of God's temporary restraint of vengeance is significantly operative also elsewhere in Romans, especially in the crucial passage, 3:25b–26: ". . . because of the passing over of the prior sins, due to God's restraint" (see his *Jesus' Death as Saving Event*, HDR 2 [Missoula, Mont.: Scholars Press, 1975], 19f.; also now his important article, " 'The Righteousness of God' in Romans," *Journal of Biblical Literature* 99 [1980]: 241–90).

In retrospect, I have come to wonder if the interpretation I give here of Rom. 12:19–21 does not give a key also to Romans 13 with its counsel to accept the Roman order. If so, that chapter would have to be seen as Paul speaking "tongue in cheek," using eschatology for the purpose of belittling the state. For it is clear that Paul's use of eschatology (cf. 13:11) is always functional rather than proclaimed for its own sake, see now Vincent L. Wimbush, *HOS ME [As If Not]: Paul's Use of an Expression in the Context of Understandings of "World" (Rom. 7:29–35)*, Ph.D. diss., Harvard University, 1983.

The observations in note 2, below, may have extensive significance for the understanding of the history of biblical interpretations of ethics through the ages, as indicated above, p. 85.

The article was published in *Harvard Theological Review* 55

(1962):345–55. That was the issue of the review set aside to celebrate the sixtieth birthday of Professor Arthur Darby Nock whose untimely death, however, made the articles a tribute to his memory. I had been working on the article for some time (see below, note 30), and Nock's precise and generous suggestions and caveats form part of it. But it was not until the last moment of writing that it dawned on me that love and nonretaliation may not be the same thing. Hence the title.

I will not return evil to anybody, with good will I pursue man, for with God rests the judgment of every living being and he is the one to repay man for his deeds. . . . And the trial of a man of perdition I will not handle until the Day of Vengeance. But my anger I will not turn away from the men of deceit, and I will not be content until He has established judgment (1 QS x, 17–20).

In these hymnic phrases the attitudes of nonretaliation and hatred are woven together in a striking manner.[1] Yet there should be nothing strange in this juxtaposition; rather it helps us to discern the structure of Qumranite ethics, even to the point where it appears that the nonretaliation is grounded in the eschatological intensity of the "eternal hatred towards the men of perdition" (1 QS ix, 21f.).

This polarity between nonretaliation and hatred may, nevertheless, have been striking even in the eyes of the contemporary observer. When Josephus speaks about the "awesome oaths" (ὅρκους φρικώδεις) which the Essenes take upon themselves he lists among them: " . . . that he will wrong no one . . . ; that he will hate always the unjust and fight with the just" (Bell. II, viii, 7).[2] This seems to be in good agreement with the manual, where we can discern the actual procedure of admission: "He shall love each one of the sons of light according to his lot in the council of God, and hate each one of the sons of darkness according to his guilt (as it stands) in the (impending) vengeance of God"[3] (1 QS i, 9–11). But we shall see how at Qumran "love" is confined to the community and, how the attitude of nonretaliation is by no means a type of love. To pursue outsiders with good is a special case of "the eternal hatred," not of love.

While the juxtaposition of nonretaliation and hatred may be a striking feature, the different elements can be readily identified as central to the OT. The hatred for the enemies, which are not only the enemies of the righteous but the enemies of God, is well known from the Psalms. "Do I not hate them that hate thee, O Lord? I hate them with perfect hatred;

I count them *my* enemies" (Ps. 139:21f.). Psalm 79 is a strong witness to the unconditional identification of the enemies of God and the enemies of Israel. In the Song of Moses (Deuteronomy 32) the evil of the enemies is stored up against them toward the day of vengeance (v. 34); and we read: "Vengeance is mine, and recompense, for the time when their foot shall slip; for the day of their calamity is at hand, and their doom comes swiftly. For the Lord will vindicate his people and have compassion on his servants" (vv. 35–36; cf. 41–43).

In the Qumran texts the sovereignty of God is stressed by the strongest language (e.g., 1 QS ix,11; 1 QH i, 20), and it is heightened by the eschatological intensity of the sect. The day of vengeance is close at hand. In such a situation one can afford to practice nonretaliation toward the enemies—the enemies of the righteous which are by definition also the enemies of God.[4] For eschatological intensity always means that all shades of grey disappear; there is only black and white. Hence the line goes not *within* the hearts of men with their good and bad inclinations as in the teaching of the Pharisees. The line is now drawn *between* the men of the Spirit of Light *and* the men of the Spirit of Darkness. With the day of vengeance at hand the proper and reasonable attitude is to forgo one's own vengeance and to leave vengeance to God. Why walk around with a little shotgun when the atomic blast is imminent? Whatever we may think about such a frame of mind, there can be little doubt that it is in such a framework that the juxtaposition of nonretaliation and hatred in the Qumran texts can be understood.

This mood and framework should be remembered when we read Paul's admonitions to the Romans:

> Repay no one evil for evil, but take thought for what is noble in the sight of all. If possible, so far as it depends upon you, live peaceably with all. Beloved, never avenge yourselves, but leave it to the wrath of God; for it is written, "Vengeance is mine, I will repay, says the Lord." No, "if your enemy is hungry, feed him; if he is thirsty, give him drink; for by so doing you will heap burning coals upon his head." Do not be overcome by evil, but overcome evil with good (12:17–21).

The interpretation of this passage depends partly on who the enemies are, and with whom the Christians are to keep peace if possible. Beginning with Rom. 12:14 the attention is shifting from the insiders to the outsiders, to the persecutors and to the attitude toward the world at large, and in 13:1–7 we are told about the role of the authorities in this world. The admonitions in verses 15–16, which repeat what has been said in verse 3, may well be understood as about the community under

139

persecution. In any case verses 19–20 speak about enemies. These must
be the outsiders. Apart from the general use in Gal. 4:16 and Phil. 3:18,
neither Paul nor the NT at large ever uses "enemy" for a fellow Christian.[5] According to 2 Thess. 3:15 even a brother who is to be totally os-
tracized by the church should not be considered an "enemy." And in
most of the NT there is little doubt that these enemies are the enemies
of God and of his Messiah.[6] They are related to the enemies mentioned
in Ps. 110:1 (one of the OT passages most quoted in the NT: Mark
12:36 parr.; Acts 2:35; 1 Cor. 15:25; Heb. 1:13; 10:13). It is only by a
clear distinction between the general question of love for one's fellow
men and the daring possibility of nonretaliation toward God's enemies,[7] that we can approach this Pauline passage.

We note that the attitude of nonretaliation is motivated by the admonition to give room for God's judgment, the wrath (v. 19).[8] This motivation is furthermore substantiated by the quotation from Deut.
32:35, which we have seen as the background to the Qumran attitude.[9]
The idea is one of *deference*, not different from the statement about
Christ (1 Pet. 2:23), "when he was reviled, he did not revile in return;
when he suffered, he did not threaten, παρεδίδου δὲ τῷ κρίνοντι
δικαίως." In its context this portrait of Christ is an example for submis-
sion to unjust treatment. It is this same deference of the final judgment
that Paul calls for, when he instructs the Christians to refrain from
avenging themselves.

He also tells his readers how this attitude should express itself positively. This he does by the quotation from Prov. 25:21f. with its rather
enigmatic reference to the coals of fire. The two main lines of Christian
interpretation were established already in patristic times. Origen and
Chrysostom, on the one hand, saw here a warning that those who re-
sisted such kind deeds were guilty of more serious punishment, which
hence was stored up against them. Augustine and Jerome, on the other
hand, understood the "coals of fire" as "burning pangs of shame"
which may produce remorse.[10] The latter interpretation has been supported in modern times by reference to the penitential practice in Egypt
described in a demotic text from the third century B.C.[11] More recently
M. J. Dahood has suggested that *ḥatâh 'al* be translated not by "heaping upon" but "remove from." While such an interpretation of the
Masoretic text may be possible, it is irrelevant to the understanding of
the LXX and of the Pauline quotation, which both read σωρεύσεις
ἐπί.[12]

The image of the burning coals is not confined to Proverbs. In Ps.

140:10 we read in a prayer for delivery from enemies: "Let burning coals fall upon them! Let them be cast into pits, no more to rise." In the Christian 5(2) Esdras 16:52–53 we find the same use of the image as one of God's judgment: "Behold, just a little while, and iniquity will be removed from the earth, and righteousness will reign over us. Let no sinner say that he has not sinned; for He (God) will burn coals of fire on the head of him who says, 'I have not sinned before God and his glory,'" For a study of Rom. 12:20 it is of interest to note that here the coals of fire imply an element of surprise. They are heaped on those who did not know that they had sinned.

Proverbs 25:21–22 has received considerable interpretative attention in the Jewish tradition. In Aboth R. Nathan 16 (6a) a quotation, which also includes the last part of verse 22 ("and the Lord will reward thee"), is annotated by the comment: "read not 'will reward thee' (*yešallem lak*) but 'will put him at peace with thee' (*yašlimennu lak*)."[13] But it should be noted that his emendation seems to go together with a consistent rabbinic interpretation of Prov. 25:21–22 where "he who hates you" is the *yetzer ha-ra'*, the evil inclination, and where the bread and the drink is the Torah which has the power of overcoming the evil inclination in man. In Pirke Aboth 2:10 (R. Eliezer) the teaching of the sages is called a fire, "but be heedful of their glowing coals lest thou be burned . . . and all their words are like coals of fire."[14]

But when the text is applied to actual enemies, it is taken in its Masoretic form and meaning. In a Baraitha in bMeg.15b the question why Esther invited Haman, is answered by R. Eliezer with a reference to the table which became a snare (Ps. 69:23) while his contemporary R. Joshua refers to Prov. 25:21f.

There is no ancient rabbinic evidence for a positive concern for the betterment of the enemy, and the awareness of an establishment of peace between the two parties is bound up with an allegorical interpretation about the evil inclination. Hence it is difficult to use this rabbinic material to support an interpretation according to which Paul would think about the function of the coals of fire as "pangs of shame" as a means toward repentance for the enemies. Already Paul's use of the LXX future tense in σωρεύσεις makes it easier to read his words in an eschatological sense: if you act in nonretaliation your good deeds are stored up as a further accusation against your enemy for the day of wrath to which you should defer all judgment.

In later Rabbinic material there are warnings against such deference and then the discussion centers around Gen. 16:5. We hear how Sarah's life was shortened since she had said to Abraham: Yahweh be the judge between us! But this discussion is concerned with tensions among Jews and has no application to the relation between the people of God and its enemies.[15]

If we return to the Qumran material with this quotation from Proverbs in our mind, we may, however, find a more explicit framework for its understanding. The norms for the member of the Qumran sect "in these times (i.e., with the day of vengeance impending), with respect to his hatred" (1 QS ix, 21) are not only described in the terms of nonretaliation as stated in the text from which we took our departure, x, 17–20. In ix.21ff. we read:

> (There shall be) eternal hatred against the men of perdition, *in a spirit of concealment*, so as to leave to them property and the labor of hands, as a slave does to his master, subdued before him who lords it over him. So he (the member) shall be a man zealous for the ordinance and its (relation to the proper knowledge of God's) time, toward the Day of Vengeance so as to do what is (God's good) pleasure in all activities and in all his ruling as He (God) has commanded. And all that is done to him he accepts willingly.[16]

The "eternal hatred" (cf. x, 20) is thus practiced in a hidden way, in that he does not interfere with the affairs of the world. He does not raise any just claims on behalf of God regarding such matters. The world is allowed to run its course, toward the day of vengeance. He conceals his hatred by appearing obedient and subdued and peaceful[17] and willing to be deprived of property and produce.

This "spirit of concealment," which here is applied to the actual behavior of the eschatological community, is better known from another, more theological context in Judaism. It is part of the theodicy in times of trouble. The Psalms of Solomon (esp. chap. 13) distinguish between the chastening of the righteous and the final destruction of the sinners.[18] More explicit is this pattern in 2 Macc. 6:12ff.:

> Now I urge those who read this book not to be depressed by such calamities, but to recognize that these punishments were designed not to destroy but to discipline our people. In fact, not to let the impious (δυσσεβοῦντας) alone for long, but to punish them immediately, is a sign of great kindness. For in the case of the other nations the Lord waits patiently to punish them until they have reached the full measure of their sins; but he does not deal in this way with us, in order that he may not take vengeance on us afterward when our sins have reached their height.

Thus only Israel is warned by chastisement and hardships, and this by the grace of God. But the other nations, the enemies, who lord it over

Israel, run unwarned and untroubled to their condemnation when their sins have reached full measure.[19] This concealment is structurally identical to the one applied to sectarian and individual behavior in the Qumran texts. The eschatological intensity of the sect makes this quite natural. The sect has drawn the consequences of "the times" and its members practice their eternal hatred for all evil in a spirit of concealment, in which they practice nonretaliation and pursue mankind with good, but their anger they will not turn away until God has accomplished judgment (1 QS x, 18ff.).

In the Testaments of the Twelve Patriarchs we find, however, a different spirit in regard to love, nonretaliation, and hatred. The most striking examples are Test. Benj. 4–5 and Test. Gad 6–7. Here the possibility of winning the enemy over by showing mercy is clearly stated. Furthermore, the righteous takes a posture of prayer, and in Test. Jos. 18:2 this is definitely a prayer for the one who seeks to harm him. In Test. Gad 6:7 the ultimate recourse is to the vengeance of God, but this is not done in a spirit of concealed eternal hatred, but with "forgiveness from the heart." The interpretation of these texts depends of course on whether the testaments address themselves to the relations between fellow Jews, or to the attitude toward outsiders, persecutors, and oppressors of the righteous. A third possibility may be the one closest to the truth: this distinction is not consciously in focus, but neither is it transcended by an explicit universalism. Hence the statements are of a general wisdom character, but primarily and immediately applied to the life in the community (cf. Ecclus. 28:1–7).[20]

This is the more natural since the great example of the spirit of humble nonretaliation is Joseph's way of handling the evil plotting of his brothers. Test. Benj. 4–5 deals with the happy end of the good man Joseph. He did not repay evil by evil, he was not jealous, and so forth. Joseph had exemplified how a good man can exert his influence and teach his brethren. "If anyone does violence to a pious man, he repents;[21] for the pious man is merciful to his reviler, and holds his peace. And if anyone betrays a righteous man, the righteous man prays; though for a little while he be humbled, yet not long after he appears much more glorious, as was Joseph my brother" (Test. Benj. 5:4–5). While the prayer in Test. Jos. 18:2 was explicitly an intercession for the offenders, this is not clearly the case here.[22] In both cases it is the rescue and exoneration of the afflicted that are important, not the conversion of the offenders.

In Test. Gad the attitude of love instead of hate against the brother (cf. Test. Sim. 4:4) is also applied to the act of hatred by which Gad and Simeon sold Joseph (2:3). Gad has been chastised and learned his lesson (chap. 5). But we note that the attitude of love and forgiveness is partly motivated by pragmatic reasons. It is more prudent and expedient to love than to hate (6:5–6; 7:1). There is little point in being jealous, since all flesh shall die and in the end the Lord has reserved the unrepentant for eternal punishment (7:2–6).

Thus we find that the Testaments of the Twelve Patriarchs have generalized the pattern of brotherly ethics; there is awareness of the wisdom of love rather than hate and retaliation; there is possibility of the good influence of love prompting repentance and betterment. All this is in accordance with the sound, relaxed, and sensitive climate of wisdom. The sharp line between the elect and the sons of perdition is not drawn. Once that happens, this margin of repentance seems to be a luxury beyond what one can afford in the last days.[23]

Theoretically we should then be able to assess the Pauline understanding about the coals of fire by deciding whether the Pauline climate comes closer to the Testaments or to Qumran. In a letter where the recipients are told that their salvation is now closer at hand than when they came to faith (Rom. 13:11), the eschatological acceleration appears considerable, and there can be little doubt that Paul assesses his time as the very last of the old eon, since he anticipates to be around at the Parousia (1 Cor. 15:52; "the dead will be raised and *we* shall be transformed"). The "gentleness" that Paul wants the Philippians to show forth (Phil. 4:5) is closely related to the attitude we have been analyzing in Rom. 12:17–21; τὸ ἐπιεικές and ἡ ἐπιείκεια signify a graciousness out of strength,[24] and the specific strength here lies in the words "the Lord is nigh." The same tone and combination may be present in Col. 4:5, ἐν σοφίᾳ περιπατεῖτε πρὸς τοὺς ἔξω, τὸν καιρὸν ἐξαγοραζόμενοι.

While it is true that the interpretation of Rom. 12:20 would have to depend to some extent on one's general understanding of Paul and the nature of his eschatology, it is nevertheless fair to ask whether the passage as it stands could reasonably be understood by its first readers in any other sense than as a word related to the vengeance of God. Even if the Testaments do count with the possibility of repentance due to the good example, there is no reference to Prov. 25:21f. in that connection. And the element in these verses from Proverbs, which were reinterpreted in Jewish exegesis toward a peaceful end, was exactly those concluding words, which are not quoted by Paul. The rabbinic exegesis shows furthermore no knowledge of the "coals of fire" as part of a penitential ritual, but goes quite different ways when a reinterpretation is needed. Hence every reference to the penitential connotation in the image as such can be totally disregarded in the Pauline context.

In Rom. 2:4–5 Paul refers to how God's kindness and forbearance to the Jews were aimed at their repentance. But when they now are unwilling to repent in the only way which Paul considers adequate in the present time, that is, by accepting Jesus as the Messiah, he addresses the Jews by saying: "But by your hard and impenitent heart you are storing up wrath for yourself on the day of wrath when God's righteous judgment will be revealed." Such enemies of God and his Messiah are dealt with in rather definite terms (cf. 1 Thess. 2:16). To be sure, Paul anticipates the ultimate salvation of Israel as the climax of history, but this is an event of quite another order (Romans 11 see below, p. 243). In actual personal relations Paul is not certain about the effect of positive influences, since salvation is according to the will of God: "Wife, how do you know whether you will save your husband? Husband, how do you know whether you will save your wife?" (1 Cor. 7:16). It is rather in 1 Peter that the missionary power of the Christian way of life is stressed (3:1–2; 2:12; cf. Matt. 5:16).

The closer study of the catechetical forms in the NT, which was begun by A. Seeberg and has been renewed and carried further by Ph. Carrington and especially by E. G. Selwyn, places Romans 12 and 13 in a complex, yet real relation, to other NT writings, especially 1 Thess. 4—5 and 1 Peter 2—3.[25] But Rom. 12:19—21 still remains without actual parallels in the NT. The quotation from Deut. 32:35 is, however, used in Heb. 10:30 with reference to apostasy, with the additional line: "It is a fearful thing to fall into the hands of the living God."[26] But to Paul the reference to judgment is a victorious one, since he speaks about the elect in their relation to the enemies. His tone is closer to Luke 18:7f.: "And will not God vindicate his elect who cry to him day and night? I tell you, he will vindicate them speedily." And he would not mind quoting James 1:20: "For the anger of man does not work the righteousness of God."

It has usually been argued that the concluding verse in Rom. 12:21, "Do not be overcome by evil, but overcome evil with good," is an unambiguous witness for reading the quotation from Proverbs as a word about the power of love to influence evil. That is by no means certain. If we were to read verses 19–20 as a deference to God's judgment, where the good deeds are stored up against the enemies—God's and those of the Christians—then that would be just as much a victory over evil, without falling for the temptation to retaliate. The motif of "moving on" rather than "insistence" is worth pursuing in the different strata of the NT and may be significant in this context (cf. Matt. 10:11–14, 23). In a church that prays not for the power to fight evil, but to be delivered from evil, this makes perfect sense. And to Paul, God's help provides an ἔκβασις, not a victory, when the temptation and trial come (1 Cor. 10:13).[27]

Much of our argument has been rather negative in nature. We have tried to refute some of the support for having Paul say what appears more in accordance with what we would hail as Christian ethics.[28] Once this has been done, and the Qumran material is placed side by side with the NT, it should become rather clear that Paul here comes very close to it at least in two respects:

1. The nonretaliation is undoubtedly based on and motivated by the deference to God's impending vengeance. It is not deduced from a principle of love or from within the wisdom tradition. Neither Qumran nor Paul speaks about love for enemies. The issue is rather how to act when all attempts to avoid conflict with the enemies of God and of his church have failed (vv. 17f.).

2. The specific answer given to this question by Paul is found in the quotations from Deuteronomy 32 and Proverbs 25. We have found no basis for thinking that this could be understood by his readers in any other sense than as a qualified form of adding to the measure of the sins of the enemy. And with the help of the Qumran texts and of Jewish material concerned with the assault of enemies we have pointed to a pattern where such an attitude of doing good to the enemies of God conforms to God's own way of handling the world and his elect within it.

Once this has been seen in Paul, it would be tempting to pursue these two points in other strata of the NT, and especially in the Sermon on the Mount. It would be reasonable to find that the command about turning the other cheek where the pressure comes from enemies and "outsiders" (Matt. 5:39: μὴ ἀντιστῆναι τῷ πονηρῷ), and the logion about not judging (7:1) have as their basis the trust in the ultimate judgment of God, as has the urgency to make friends with your adversary (5:25: ἀντίδικος, not an enemy of God). And we would have to ask whether the image about God who treats the righteous and the unrighteous equally by his sun and his rain is not possibly of one piece with the pattern of not giving warning to the enemies (5:45). Even if that were so, we find in Matt. 5:44–48 elements that seem to transcend such an interpretation. There is the emphasis on prayer for the persecutors.

And there is here, and only here, the explicit words about ἀγαπαν τὸν ἐχθρόν σου—not only treating him well. But it should also be noted that there is no intimation that such an attitude is envisaged as a means to cause repentance or toward overcoming enmity.[29] It is rather seen as the right attitude in an unfriendly world, and it is right and beyond human calculation since it is congruous to the attitude of God.[30]

NOTES

1. On "hatred" in Qumran, see E. F. Sutcliff, *Rev. Qum.* 2 (1960), 345–56, cf. idem, *The Monks of Qumran* (1960), 81f.

2. This passage in Josephus is closely related to 1 QS i also in its stress on the right relation to those in power (μάλιστα δὲ τοῖς κρατοῦσιν). Hence Josephus may refer to the leaders of the community; or, and what is more probable, he consciously generalizes the community attitudes to have them serve as an ideal for common social virtues. This seems to be the case also when he describes them as "holding righteous indignation in reserve (ὀργῆς ταμίαι δί-καιοι—lit.: righteous controllers of wrath), being masters of their temper, champions of fidelity, very ministers of peace" (viii,6). For the more specific and colorful nature of this attitude at Qumran, see below note 17.

3. *běniqmāt 'el*. On *naqam* in the OT, see G. E. Mendenhall, in the *Wittenberg Bulletin* (Dec. 1948): 37–42.

4. It should be noted that the "enemies," the men of perdition and deceit, are the sons of darkness and are always outsiders; the tensions between members of the community are handled with a different terminology, see, e.g., v, 24–vi, 1 and vi, 24–vii, 25. See also CDC vi, 20ff. and ix, 2.

5. For Matt. 5:43–48, see above, pp. 146–147.

6. Cf. O. Michel, *Der Brief an die Römer* (Meyer Komm, 1955), "Bei dem 'Feind' hat man an den konkreten Widersacher der christlichen Gemeinde zu denken, der in seiner Person das 'Böse' verkörpern kann" (278).

7. Michel, ibid., uses the adequate term *das Wagnis der Feindesliebe*. It remains to be seen whether we should not actually speak about nonretaliation rather than "love of enemies" also in Paul, but the element of daring and of risk is obvious, and is the point at which the impending judgment makes a difference.

8. Cf. Rom. 5:9. See G. H. C. MacGregor, "The Concept of the Wrath of God in the New Testament," *N.T. Studies* 7 (1960/61): 101–9; and A. T. Hanson, *The Wrath of the Lamb* (1957), 91, 97, and 101.

9. This quotation is used also in Heb. 10:30. Its occurrence in the context of church discipline would argue against our definition of "enemies" as outsiders, were it not for the fact that the ultimate and irrevocable apostasy in Hebrews 10 makes such a "brother" worse than the enemies. This passage is the more significant, since the apostasy here seems to be one under the pressure of persecution.

10. The New English Bible ties the reader to this alternative by making full use of ἀλλά as adversative and translates: "But there is another text: 'If your en-

emy . . . ' " Such an adversative relation between two scriptural quotations would be odd and I cannot find any instance in support. Hence the ἀλλά is either adversative in relation to the main alternative (to seek one's own vengeance), or generally heightening (so Michel, *Der Brief*, 278).

11. Latest and fullest discussion in S. Morenz, *Th. L.Z.* 78 (1953): 187–92; for the text see F. L. Griffith, *Stories of the High Priests of Memphis* (1900). Less attention has been given to a most intriguing passage in The Babylonian Book of Proverbs: "Verily, if it is thy quarrel which has flamed up, quench thou it. But be it a quarrel which is just, it is a bulwark, a protecting wall which (establishes) the shame of his adversary, so that his oppressor will act according to the mind of a friend.—In thine adversary not shalt thou place thy whole confidence. Unto him that doeth thee evil shalt thou return good. Unto thine enemy justice shalt thou mete out." S. Langdon, *Babylonian Wisdom* (1923), 90.

12. *Catholic Biblical Quarterly* 17 (1955): 19–23. Dahood must think that his suggestion has ramifications for Rom. 12:20, since his article bears the title "Two Pauline Quotations from the Old Testament," but he does not indicate how his interpretation could suggest itself to a reader of LXX or Romans.

13. So translates J. Goldin, *The Fathers according to Rabbi Nathan* (Yale Judaica Ser. 10, 1955), 85; lit.: "he will surrender him to you." For further references to this widespread emendation see Str.-B. III, 302. Later in chap. 16 of Aboth R. Nathan (Goldin, p. 86), we hear about the hate toward the sectarians, apostates, and informers. The proof-text is Ps. 139:21f., which we quoted above.

14. This imagery is used also in a setting of theodicy, where God's dealing with mankind is seen in the parable of the baker who from the same fire places coals of fire on his enemy's head and gives bread to his friend, i.e., from the one God came the fire of Sodom and the Manna to Israel. Str.-B. III, 303; Tanh. B § 20(33b).

15. Str.-B. III, 301 from GenR 45 (28c). Cf. Paul's cautious addition "but thereby I am not declared just" in 1 Cor. 4:4, although the context indicates that he is rather certain of the outcome, as he is also in 2 Cor. 5:11.

16. Prof. Frank Cross assisted me in arriving at this translation; for "done to him," cf. Dan. 9:12.

17. It may be this attitude which, translated into general terms of ethics, is described by Josephus as quoted in note 2 above.

18. For a reconstruction of the text, see K. G. Kuhn, *Die älteste Textgestalt des Psalmen Salomos* (Beitr. z. Wiss. d. A.u.N.T. 4:21; 1937).

19. Cf. Gen. 15:16. In 1 Thess. 2:16 Paul speaks about the resistance to his mission to the gentiles as being εἰς τὸ ἀναπληρῶσαι αὐτῶν τὰς ἁμαρτίας πάντοτε. ἔφθασεν δὲ ἐπ' αὐτοὺς ἡ ὀργὴ εἰς τέλος—cf. also Matt. 23:32f.; and 1 Cor. 11:31f.

20. R. Eppel, *Le piétisme juif dans les Testaments des Douze Patriarches* (1930), 157–62, notes the limits of universalism, but has not raised the question about the *Sitz in Leben*. Hence he treats the sayings from the point of view of ethical enlightenment.

21. While the text here, as in many places in the Testaments, is quite uncertain, μετανοεῖ seems to refer to the violator, and has to mean that he can and

does use the opportunity of repentance when the "pious man" shows mercy toward him by not retaliating.

22. In Test. Gad 5:9 it is the prayers of Jacob which rescue Gad from the punishment inflicted by God.

23. M. Buber has analyzed this difference from the perspective of two different types of faith (the actuality of faith as trust, and "believing that . . . "); cf. also his examples from rabbinic sources, *Two Types of Faith* (Eng. trans., 1951), 73–75.

24. See H. Preisker, in Th.W.B.II, 586.

25. See Essay II in E. G. Selwyn, *The First Epistle of St. Peter* (1949).

26. Cf. above, note 9.

27. Cf. 2 Pet. 2:9 where the sentence "The Lord knows (how) to deliver the godly out of temptation" is continued by a statement much akin to the thought expressed in Rom. 12:19–20, "but to preserve the unrighteous unto the day of judgment to be punished."

28. Indicative for the tone of most commentaries is the way in which, e.g., Sanday and Headlam (ICC, p. 365) rule out a harsh interpretation since it is harsh. I have found Michel, *Der Brief,* to be the most adequate of the modern commentaries; while he finally comes out on the Augustinian side, he gives a full and unbiased presentation of the comparative material and of the alternatives involved. H. Preisker, *Das Ethos des Urchristentums* (1949), on the other hand, reads Rom. 12:20 in the judgmental way and adds: "Ganz offensichtlich ist ein völlig anderer Geist in die christliche Liebe eingedrungen" (184).

29. Cf. *Didache* 1:3: "But you should love those who hate you, and you will have no enemies." M. Dibelius, *Die Formgeschichte des Evangeliums* (1933²), 249, calls this rightly a rationalized form of the logion; see also H. Köster, *Synoptische Überlieferung bei den Apostolischen Vätern* (T.U. 65; 1957), 221, 263, who ascribes this form to the editorial activity in *Didache*. Cf. Epict. Enchir. 1, and we are reminded of the tendency which expressed itself in the Test. XII Patr., e.g., Test. Benj. 5:1–3. For a discussion of Rom. 12:19–21 in comparison with Seneca, see J. N. Sevenster, *Paul and Seneca* (Suppl. to Novum Testamentum, vol. 5, 1961), 183–85.

30. The substance of this article was presented as a paper at the World Jewish Congress for Jewish Studies, in Jerusalem, July 1961, and to the Society of Biblical Literature and Exegesis, December 1961. At the latter meeting William Klassen read a paper on the very same topic. He comes to very different conclusions, quite opposite to mine. In addition, he gives a rich survey of the history of interpretation. "'Coals of Fire': Sign of Repentance or Revenge?" *NTS* 9 (1962): 337–50. He discusses my article on p. 346.

11

Paul
at Prayer

Introductory Note: Luke had the gift for graphic images of the people he wrote about. Of Paul it is said "for behold he is praying" (Acts 9:11). It becomes an intriguing task to get on the inside of Paul's mind and soul by using his own letters as far as they allow us to guess about Paul at prayer.

This essay from the journal *Interpretation* (published in *Interpretation* 34 [1980]:240–49) formed part of an issue dedicated to the subject of prayer. Only too late did I come across two extensive studies of the topic: David M. Stanley, *Boasting in the Lord: The Phenomenon of Prayer in St. Paul* (New York: Paulist Press, 1973), and Gordon Wiles, *Paul's Intercessory Prayers* (Cambridge: Cambridge University Press, 1974).

In his book *The Prayers of the New Testament*, Donald Coggan, the former archbishop of Canterbury, has gathered and commented upon what could be found as the most significant prayers of Paul.[1] It is instructive that none of the thirty or forty Pauline entries is what we would call a prayer. What we have in Paul is rather a style of writing that is saturated by prayerful language. His gratitude, his greetings, his farewells, his hopes, his admonitions, his worries, his travel plans are all often cast in a language that borders on prayer, a language shaped and informed by his awareness of divine presence, divine activity.

Much common thinking about prayer is dominated by the understanding of prayer as dialogue. That perspective is intensified in special ways by the dominance of anthropomorphism in the piety of the nineteenth century and into the twentieth. Romanticism, pietism, and liberalism all combine in an understanding of a "personal God" that actually sees God in an enlarged human-father image, without the transcending interplay between the three "persons" in the trinitarian mystery. And

Jesus is the one with whom we "walk and talk." In its own way, the I-Thou imagery of Martin Buber becomes a more academic form of this anthropomorphism. The numinous and God as power are often seen as sub-Christian or even subreligious.[2]

Such a perspective carries with it a tendency to find the center of Paul's prayer in his assertion of how we say Abba-Father (Gal. 4:6; Rom. 8:15);[3] but as we shall see, for Paul the reference to Abba-language is not part of his own prayers but rather a part of his quite specific arguments about what it means for Christians, and especially gentile Christians, to be heirs to the promises of God and about the way in which the Spirit gives and assures this status. Here Paul uses observations about the actual prayer life of the church as illustrations for a theological argument.

But first we must get hold of Paul's prayerful language. It expresses itself most pervasively in his greetings, doxologies, and confessional language. In all these cases the primary mood and mode is that of thanksgiving.

The typical greeting of Paul is one of grace (*charis*) and peace. In its shortest form it is found in the oldest of Paul's epistles, 1 Thess. 1:1: "Grace to you and peace." The conventional Greek greeting was *chaire/ chairete*, which had lost its etymological force of "rejoice" and had come to mean just "Good day," or "Greetings!"[4] Conscious of the assonance of *charis/chaire*, Paul uses a formula with *charis* and combines it with the pervasive Semitic greeting *shalom/eirene*. In the later epistles this greeting is further developed by the reference " . . . from God our Father and the Lord Jesus Christ" (Rom. 1:7; 1 Cor. 1:3; 2 Cor. 1:2; Gal. 1:3; Phil. 1:2; Philemon 3).

Since the now classic study by Paul Schubert on *Form and Function of the Pauline Thanksgiving*,[5] the greetings and introductory sections of Paul's letters have been well placed in relation to contemporary literary conventions. Here it becomes clear that Paul is quite a master of using literary conventions, but he transcends the stereotypic language in such a manner that each introduction—with its traditional giving thanks for and expressing one's remembrance of the addresses—becomes a true introduction to the very specific themes and concerns that follow in his letter. And in Galatians, where Paul sees little reason for thanks and much need for asserting divine authority, the very greeting of grace and peace turns into a doxological ascription to the acts of God in Christ and is concluded with an assertive "Amen!" (1:3–5). Thus the tone is

set for this stark letter of assertive authority and of Paul's direct relation
to Christ.

In the introductions we thus have a good guide to the mind-set of
Paul.[6] It is as apostle that Paul speaks a language that constantly borders on prayer and doxological confession.[7] And all his letters end with
farewell formulas similar to those of the greetings, again with attention
to themes and concerns of the specific letters. So, for example, 1 Corinthians ends (16:21–24) on the note of strong warning against a lack of
love (apparently with special attention to lack of equality at the common meals).[8] Then follows the greeting of grace, and last his "My love
be with you all in Christ Jesus," echoing the love theme which is so decisive in that epistle. For it is striking that there is no attention to God's
love in 1 Corinthians, but love, agape, is the quality that binds the
church together (1 Corinthians 13) and builds it up as over against the
gnosis that puffs up (8:1).

Paul's epistles are an integral part of his apostolic mission, and they
deal overtly with that mission to a far greater extent than traditional interpretation recognizes. The same is true about his "prayers." Thus the
requests to his congregations and their leaders for intercessory prayers
are dominated by his concern for that mission. Only in 1 Thess. 5:25 is
the request a general one, as part of the final greeting. More typical is 2
Cor. 1:11 where Paul places the struggles and vicissitudes of his life as
an apostle "for your comfort and salvation" (v. 6) before the Corinthians with the concluding words: " . . . and (God) will deliver (us) as you
cooperate by prayer for us in order that there be many to give thanks
on our behalf for the blessings granted us in answer to many who
prayed." Also in Philippians Paul counts on the prayers of the congregation as he faces martyrdom (1:19). And as Paul anticipates with fear
and trembling his visit to Jerusalem he writes to the Romans: "Join
with me in the struggle by your prayers to God" for a successful and
nonviolent outcome of the visit and a happy arrival in Rome in due
time (15:30–32). The same perspective becomes part of the Pauline tradition (2 Thess. 3:1; Col. 4:3; Eph. 6:18–20).

Paul's apostolic ministry is one of travels. There are many indications
that Paul's hopes and disappointments about his travels and plans
played a significant role in his life of prayer, as prayer did in his very
understanding of his ministry. The invitation to the Roman Christians
to join in his prayer-struggle (Rom. 15:30) was not just rhetoric. Time
and again he speaks of his frustration as to his itinerary (see, e.g., 1

Thess. 2:18; 3:10–11; Rom. 15:23; cf. 1:10); and in Philemon 22 he hopes that by their prayers it will be possible for him to make use of their hospitality. Once much blessing came out of an illness that changed his plans. The illness that stranded him in Galatia proved to be a blessing both to the results of that mission and to a right understanding of the nature of the mission itself (Gal. 4:12–14). It is interesting indeed that as Luke reconstructs Paul's missionary travels in his Acts, it is exactly with reference to Galatia that we hear how the Holy Spirit/the Spirit of Jesus "hindered" them to move on according to plan (Acts 16:6f.).[9] But in 1 Thess. 2:18 the reason for dashed travel plans has the stark designation: "Satan hindered us." What to Luke's more distant and pious eye is the beautiful guidance of the Spirit has to Paul been a struggle of intense frustration.

It even seems as if it was exactly in connection with his frustrated effectiveness as a traveling apostle that we find the most intensive and extensive evidence of Paul's own life of prayer, both in terms of the highest experiences and the most intensive prayer-struggle, that is, concerning his heavenly revelations and concerning the thorn in the flesh, the angel of Satan (2 Cor. 12:1–9). In reading about Paul's visit to Paradise and the following maimedness, one is reminded of the Talmudic story about the four great scholars of the early second century who ascended into heaven and saw Paradise: all but one—the great and revered Rabbi Akiba—suffered calamities, death, and mental illness.[10] Paul was not as lucky as Akiba, and he interprets his handicap—no doubt a medical condition that interferes with his apostolic effectiveness[11]—as God's own way of teaching him the way of strength through weakness (vv. 9–10; cf. also 2 Cor. 4:7 about the treasure in earthen vessels, again right after a passage of intense and visual religious experiences, 2 Cor. 3:18; 4:6).

This insight, says Paul, came out of prayer (2 Cor. 12:8). "Three times" he has pleaded with the Lord to rid him of his handicap. I am inclined to take the mention of the "three times" literally, that is, on three separate occasions he has had it out with the Lord, perhaps in a prayer-fast. But now he has learned to accept his handicap as a divine lesson about how his weakness bars him from self-glory. Thus this insight, won through prayer, becomes a key to his whole theology. Here in the very prayer life of Paul is the root of his famous theology of the cross (cf. 2 Cor. 13:4). We owe, of course, this report on Paul's life of prayer to his conflict in Corinth with the more healthy and triumphalist apostles (2 Corinthians 10—12). Yet it is significant that it is out of his

154

struggle with his work and his mission that this deep prayer experience of Paul comes. It is not part of a supposed existential concern for his private status as a "justified" Christian.

The other striking experience of personal prayer of which Paul speaks is equally triggered by the problems his mission had encountered in Corinth, that is, the right role of glossolalia.[12] In his discussion of this phenomenon in Corinth, Paul assures the Corinthians that he himself does speak in tongues (1 Cor. 14:18). He is grateful for that gift, but he does not consider it helpful in public. It is a family matter and should not be used to try to impress others, especially not outsiders. But Paul does refer to glossolalia once more, and then specifically in the context of prayer (Rom. 8:26–27): when we do not know how or what to pray, then the Spirit comes to our help, interceding for us in nonverbal groans; but God, who searches the hearts, knows the mind of the Spirit. Here Paul understands glossolalia as the Spirit praying in us. In a typically Pauline manner he sees this phenomenon not as a sign of high spiritual achievement, but as God's antidote to human weakness.

This eighth chapter of Romans is unusually rich as background for Paul's spirituality. It begins with exuberant language about the indwelling of the Spirit of God and of Christ, both expressions side by side in verse 9. It is this Spirit that witnesses—in the Abba-cry—to the adoption to be as children and heirs of God and coheirs with Christ. Then the tone shifts with the stress on suffering and weakness, climaxed by the glossolalia as a sign of our helplessness. And then on to the trust in God's power to see us through it all—unsevered from the love of God in Christ our Lord. As the chapter progresses the language is more and more colored by Paul's hardships and potential martyrdom (for example, vv. 35f.) in his mission on behalf of the gentiles, the topic on which he is to reflect in great depth in what follows next (Romans 9–11). Thus this whole chapter is theological reflection at the heart of Paul's life of prayer, full of exuberant language, mingled with hard-learned realism as to weakness and trust in God in the midst of suffering.

Paul knows of the acclamation "Abba-Father." His two references to this expression (Rom. 8:15; Gal. 4:6) make it clear that his audiences are familiar with it, and the bilingual form represents the manner in which the acclamation was actually used. Thus it seems to have had a liturgical and confessional function similar to the *Kyrios Iesous* (1 Cor. 12:3), and Paul sees both as the blessed result of the presence of the Spirit in the body of the believers. Furthermore, in both cases he uses these expressions, well known in worship practice, for making a point important for his argument. In the case of "Jesus (is) Lord," the point is the one-ness in the diversity of spiritual gifts. In the case of "Abba-Father," the point is the common status of heirs, coheirs with Christ.

As we said above, this reference to Abba has often been taken as the key to Paul's spirituality of prayer and the link to the spirituality of Jesus, be it in the Lord's Prayer (Matthew 6; Luke 11) or in Jesus' prayer in Gethsemane (Mark 14:36 parr.). The emphasis then falls on what is seen as a tone of informality and emotional warmth in the relation between the believer and God.[13] I would proceed with more caution. To begin with, the verb used both in Galatians and Romans (*krazomen*/we cry out) does not signal a warm Fatherhood-of-God piety. Rather, it has the ring of ecstasy, almost akin to the glossolalia. The only other time Paul uses that verb is for a mighty and inspired prophecy from Isaiah (Rom. 9:27).[14]

It must also be noted that Paul's own language of prayer to the Father is not marked by such informality or emotional warmth. As we saw, and as we shall see further, Paul's most intimate expression of prayer is rather the one where he pleads with the Lord Jesus Christ for relief (2 Corinthians 12), or where the Spirit intercedes (Rom. 8:26), or Christ Jesus intercedes on our behalf (8:34). The unmediated Abba-language does not seem to be his own natural prayer expression. For him that is an acclamation that he can take for granted as part of the language of his churches and that allows him to make a theological point as to the eschatological status of Christians, a status which in Paul does not translate into a new or more direct language of prayer.

It could even be argued that the Pauline language of prayer moves in a direction opposite to that of immediate Father-language. It is in Jewish prayer and prayerful language, exactly in the period *before* and after the birth of Christianity, that we find a marked increase in Father-language.[15] Representative is the passage in Wisdom of Solomon 2:16, where the enemies of the righteous take offense at his "boasting that God is his father"—a passage to which Matthew makes reference in his passion narrative (27:40).

In Paul's language the emphasis is rather on the "through Jesus Christ," which leads us to give careful attention to the role of Jesus Christ in the prayer-language of Paul.

Our starting point must be that the object of prayer for Paul is God, not Christ. This also holds for doxologies, thanksgivings, and the very structure of Paul's life of prayer. Second, it is clear that it is natural for Paul to refer to God as father, father of our Lord Jesus Christ, and hence our father. It seems to follow that Paul's basic address of prayer is not the simple Abba-Father but, in the title words of a recent study *Per Christum in Deum*, through Christ to God.[16] In this respect it is interesting to note that the collects of the Western church have retained the Pauline stance. They are all directed to God, in the name of Jesus Christ, they are never prayers to Christ.[17]

Furthermore, this is so in spite of the fact that Paul takes over and makes significant theological use of the title "*Kyrios*/Lord" for Jesus Christ. The most significant evidence for this development is the Christ hymn in Phil. 2:6–11 with its final acclamation: "and all tongues confess: *Kyrios Iesous Christos*"—but mark also the theocentric continuation by which the hymn ends: "to the glory of God the Father." It is reasonable to follow Lohmeyer and others in recognizing this hymn as having been shaped prior to Paul.[18]

It is clear that the title *Kyrios* in Paul refers consistently to Jesus Christ, and Paul sees his mission as "preaching Jesus Christ as Lord" (2 Cor. 4:5). There is no clear designation of God as *Kyrios* in Paul's own language. This fact is the more striking when Paul (different from Acts 2:21) applies the quotation from Joel 3:5 (where the Septuagint has *Kyrios* for *Yahweh/Adonai*) to Jesus Christ: "Everyone who calls upon the name of the Lord will be saved" (Rom. 10:13; cf. also 2 Cor. 3:16; 10:17; 1 Cor. 2:16).

The question before us is how Paul understands this title *Kyrios*. In the later developments—due to the coincidence with the later[19] Septuagint *Kyrios/Yahweh/Adonai*—this title opened up mighty theological avenues. But in Paul there is still a marked distinction which does not allow for an easy affirmation that Christ hence "is God." Rather, the Lord Jesus Christ is the Son of the Father who has brought us into a new and saving relation to God. It is by calling on the name Jesus Christ that we are what we are. This "calling" is not so much prayer as confession, the expression of faith in what God has done in and through Christ, *per Christum in Deum*.

This state of affairs lends much weight to the position of Bultmann, Conzelmann, and others that the *Kyrios* terminology of the early church cannot be understood just as an application of a "Septuagint" *Kyrios* for *Yahweh*, but grows out of the cultic acclamation of Hellenistic Christianity, whether Jewish or gentile.

The question here under discussion has been anachronistically distorted by later christological and trinitarian perspectives and concerns. The gauging of "degrees of divinity" in Christ is a misleading approach, not least when we try to understand Paul at prayer. He prays to God. His life and mission are totally conditioned by what God has done in and through Jesus Christ whom God raised from the dead, who is hence the Risen Lord. Paul communicates with this Risen Lord whose apostle he is. Especially when it comes to his mission and its obstacles, Paul naturally argues with the Lord (2 Corinthians 12)—whose emissary he was. If we were to ask Paul why he did not argue "directly" with God, he would presumably not understand our question. For to him the later questions, both Jewish and Christian, concerning monotheism versus Christology, are nowhere present in his letters. When he affirms "monotheism" versus idol worship he can do so in an almost unreflective manner by saying: there is no idol in the world and no God but One (cf. the *Shema'*, Deut. 6:4), and even if there be so-called gods in heaven or on earth as there surely are many gods and many lords (*kyrioi*), for us, nevertheless, it is: One God, the Father from whom (is) everything and we in and toward him, *and* One Lord Jesus Christ through whom (is) everything and we through him (1 Cor. 8:4–6). I cannot see that this expanded *Shema'* has any corrective function over against Jewish monotheism. The point is not that now we must "add" the Lord Jesus Christ. The Lord Jesus Christ just affirms in his oneness and uniqueness the oneness of God over against all idolatry.

It is in this light that we can better understand the full spectrum of Paul's language. As God's apostle of Jesus Christ he can communicate with Christ, he is ever conscious of how his mission is the same as Christ's, as is the status before God of his followers. In Romans and Galatians this status is developed and argued with special attention to the gentiles, who would be nowhere were it not for their faith in Christ. In 1 Corinthians the act of excommunication is carried out by an act of prayer where Paul and the Corinthians join "in the name of the Lord Jesus . . . with the power of our Lord Jesus, you are to deliver this man to Satan for the destruction of the flesh, that his spirit may be saved in the day of the Lord Jesus" (5:3–6).

We saw above that Paul's doxologies and greetings are carefully shaped by the issues and concerns at hand.[20] He does not just mouth traditional language. Thus it is worth special attention when Paul once writes a doxology in pure God-language, without any reference to Christ. He does so in Rom. 11:33–36. It is reasonable to suggest that Paul—either consciously or unconsciously—writes his doxology this way since his concern here is the mystery of God's salvation of Israel in a manner beyond Christian conceit toward the Jews (11:21–25). Thus he speaks straight God-language—as he actually has done in Romans ever since 10:17. The absence of Christ-language on those pages is motivated by Paul's intention. These gentile (see 11:13) Christians need to "learn" to pray and think in God-language. Paul surely has no feeling that his doxology is thereby incomplete or not truly Christian.

In his review of von der Goltz's book on prayer in early Christianity, W. Bousset draws attention to the fact that in Pauline—and by and large in NT—prayers and doxologies the attributes and names of God express what he calls "the specific Christian mood of prayer"; and he seems to refer to Father- and Christ-language in the context of grace.[21] On the other hand, the praise of God the Creator (which played and plays a great role in Jewish liturgical prayers) is not present. He further points out how the latter language asserts itself in postapostolic books. I find that observation—which is correct—to be both interesting and challenging. As Bousset uses this observation, it has a Marcionite ring. Should we draw the conclusion that Christian prayer is more Christian if it stays away from God as Creator?

I like to raise the question for a very special reason. My essay is meant to trigger some theological reflections, and hence it is important to ask in what sense Paul's prayer (or more correctly, the prayerful attitude of Paul as evidenced by his language—for we do not really know how he said his prayers) is normative for the church. We are not Paul, nor are we apostles as he was an apostle. He had seen the Lord in a way that we have not (1 Cor. 9:1). Nor is our world his world. But we can learn from him, be inspired by him, pray with his language. We can learn, as he learned, not to pray for a bliss and a health that is not to be given us; we can learn to become a mutually supportive community of intercession. We can rejoice in ecstasy, our own and that of others.

But we must remember that Paul's epistles are closely tied to this mission, and it would be stifling and wrong to say that Paul taught us what it is proper for a Christian to pray about. It could perhaps even be argued that Paul was "too caught up in his work," and his prayers were also. They are the prayers of an apostle, a missionary with eschatological urgency (Romans 15). They have in them the signs of joy and gratitude for the great new act of God in Jesus Christ.

As Christians we have deep and everlasting reasons to share that joy and gratitude. But there is also something sound and rich in the way in which later generations found again the importance, the necessity, the urge, and the beauty in lifting up their eyes to God the Creator of heaven and earth. Or, come to think of it, we could ask what role the

Psalms played in Paul's own life of prayer and worship. Yes, we can wonder how it really sounded when Paul was at prayer. That we do not know.

NOTES

1. *The Prayers of the New Testament* (New York: Harper & Row, 1967), 87ff.

2. For a broader perspective on prayer few things are more helpful than G. van der Leeuw's masterpiece *Religion in Essence and Manifestation: A Study in Phenomenology*, 2 vols. (New York: Harper & Row, 1963), II, 422–34.

3. This is the perspective that informs the pioneering study by E. von der Goltz, *Das Gebet in der ältesten Christenheit* (Leipzig: Hinrichs, 1901).

4. See Bauer-Arndt-Gingrich, *A Greek-English Lexicon of the New Testament* (Chicago: University of Chicago Press, 1957), 882.

5. Beiheft 20, *ZNW* (Berlin, 1939).

6. On the truly creative role of Paul for the formation of the Christian letter styles, see now Helmut Koester, "I Thessalonians—Experiment in Christian Writing," *Continuity and Discontinuity in Church History. Essays Presented to G. H. Williams* (Leiden: E. J. Brill, 1979), 33–44.

We now have a commentary (to Galatians) that gives maximum attention to the literary structure of a Pauline epistle and that in a manner which yields significant insight to the theology of Paul. Otherwise, formal and stylistic observations often remain unrelated to genuine exegesis. See Hans-Dieter Betz, *Galatians;* Hermeneia (Philadelphia: Fortress Press, 1979).

7. Note how the specific problem of the Galatians is present already in Paul's way of adapting his constant self-designation in the greeting in Gal. 1:1, Paul, apostle—not from humans, nor through humans, but through Jesus Christ . . . i.e., the very theme of Galatians, cf. 1:11ff.

8. The Maranatha in 1 Cor. 16:22 functions in *Didache* 9 and 10 as the fence around the community meals, at which, according to 1 Corinthians 11, the Corinthians are behaving in a loveless, i.e., inconsiderate, manner. See C. F. D. Moule, "The Judgment Theme in the Sacraments," in W. D. Davies and D. Daube, eds., *The Background of the New Testament and Its Eschatology* (New York and London: Cambridge University Press, 1956), 474.

9. But in Acts the outcome is not a successful stay in Galatia instead of moving west to Asia (i.e., to cities like Ephesus, etc.), or north to Bithynia. No, for Luke this is the important movement across to Europe—through the night-vision of the Macedonian who begged: Come over and help us (16:9–10). According to Luke, another night vision had produced the quantum jump into baptizing gentiles (the Cornelius story, Acts 10). See Ernst Haenchen, *The Acts of the Apostles* (Philadelphia: Westminster Press, 1971), 484–87.

10. Hagigah 14b. The context is the rules for instruction about mysticism (later, Kabalah). See G. F. Moore, *Judaism*, 2 vols. (Cambridge: Harvard University Press, 1950), I, 413. Elisha ben Abuya "cut down the plants," a term for becoming a heretic. Simeon ben Zoma lost his mind, and Simon ben Azzai died. Only Akiba made his exit safely.

11. See my *Paul Among Jews and Gentiles* (Philadelphia: Fortress Press, 1976), 42, where I made the guess that an epileptic condition may well best fit the evidence. Tertullian suggested neuralgia and many other guesses have been made.

12. For a more extensive treatment, see *Paul Among Jews and Gentiles,* 108–24.

13. The romantic interpretation of Abba as an endearing term for God, with the informal and familial connotation of "Dad" rather than "Father," is presumably without firm foundation. The Aramaic Abba "is as much a literary form of the language as that of the Qumran texts," see J. A. Fitzmyer, *A Wandering Aramean* (SBL Monograph Series 25; Missoula, Mont.: Scholars Press, 1979), 135.

14. On both *krazein*, acclamation, and Abba, the pertinent issues and literature are well stated by Betz, *Galatians*, 211.

15. On Father-language in Judaism of this period, including the famous standard prayers of Judaism, see G. F. Moore, *Judaism*, II, 203.

16. W. Thüsing, *Per Christum in Deum. Studien zum Verhältnis von Christozentrik und Theozentrik in den paulinischen Hauptbriefen.* NTA, N.S. 1 (1965).

17. See J. A. Jungmann, *The Mass* (Collegeville, Minn.: Liturgical Press, 1976), 172.

18. Ernst Lohmeyer in his commentary, Meyer Series (Göttingen, 1956, 11th ed.). On later discussion see the *Beiheft* by W. Schmauch (1964); cf. R. Bultmann, *Theology of the New Testament*, 2 vols. (New York: Charles Scribner's Sons, 1951), I, 125.

19. I say "later," since it is now increasingly clear that the pre-Christian Greek translations, including the Septuagint, actually had not established the standard translation *Kyrios* for Yahweh. See Fitzmyer, *A Wandering Aramean*, 119ff.; also Hans Conzelmann, *An Outline of the Theology of the New Testament* (New York: Harper & Row, 1969), 82–86.

20. Even here it is reasonable that Paul thinks of Christ as the Lord on judgment day, thus another example of how (like Rom. 10:13) OT references become filled with *Kyrios Iesous* meaning. Where this process becomes strained, Paul offers exegetical basis for it, as in 2 Cor. 3:16f.

21. In *Göttingsche gelehrte Anzeigen* 165 (1903), 272.

12

The Church
in Early Christianity

Introductory Note: In the process of translating this article from the German original, I revised it somewhat to make it more readable than could be the case with its encyclopedia style in *Religion in Geschichte und Gegenwart* (Dritte Auflage, vol. III, cols. 1297–1304, "Kirche: II Urchristentum." Tübingen: J. C. B. Mohr [Paul Siebeck], 1959). The original includes an extensive bibliography which is not reproduced here.

As I read the essay twenty-five years after writing it, I recognize how relatively naive I was at that time in my use of Jesus material. Theoretically I knew of layers of meaning, and the diverse trajectories of traditions and theologies, but it seems now that I was not too good at applying it when called upon to give a wholistic picture, a picture which I liked but which blinded me to the full diversity. My understandings of eschatology and salvation history are somewhat precritical. With that caveat, however, the article strikes me as still useful.

THE OLD AND
THE NEW CONSENSUS

In 1932 Olof Linton wrote his famous *Das Problem der Urkirche in der neueren Forschung* (The Problem of the Primitive Church in Recent Scholarship). He spoke about an old consensus, but not yet about a new one. In 1942 F. M. Brown found it quite proper to present such a new consensus. The Ecumenical Movement (WCC since 1948) had given incentive to such a development as well as profited from that short and intensive period of research. The hope for guidance from the Bible as that which all churches had in common was a mighty force in the Ecumenical Movement, and coincided with the great efforts and expectations of the emerging biblical theology, perhaps most monumentally enshrined in Kittel's (et al.) *Theological Dictionary of the New Testament* (the German original published from 1933 to 1979).

The old consensus was dominated by constitutional questions, for example, questions of structure. The two foci were (1) the church as a totality and/or individual congregations; and (2) the development of offices. The church as a totality was seen as a federation of local congregations, and episcopacy as a development out of an originally collegial structure of church leadership.

An indicator of the consensus is the 1917 Swedish translation of the Bible, in which *ekklesia(i)* is consistently rendered "congregation(s)," thereby accepting the language of the free churches. My generation of Swedes has had no church in its Bibles.

The new elements in the discussion which came from Harnack and Sohm did not break through this framework. But already Sohm together with Schürer and Weizsäcker saw the OT *qahal/ekklesia* as the root of the NT concept of the church, and thereby questioned whether the problem could be approached from another angle. Especially Sohm's consistent distinction between spirit and rights, charisma and organization, religion and constitution, turned out to be a significant step in the direction toward the new consensus—although it still functioned within the framework and the presuppositions of the old consensus.

The new perspective presupposes the rediscovery of NT eschatology. When F. Kattenbusch (1921) made his programmatic attempt at finding the roots for the idea of the church, he moved in quite a different thought world than had Hatch, Harnack, and Sohm. Kattenbusch located the idea of church in the messsianism of the NT. Thus ecclesiology is rooted a priori in Christology. The picture that Kattenbusch and K. L. Schmidt drew with such a perception became by and large a commonly accepted view.

A crucial question remains open, however, and hotly debated, that is, if and/or in what sense Jesus himself "intended" a church. The answers depend partly on how one assesses Jesus' self-understanding. Did he think of himself as the Messiah, a Messiah, or the forerunner, or neither . . . ?

The decisive presuppositions in the new consensus are: (a) *he ekklesia* (*tou theou*) must be understood as the LXX translation of *qehal* (YHWH). When the NT consciously uses this term, it wants to present

164

the church as the people of God in the last times, in the *eschaton*; (b) A Messiah without such a church is incomprehensible. If one says "Messiah" then one also means "church"; (c) Thereby a right understanding of the relation between the kingdom of God and the church becomes decisive.

To be sure, these three theses, or presuppositions, can be stated and worked out in quite different ways. But the discussion is carried on within the framework that they constitute.

THE WORD *EKKLESIA*

The common Greek usage of *ekklesia* as "meeting of an assembly" is found also in the NT (Acts 19:32, 39, 40). It refers only to an actual session—between sessions there is no *ekklesia*. Therein lies the basic difference between the common Greek word and its use for the church, a usage that cannot be directly deduced from contemporary Greek. The etymology suggests "something called out," and *hoi ekkletoi* are "the citizens called to meeting by a herald."

It is quite wrong to make theological use of this etymological meaning (e.g., "In Christ God calls persons out of the world," or similar more or less kerygmatic statements). Neither *ekkalein* (to call out) or *ekkletoi* (those called out) occur in the NT or in the apostolic fathers. Even more strikingly, *ekklesia* never occurs in a context which indicates awareness of such an etymological meaning.

The LXX has *ekklesia* about one hundred times, always for the Hebrew *qahal*. Especially as *ekklesia tou kyriou/qahal* YHWH in Deuteronomy and 1 and 2 Chronicles, it is a technical term for the "assembly of the Lord" (e.g., Deuteronomy 23).

The Qumran texts use primarily *'eda* (LXX: *synagoge*) and *yahad* for the community in its totality, often with an OT ring that indicates that the true Israel in the *eschaton* is meant. *Yahad* is the Brotherhood, the nucleus of the movement, seen historically or geographically (1QS). *Qahal* is rare, but of interest. In 1QSa 1:4 it refers to the eschatological grand assembly of those who have kept God's covenant in order to atone for the land. All, including small children and women, will gather. 2:4 deals with the question of access to the community, using Deuteronomy 23. The Damascus Document has *qahal* five times and *'eda* 15. In 12:6 *qahal* is also used in connection with Deuteronomy 23 (the setting is similar to Matt. 18:7; cf. 15:17). 14:18 is unfortunately fragmentary, but the parallel with 1QSa makes it reasonable to suppose that it refers to the eschatological assembly of the messianic time. In both passages there is emphasis on atonement.

In texts from Greek-speaking Judaism two tendencies are important: (a) *ekklesia* is influenced by the common Greek usage; and (b) when used in biblical and religious contexts it takes on an archaic tone and is connected with the question of belonging to the true Israel—as with the Hebrew *qahal*. This question has its center in reflection on Deuteronomy 23 in the first centuries B.C.E. and C.E.

The Qumran texts witness to the importance of these tendencies. *Qahal* is not one of its central theological terms, but when it occurs, it expresses a future eschatological perspective. Both *ʿeda* and *yahad* have eschatological connotations but describe the community as established here and now. (*Qahal* and *ʿeda* seem to be somewhat archaic words in the Mishnah.) In Greek-speaking Judaism the word *synagoge* becomes increasingly used for the building where the congregation gathers, as well as for the local congregation itself.

All this lends support to the view that early Christianity, in using the word *ekklesia*, consciously expressed its claim to be the true people of God. It remains surprising that the church opted for *ekklesia tou theou* (. . . of God) rather than the septuagintal *ekklesia tou kyriou* (. . . of the Lord), which might have been more natural, not least in light of the earliest Christian identification of Christ as Lord. The missing piece in this puzzle is the term *qahal el* at Qumran (1QM4:10; 1QSa 1:25).

It is then most surprising to find—as J. Y. Campbell has pointed out (in *Journal of Theological Studies* 49 [1948]: 130–42)—that we have hardly any evidence in the NT of the word *ekklesia* used in the overt meaning of "the true Assembly of God." Acts 7:38 may be a case, but it refers to Moses and the people in the wilderness. Hebrews 12:23 could be such a case, but it stands alone in the NT and again in an OT midrash. K. L. Schmidt considers it doubtful as an example of the technical Christian use of *ekklesia*. In 1 Peter 2:4–10 the church is pictured as the true eschatological people of God, but without the word *ekklesia*. Never is there a reference, or allusion, to the OT where *qahal/ekklesia* is used in that sense; Heb. 2:12//Ps. 22:23 is not quite it. One could mention Acts 20:28 with its possible allusion to Ps. 74:2, but there we find *synagoge/ʿeda*. Except for the *soma* (body) passages in Eph. 3:10, 21, and 1 Tim. 3:15, there are actually no occurrences of *ekklesia* where the context suggests that the word has a specific theological ring.

Ekklesia is used interchangeably in singular and plural, also in the "full form" *ekklesia tou theou* (Singular: Acts 20:28; 1 Cor. 1:2; 10:32; 11:22; 15:9; 2 Cor. 1:1; Gal. 1:13; 1 Tim. 3:5, 15. Plural: 1 Cor. 11:16; 1 Thess. 2:14; 2 Thess. 1:4). Thus it is clear that its singular form can refer both to the local church and to the church in its totality. But such usage does not prove that *ekklesia* evinces the heavy idea of an eschatological reality manifested in the local churches.

Ekklesia has consequently become a technical term already in the NT, but without conscious or expressed connection with the OT idea of the true people of God. This somewhat surprising fact is corroborated by the ways in which the earliest theological reflection on the church goes in distinctly different directions. We need only mention the images of the body and the house and its building up (*oikodome*). The former comes from the need for unity and has no OT background. There the unity of the people is a given—not so in the church of Jews and gentiles. The images of house and building make use of OT elements but develop along different lines.

Thus we should understand the NT term *ekklesia* as a mere word, without theological connotations. This was so for the Greek ears of the early church even if perhaps the choice of the word had been prompted by the OT *qahal/ekklesia*. The NT shows no awareness of that history. Now it is a mere word. And, after all, the alternative *synagoge* was otherwise occupied.

HOW DID THE CHURCH UNDERSTAND ITSELF?

The author of Acts gave the first sustained interpretation of the church as a historical entity. When he anchors the community whose history he writes in the manifestations of the Holy Spirit, his picture coincides at a significant point with Paul's perception (1 Corinthians 3 and 12). Also the Johannine church is placed in the time of the Spirit (the *parakletos*/Advocate/Helper/Intercessor), a situation which is superior to that of the historical Jesus (John 16:17).

Membership in the Qumran community as the "new covenant" meant a realized participation in the age to come and hence the ultimate belonging to the true Israel. In that respect there is a fundamental similarity between Qumran and the NT church. This similarity extends to the fact that both operate with an anticipation, and in both communities this anticipation is based on events in the recent past. In the NT the degree of anticipation is heightened by the heavenly enthronement of the

Messiah (Acts 2:34–36; interpreting Ps. 110:1) He will remain in heaven until the Parousia, until his coming (n.b., not "second" coming), but he is not an unknown, for he is Jesus whose life and work and death on earth is known (3:20f.). His lordship in the church is manifested by the eschatological gift of the Spirit which enlivens the church's witness (2:33).

The Spirit is here seen as the promised Spirit which Joel had prophesied (Acts 2:17–21; Joel 3:1–5) but which had been withheld from God's people since the last of the prophets, as some Jewish sages also taught (e.g., Sotah 48b). That Spirit of God had now made its comeback. Therefore the church could be sure not only that the new age was a matter of hope and faith, but also that it was present in the Spirit.

Such an understanding of the church and the Spirit may well represent a developed stage of early ecclesiology, and it is often suggested that it may be a response to the delay of the Parousia (see now R. J. Maddox, *The Purpose of Luke—Acts* [1982]). But already in Paul the Spirit is the anticipatory manifestation, the first fruit of our inheritance (Rom. 8:23; Gal. 4:6; cf. Eph. 1:14), the down payment on our salvation (2 Cor. 5:5; cf. 1:22), while also being the organizing energy of the church (1 Corinthians 12).

A member of the Qumran community who lies and cheats when he transfers his possessions to the community is excommunicated for one year (1QS 6:25); those who do the same in the church are killed (Acts 5:1–11) for they have lied against the Holy Spirit. Even if Acts gives us an exaggerated and "idealized" picture of the time of the earliest church, this story serves well as an indicator of the higher intensity of realized anticipation in the church. Once the Spirit has come there is no room anymore for the gracious mercy of the graded punishments case by case (cf. also Matt. 12:32).

Such a self-understanding of the church can be seen elsewhere also. In Gal. 3:22f. the history of Israel under the Torah is seen as a period in which God withholds the eschatological salvation from his people until the faith in Jesus Christ is available (cf. Heb. 11:40; for Paul the point of the argument is that this faith is open to gentiles). First Peter 1:10–12 places the church in the same pattern of redemptive history. A picture of the early church thus emerges: a community of salvation and redemption that knows itself to have newly come into existence, a community in which the old prophecies begin to be fulfilled.

Within such an overall understanding the NT shows variations and tensions. There is, for example, the question of Jews and gentiles. The issue was not *whether* gentiles were to be included but *how* and on what terms. How that issue would have been worked out without Paul's influence is an interesting hypothetical question. Paul rests his authority as *the* apostle to the gentiles on a special and personal revelation (Gal. 1:10ff.). He sees the church in the light of a redemptive history in which God and Israel are the primary dramatis personae. The gentile Christians are grafted on to the authentic olive tree (Rom. 11:24). The whole Pauline correspondence is devoted to the problems caused by the gentile mission. It gives to his concern for the unity of the church an importance and a shape that it could not have for Jewish Christians. It makes unity a theme that has few roots in the OT or in Israel's earlier experience. This unity could not be easily argued from the self-evident and nonproblematic unity of Israel as the people of God. His opponents could easily argue that it was exactly this unity that he exploded.

Paul finds the unity in Christ, and we can understand better why Paul—and only he—speaks of the church from an explicit christological perspective. The image of the body is decisive (1 Cor. 12:13–27; Rom. 12:5; cf. 1 Cor. 10:17; 11:29). This image has no relation to the idea of a people of God, but is known from stoic political rhetoric. It is of singular importance for the Pauline idea of the church. It comes to play an even-greater role in later theology, especially when it becomes intertwined with the idea of incarnation (e.g., 2 Clement 14).

For Paul Jew and gentile, slave and free, speakers of tongues and administrators are all baptized into one body, into Christ (1 Cor. 12:12f.). In Colossians and Ephesians the relation between Christ and the church is seen differently: Christ is the head and the Christians are the limbs/members. Gnostic influence may have played its role. In any case, the door opens up toward speculation. Yet, the concern for unity which is the point in 1 Corinthians 12 (and Romans 12) remains central. The new cosmic dimension in Colossians and Ephesians has interesting parallels in the absolute claims to redemptive history which find expression, for example, in 1 Pet. 1:10–12.

The Johannine traditions stress unity in a different manner. It is not grounded in purely christological terms, but in the unity of the Father and the Son (John 17). The believers are the disciples (13:35; 15:8), the friends (15:13ff.), "his own" (13:1; cf. 10:3f.), given him by the Father (6:37–39), by their faith, drawn by the Father (6:44). By their hearing and loving they show themselves to belong to the flock and the vine. The word *ekklesia* occurs only in 3 John.

The more speculative modes of thinking carry with them a significant shift, or even dislocation, in the understanding of the church. To be sure, in Acts the church is the object of historical reflection, but has not yet become "a thing in itself." The Christians *are* the church; they are not *in* the church. The Pauline image of the body (1 Corinthians 12 and Romans 12), and perhaps also the Johannine images of a more "ontological" unity, retains such a function. But once the images have a life of their own and begin to function as suggestive theological *topoi*— begin to grow legs and walk around on their own, so to speak—then the church becomes a reality in its own right, over against the members. Colossians and Ephesians show the first steps in that direction.

This development is often described as "institutionalization." But it should not be overlooked that in this process of self-engendering thinking the motifs of redemption history and cosmic/eschatological awareness are retained in their own right and not only as institutional props. There is the creative joy in amassing glorifying participles and adjectives (e.g., in Ignatius), not only out of theological concerns but partly for reasons of style, the labored style of so-called Asianism. The unity of the geographically dispersed church is seen as a diaspora (James 1:1; 1 Pet. 1:1; 1 Clement). In the *Didache* the bread of the Eucharist prefigures the geographically scattered church (*Didache* 9). The eschatological understanding of the church is both retained and transformed in the preexistence of the church (2 Clement 14; cf. Eph. 1:3ff.), and in the idea that the world was created for the sake of the church (Herm. Vis. 1, 1,6). The early eschatological view—that God's plan of salvation goes toward its fulfillment—is elaborated theologically and thereby the church becomes a major object for faith and for speculative thought. The church is not any longer merely the self-evident and obvious framework for the life of Christians.

Theological reflection about the sacraments is part of, and contributes to, such a new understanding of the church. What originally expressed the closeness and anticipation of the age to come (Qumran and still in Acts) is increasingly interpreted theologically in relation to the work of Christ. Already Paul moves in that direction (Gal. 3:27f.; 1 Corinthians 10 and 11; 12:13; Romans 6).

A parallel—one could say: an intrinsically necessary—development takes place in the understanding of the offices of the church. Also here the problem of unity governs the theological and ecclesiological moves. In Ignatius's letters this unity ultimately is grounded in the relation between the church and Christ, and Christ and God (Ign. Eph. 5). Earlier (e.g., Acts 15; 1 Corinthians 3 and 12) the organizational structure and relation of leaders remained less precise and less hierarchical. When the offices receive more profile—as is the case in, for example, the pastoral epistles—the Pauline favorite word "faith" becomes a word expressing a content (1 Tim. 4:6; Tit. 1:13), rather than an affirmation and an attitude. Now the church knows of her faith as a set of doctrines.

JESUS AND THE CHURCH

The second main thesis of the new consensus insists that a Messiah without a people would be an absurd idea. Thus the church is implicit already in the faith in the Messiah. This view was originally argued on the basis of Daniel 7 (see esp. Kattenbusch; cf. T. W. Manson). But it can be better understood in the light of our earlier presentation. Schlatter and Oepke both argued that a church is there regardless of whether Jesus founded "his" church or not. The issue is not whether or not Jesus instituted a church. It is rather how Jesus' eschatological self-understanding played into the life and constitution of the people of God. The given is "the people," the Messiah is its Messiah. It is against the organic nature of the case to first ask about Jesus and only then about the church.

The word *ekklesia* occurs only three times in the gospels: Matt. 18:17, where the word occurs twice, is of secondary importance since it refers to a concrete congregation (cf. 1QS 6:1, "the many," those with full membership). The third and remaining case is Matt. 16:18. Here Peter is the rock on whom/which Jesus will build his *ekklesia*. Presumably the Aramaic to be posited as equivalent is *kenishta*, which relates more to *'eda/synagoge* than to *qahal/ekklesia*. If treated as an authentic (Aramaic) word of Jesus, the saying refers to a distinct synagogue, but one with an eschatological claim (16:19), and hence with little similarity to the local synagogues in Palestine. In view of the translation problem it is more probable to see the word *ekklesia* here as part of a Greek-speaking tradition.

Of great importance is the future tense of the saying: I shall build. Whether a word of Jesus or the language of the church, this *ekklesia* belongs to the future—when seen from the perspective of the historical Jesus. The question must be: In Jesus' view of the future, was there a period after his death yet before a final Parousia in which he envisaged a duly constituted congregation of his disciples? Or should all texts that speak of an interim period be seen as the fruits of the embarrassment in the delay of the Parousia? It is certainly clear that Jesus during his earthly ministry did not establish a clearly delineated community. To be sure, the Twelve are promised the thrones of eschatological Israel; they are the nucleus of the true people of God. But the question remains an open one whether they are to play these or analogous roles in a church, for the sayings refer not only to the future but to the ultimate future, the *eschaton* of the world (Matt. 19:28; Luke 22:29f.).

The very first members and leaders of the church are by and large identical with the disciples of Jesus from Nazareth. And he had urged them to watch, for soon the kingdom was to come. They should not just repeat his teachings. Thus it is not so surprising that in the light of his death and resurrection and the experiences of the Holy Spirit they came to think of themselves as what they called the *ekklesia*. For in it the power and manifestations of the kingdom seemed present. In it the participation of the kingdom was anticipated in Jesus' name. Whether Jesus had predicted exactly that, perhaps they did not know, nor did they at first ask that question. They were lifted and carried forward on the mighty wave of eschatological events. If Matt. 16:18 were authentic words of Jesus, then his thoughts had once gone in that direction. That is not impossible—nor possible to prove.

As the picture of the church emerges from the pages of the NT, it is clearly the response of the disciples to what God did in the life, death, and resurrection of Jesus Christ. The question concerning whether Jesus wanted or foresaw a church actually removes itself from the center of the discussion, since it fits poorly into the situation in which the disciples found themselves. And they certainly did not experience the church as "a second best," a cover-up construction out of the delay of the Parousia. They were too thankful for what they now experienced in the church, and that gratitude was not the climate for feeling deprived of or lacking anything.

13

The New Testament Background for the Doctrine of the Sacraments

Introductory Note: Vatican II is certainly a milestone in the history of all Christian churches. Protestants had tended to think that Rome was unchangeable by definition, and that nothing significant had happened since the Council of Trent in the sixteenth century—at least nothing good or hopeful for ecumenism. Now it seemed that all questions were reopened, and a spate of consultations between Roman Catholics and the various Protestant churches began. This essay belongs to the reflections of Lutherans in that new climate—as did also the essay "One Canon is Enough" (see above, pp. 55–70).

The thrust of the essay is simple, grounded in a choice of starting points: baptism as an act of initiation and the Eucharist as a meal. By that choice one can cut through many layers of obfuscation and allow the theological reflections to be just that: reflections on the acts which are the two constants.

The original was (in English) in *Evangile et Sacrement—Oecumenica* (1970), 41–60. *Oecumenica* is the Annual Volume published by the (Strasbourg) Centre d'études oecuméniques of the Lutheran World Federation.

There is a slight Marcionite tendency—common in Lutheran circles—to begin a lecture not on the OT background, but to proceed immediately to the NT.[1] Had we met under more Calvinist auspices this may not have been so.

And yet I shall not try to make up for that by references to the OT. I shall rather warn myself and you about the dangers of biblical imperialism in the theological world. I mean this seriously. It is of course obvious that when one starts a series of presentations and lectures around the theme "Gospel and Sacrament," one naturally takes the place of departure in the Bible. It is not always clear whether one takes that point of departure because the Bible is the Bible, or because the Bible contains the historically earliest material that is available for the assessment of the problem at hand; whether the approach is theological or historical, historical and genetic. We have just lived through a period in Christian theology—fifty years roughly as far as Protestants are concerned, and a little less as far as Roman Catholics are concerned—a period that really can be described as the time when the biblical theologians could say to each other "We never had it so good." Our information, evaluation, and research were the obvious point of departure and *pièce de résistance* for theological work. I am referring to what we may call the "World Council of Churches biblical theology." It is the type of biblical theology that was presented and sought on the presupposition that once we knew what the Bible said, we had the basis on which we could assess future historical and dogmatic developments, and we would really have, in a rather easy way, the properly ecumenical basis for the discussion at hand. I am happy to note that my title today is not the NT *basis* for treating Gospel and Sacrament, but the NT *background*. I do not know to what extent this formulation is conscious in a very specific way, but, as you will see as I progress, I like it.

The time has come when those of us who work primarily with the biblical material have to give more reasons for why and how our material is to be used. We have lived through an era that in its latest stages has been characterized by the title "hermeneutics." That is the word that the contemporary theologian uses to prove that he is a member of the club. If he can spell it and use it right he is in, just as the former generation did the same with the word "kerygma" and the one before that with the word "eschatology." For a while now the word has been "hermeneutics." What we—and especially those of us of a Lutheran brand—should notice is that much of this hermeneutics discussion is a very continental Protestant or even Lutheran phenomenon that somehow builds upon the presupposition *im Anfang war der Text*, "in the beginning was the text." The theological task is consequently thought of as the production of the right kind of translation. It is a problem of translation into the "languages" of new cultures and situations. This whole approach is highly verbal in its understanding of Christianity, and that is worth noting since we are here to deal with that very area of theology where the verbal is to some extent called into question: sacra-

174

ments, that is, things so nonverbal that modern man might even have to use the word "magic" in order to convey the meaning to ververbalized Western man.

So my *first* point is plain and simple: when we now speak about the biblical material concerning the sacraments, the question of how this biblical material is related to systematic theology of the past and of the present and of the future should remain an open question. I am not giving you the following observations to tell you how it should be. I am not practicing biblical imperialism. I count on the creative power and inspiration of our systematic theologians.

My *second* general observation is this: I have been asked to speak about the NT material and for that reason I am not interested in "sacraments"; I am not interested in the term "sacrament." We have found in our negotiations between the Roman Catholics and Lutherans in the United States that a totally new and better state of affairs for that dialogue occurs at the moment when we bracket or even drop the word "sacrament." We all know that such a terminology came in later. If we try to begin by defining what a sacrament is or by reflecting on "the sacramental" and take such a conceptuality into the reading of the NT text then we have already closed a lot of doors and complicated much simplicity. For that reason we should rather discuss the actual acts that later on came to be called "sacraments" or "sacramental"; that is, the Eucharist, Penance, Marriage, Unction for Healing—rather than *in extremis*—Ordination, Exorcisms, Foot Washing. The last never became much of a sacramental act, although it is the only one that has all the requirements that the church has ever thought about for a sacrament. Perhaps speaking in tongues should be included also.

We should look at these acts and defer to the later discussions the most intriguing problem of how the Greek word *mysterion* came— much by chance, I think—to be translated *sacramentum*. These two words must have had a point where they did intersect, but they also had large areas where they certainly had totally different meanings. That has caused one of the rifts between the Greek-speaking and Latin-speaking parts of Christendom. A sacrament in Greek is *theion mysterion*, or just *mysterion*. The modern Greek word for "sacramental" is *mystagogikos*, *mystagogia* being a sacred ceremony.

The first evidence for *sacramentum* = *mysterion* is in African manuscripts of the Vetus Latina. It was picked up and utilized by Tertullian, and thus started a development of thought in Western Christendom that has as one of its elements this happenstance of word choice. I find Christine Mohrmann's discussion in the *Harvard Theological Review* 47 (1954), 141–52, correct as she criticizes Odo Casel et al. for bringing the full meaning of "mysteries" into the term *sacramentum*. She insists rightly on the common language meaning of *sacramentum*. Her article is a good example of how theologians need to be criticized for their exploitation of word studies. As you know, etymology is the poor man's theology. And one must warn students constantly against etymological gamesmanship. Theologians love it. A common example of bad habits in this area is when the Greek word for church, *ekklesia*, is interpreted as the community "called out." But I am sure that nobody in the first-century church had ever thought of the fact that the word *ekklesia* was composed by the words *ek* and *kalein*.[2]

Ekklesia just a word that meant assembly. To that point one can give the example of the thesis to be written at the University of the Moon a thousand years from now where somebody gets a doctorate for proving that English-speaking people on earth understood love as a way one walked together. How is that proven? Because in sixty of a hundred love letters that had been rescued to the moon the phrase occurred "I love you *al-ways*." That is a rather good example because that shows exactly how theologians use etymology to get a kind of theological mileage that they feel they need. *Mysterium* and *mysteria* are good Latin words prior to Christianity. But *mysteria* in plural means pagan mysteries, while *mysterium* in singular means just any kind of secret. And we cannot do word studies without doing actual idiomatic studies where we even distinguish totally between plural and singular.

But the basic touch point between *mysterion* and *sacramentum* seems to have been the idea of rite, ritual, often with a primary initiation context. The meaning seems to be clear. One should not overdo, as far as I can judge, the meaning of *sacramentum* = oath. That interpretation depends on the fact that the most-quoted and popular passage in Tertullian is one where he plays on the word in this direction.

And now a *third* observation that is of importance when we are to deal with the nonverbal, with sacraments. We can see how the verbalization wins out when terms like *verbum visibile* are used, or when the sermon is thought of as a *sacramentum verbale*. It is equally important to see the sacraments as distinctly nonverbal, as sacred acts. In that connection we should not fall for the "1000 B.C. Hebrew psychology" as to the meaning of the word *dabar*. It is often said that in the Bible the word is not only a word because the Hebrew word *dabar* also means "thing" or that the true prophet does not only foretell and forthtell, but that, if he has the right kind of word, his word creates.

It is my conviction that such an interpretation, so popular from Pedersen's *Israel*, is positively dangerous unless it is clearly dated as to the times and the periods in history when such a concept was operative. They are not "timeless" and if I understand it right, it does not apply to the period of Christian creativity in the first century A.D.

Biblical theologians should always be warned against this kind of an ahistorical tendency. And when I give the NT introduction lecture to my students, the first thing I always have to say is "Now you have an excellent introduction to OT studies. But when you come to the NT, you have to forget it all." For neither Jesus nor Paul nor any of the others had profited from the instruction of William Foxwell Albright, or Johannes Pedersen, or other glorious OT scholars of our time. The guides to the understanding of the OT as the NT time read it are rather in intertestamental literature on the one hand, in Philo and Josephus on the other (and with some precaution one can also use the Rabbinic material). And any ahistorical use—however productive it may be from a theological point of view—one can make of this kind of OT primitivism must be ruled out of court. I take it that this goes also for much of the speculation about the relation between Jesus as the Logos and his healing or instructing *logoi*. In the NT there is no connection between the "Logos" with capital L and the *logoi* that Jesus spoke. When Jesus healed by mere word, the power was in him, not in the words as such. They were "mere words." So also with Paul's gospel; it is his messsage, the one especially revealed to him, and what was special about it was the news as to the relation between Jews and gentiles in the plan of God. The gospel was authoritative as many scholars prove today, and I think rightly. There is nothing "good" in the gospel. The word *euaggelion* in the Greek of that time means an authoritative, official message and it is only by secondary reflection upon the word *euaggelion* that you get an exploitation of the "eu" in terms of "good."[3]

The gospel is the announcement of a new era and a new state of affairs, and we should be critical of any romanticism by which one tries to say that this announcement is qualitatively different from telling anything else. But what about passages like Rom. 1:16? Here we are told that Paul is not ashamed of the gospel since it is the power of God toward salvation. How hard should one press Paul's rhetoric at this point? Should one romanticize—as I would say—the pronouncement of the

177

gospel, the announcement of the gospel into something dynamic in itself or should one rather say: No, what Paul is saying is that in the data which constitute that message, in the data properly appropriated, lies salvation. But to romanticize the actual communication into a frightfully dynamic thing, is, I think, to complicate what should not be complicated and to build up a word mysticism or a kerygma mysticism or a gospel mysticism that helps nobody.

I am speaking against a whole range of kerygma speculation. The more I read about it and the more I read the NT, the more puzzled I am; the more surprised I become that we could get into such a tizzy and such a theological reverberation as we have had in the so-called kerygmatic approach. It is made up of some of the things I have just mentioned, romantic and anachronistic interpretation of the Hebrew *dabar*, made up of some kind of word mysticism.

And furthermore—and this leads over specifically to the sacramental material—most kerygmatic theology has overlooked one simple fact. We can not find a single example in the NT for the kerygma being *addressed* to Christians. If the kerygma is to mean the announcement of God's available salvation in Jesus Christ, then this announcement is and remains confined to the missionary situation. And in early Christianity as far as I can see, there is an absolutely sharp distinction between the outsiders and the insiders, between the missionary activity and the dealing with the insiders whether they are on the right track or not.

Christians are not addressed by a missionary message, a missionary kerygma, an announcement. They are dealt with as members of the church. What the kerygma is to the outsiders, the sacraments are to the insiders. We note that when the Eucharist is celebrated in Corinth (1 Corinthians 11) that very act pronounces the kerygma, celebrates it "until he come," but the church is not the object for that kerygma but the subject that "does it." In the "sacramental acts" of the church, the Christians experience the grace and power of the new situation that they had met and accepted when first approached by the kerygma.[4]

Let us now turn to the *act of baptism* in the NT. For pedagogical reasons I like to begin where one should not begin, that is, with the discussion about infant baptism. This is one of the classical points of discussion recently renewed by Joachim Jeremias and Kurt Aland. I am convinced that Kurt Aland is correct in his critique of Jeremias and that a conscious practice of infant baptism emerged in the church around A.D. 200. One can argue this on different grounds. To me it seems that even if Jeremias was right as to the archaeological evidence, it would be clear, I think, that this was due to a certain view of parents, of the family unit which would be hard to argue as being a specifically Christian way of looking at parents. Is this underlying view of family unity one which we would really accept that easily? In any case the evidence for infant baptism is and remains extremely shaky, and where it occurs it is perhaps not as revealing and binding as some have thought.

When one approaches baptism and the Eucharist, I think that the right approach is to inquire about the *primary function*, as I would call it, or the *primary meaning* of these rituals. And as to baptism then I would take my point of departure in the fact that everything that we know about baptism indicates that in the early church it is always an *act of initiation*. Such an act is capable of many interpretations. But the force and function of initiation are the sine qua non, that which makes baptism baptism.

One cannot understand baptism by combining such elements as purification, death and resurrection, regeneration, receiving the Spirit, incorporation in the body of Christ, and so forth and so on. One must begin with the fact that in all cases the practice of baptism is the rite by which *initiation* takes place. This Christian use of baptism has roots in the activities of John the Baptist. And baptism may be a radicalized form of the initiatory baptisms, or "lustrations," now known from the Qumran community.

In the Dead Sea Scrolls one can see how these lustrations grew out of a certain interpretation of the priestly lustrations at the Temple. But in Christian circles, it seems that it is exactly the initiation, the *rite de passage* element that is always present. Otherwise the line of demarcation between lustration and baptism is not so clear. There were a lot of washings going on in those times. But even where we have weekly baptizers and where we go into the Mandean material with the repeated baptisms, and so forth, the interpretation seems to be in Christian circles that the initiatory baptism is the *rite de passage*. So we start with initiation.

My third point would be that the eschatological dimension in this baptism is a decisive one. It has become increasingly precarious to see the Jewish proselyte baptism as the proper background for the understanding of Christian baptism. This is a very complex question. One of the ways in which Christian theologians and historians have tried to come to grips with Christian baptism is to say that Christians took this proselyte baptism and applied it both to gentiles and to the Jews. But to those who are drawn to this argument I would reply that it is highly questionable whether the Jews practiced proselyte baptism in the first century A.D.

So the difference—and this is my fourth point—between Christian baptism and that of John or of Qumran is described in the NT as the difference in anticipation, or a difference in eschatological intensity. Also Christian baptism retains the element of anticipation, of course. Paul's *arrabōn* (down payment) or his *aparché* (first fruits) are indications thereof. The decisive difference between the Christian baptism as interpreted in the NT and anything that proceeds it is the Spirit. And here the sayings from the gospel are familiar to you, for example, that there is a difference between John's baptism in water and Christ's baptism in Spirit. This is clear both from the synoptic gospels as they distinguish between John and Jesus (Mark 1:8 parr.) and, I take it, from the discussion in the book of Acts. The material about Cornelius, about Philip and the eunuch, and about the case in Acts 19 all revolve around the problem of the relation between the Spirit and baptism. The church claims a more definite anticipation of the age to come, and it sees baptism as the rite by which man becomes a participant in the new age with the Holy Spirit.

Now this is just part of the initiation and the initiation so interpreted. I think that all other references to baptism can be understood from its function of initiation. Paul's interpretation of baptism as death with Christ toward a future resurrection may well be Paul's own constructive interpretation. We are of course at a stage in Pauline studies where the tide is going in the opposite direction. We are learning to see more and more the common Christian tradition behind Paul. And that might be the case here too. But I am intrigued by the idea that this is Paul's own interpretation in Romans 6 and perhaps even an ad hoc interpretation, one which came to him just as he was writing this specific chapter. After all, you know, Paul was capable of new ideas, plenty of them! Why do I say that? The first thing to note is of course that this play on *baptizesthai* (to be baptized) is very natural in the Greek-speaking world. If you go to Liddell and Scott, you will find that the first and basic meaning of *baptizesthai* given in secular Greek is "to be drowned," with the death connotation, and that it is especially in Jewish Greek that this meaning of sprinkling and washing and so forth is the other meaning. So that the play on baptism and death becomes so much more natural in the Greek-speaking world.[5] In any case this

180

powerful interpretation cannot, could not, and should not be the starting point of our interpretation of baptism.

Now if I say what I say, and if I place this Romans 6 in this kind of limited and interpretative line of Paul, then you can see that I am critical of Oscar Cullmann's interpretation of Jesus' death as the *Generaltaufe*—as the "general baptism." Oscar Cullmann's interpretation of baptism starts with the death of Jesus as the *Generaltaufe*. And this is also based on a strange interpretation of Jesus' own baptism. Cullmann notes that the quotation from Isaiah 42, "This is my son, the beloved one, with whom I am well pleased" is from the servant songs. And the servant songs in modern exegetical literature are under the heading of the suffering servant. And thereby it follows, according to Cullmann, that this is a reference to the suffering and death of Jesus. But I have always found it interesting to note that this reading of Isaiah 42 as having to do with suffering presupposes Duhm's commentary at the end of the last century, which lumped the servant songs under the heading of the suffering servant. Yet there is nothing about suffering whatsoever in Isaiah 42, and in this kind of setting which we are dealing with here. So that there is no reason in the world to see any reference to a *Generaltaufe* here. We have no right to hear Isaiah 53 when we read Isaiah 42. Of course we can argue that the idea of the suffering servant held these texts together prior to the identification of the songs on form-critical grounds. But then it would be even more mandatory to have the *ebed*, the child-servant, retained in the quotation from Isaiah 42 instead of *huios* which now prevails the textual traditions. That is to say, if Cullmann were right in saying that this is a hint toward the suffering servant, why do we not have the texts straight with a reference for the servant? Why do we then have the son instead of the servant? Now I take this seriously because this way of going about arguing from the biblical basis is extremely objectionable, where one takes a loaded concept, combined in good Lutheran fashion with Paul's interpretation in Romans 6 (which might in itself be very appropriate as we have tried to show), plus a highly complex interpretation of the baptism of Jesus, and makes this a basis for the understanding of baptism.[6]

These observations would suggest that all discussion about baptism in the NT must begin with the element of initiation. The meaning of baptism cannot be found by exploiting any one specific interpretation of this rite, be it the element of free gift, or the relation to death-resurrection, or any of the other motifs which condition and enrich, but never overshadow the rite of initiation.

The discussion from hereon should, I think, go in the direction of seeing the rite of initiation in its various theological interpretations (cleansing, death, resurrection, etc.). These are specific interpretations conditioned by specific problems. We have so many motifs and so many riches, and we are tempted to account for them all so that the complexity becomes such that one gets overloaded. But one should rather examine those six or seven ways in which this rite of initiation was spoken about, and ask oneself which should be particularly stressed. In any case, the point of departure is baptism as the right of initiation into the church of Jesus Christ.

As you have found, I am not giving a systematic, all-inclusive presentation, but I am indicating to you how I think that we can use the can opener, so to speak, for all the canonical material—how we should open up from a biblical point of view the study and the discussion into the biblical basis for the sacraments. And I would like to demonstrate this on the sacraments, as the history of the Eucharist has evolved. "A beloved child is called by many names," says a Swedish proverb, and this is certainly true here; the Lord's Supper, the Last Supper, the Communion, the Mass in the narrow sense, the Sacrifice of the Mass, the Sacrament of the Altar, the Eucharist, and many other names, names which often in the history of the church have had the character of a banner under which and by which one has given one's specific accent to the interpretation and the presentation of this sacrament.

Thus, when I call it the Eucharist I am not saying that this is the best way of speaking. I do it, I guess, as a child of my time and at this very juncture in the history of theology, liturgy, and ecumenism. Many of us fell in love with this kind of accent to rescue this act from the somber overinterpretation of its sacrificial and penitential aspect, as we knew it in many of the Lutheran churches when we were young, and for me that is now long ago.

The Eucharist then is our topic. As I asked in relation to baptism, so I want to ask in relation to the Eucharist: What is the central function and the coordinating substance of this act? In baptism, we said, it is initiation; in the Eucharist, I say, it is the meal. And it is there, I think, that we should begin. That sounds naive but all good theology is naive, because if it is not naive we do not really understand what we are saying. That is a deep theological statement based on the basic understanding of Christian existence as being a child of God.

The meal, communal and eschatological, is what holds all practice and all primary thinking together in relation to this act. By that I also mean, or I think it follows, that the relation to the Jewish Passover is not essential to the understanding of the Eucharist, even if it may be highly significant. I hope that Prof. Reicke will agree with me that we do have evidence of this meal being celebrated in the early church, a rather ample evidence where the tie-in with the Jewish Passover is not essential, where we have a reason to say, "Yes, it can be so seen, but it is not obviously so." The meal itself could be both celebrated and talked about, and theologized about, with or without conscious attention to the Jewish Passover. The reference to "the night in which he was betrayed" does not need to mean—and in my judgment very often does not mean—a specific reference to the Jewish Passover.

But the relation between this meal and Jesus as the messianic figure is and remains essential. Its character of an eschatological meal is expressed and is understood in relation to Jesus Christ, Jesus the Messiah as being central in the meal itself. And so I belong to those who read the earliest material about the Eucharist in the light of what we have come to call the messianic banquet. This messianic banquet is a banquet for the brotherhood; and this communal aspect is just as essential as is its messianic and eschatological aspects. Or as some of the good biblical theologians used to say: Jesus cannot be the Messiah unless his followers are the people of God; a Messiah without a people is not a Messiah.

From these observations it also follows—and this I find of great significance—that we do not see this meal as growing out of the Temple cult. It is not in the prolongation of the Temple and its activities that this cult act is to be understood. It is rather out of that significant segment of Jewish cult which was centered in the family. That is implicit in its character of a meal, of a real meal, of a family meal for sustenance. This is of course to be expected with the type of Jewish background to which the NT witnesses in general. And somehow here is one of the lines of demarcation between the similar features in the Qumran community where the priestly element was always strong due to the very constitution of that community, which by definition had to have 10 percent priests, and, due to its very ethos, which although separated from the Temple physically was highly inspired by Temple and priestly ideology. The early Christian structure grows out of the dispersion sentiment with synagogue and home. (I would here stress home since so much of the discussion about Christian origins has usually only counted with the two possibilities: is it synagogue or is it Temple?) But anyone who knows anything about contemporary Jewish religious life as well as the history of Jewish existence knows that it is one of those traditions in the history of religions which has been most home-centered in many of its most central religious observances. And I find it striking that this fits well with the evidence of the early Christian material, so much so that this might also throw light on the famous quote from Acts 2:46 how these early Christians participated in the prayers in the Temple but at home they broke bread with joy. Now I am not saying that that proves they were always home-centered, because I guess that a little "eucharist" in the halls of the Temple would not have gone over too well in those late thirties for other reasons as well! But the *klasis tou artou* (breaking of bread) as a home activity is of significance.

And there, since I was previously critical of Oscar Cullmann, one of the sons of the faculty in this city, I shall be complimentary to him now. I think that one of the lasting contributions of Cullmann to the understanding of early liturgical life is his insistence on the fact that we have labored with a wrong image when we have seen the origin of Christian liturgy in the form of inheriting the synagogue structure as the Service of the Word and then seeing another line of the meal and the Eucharist as joining in some kind of way with the synagogue service of the Word. Anyone who was a young student in my days in Lutheran Uppsala, Sweden, is aware of the fact that this old argument from Bauer and others sounds a little too much as the classical discussion in the Lutheran tradition whether one should have a main service on Sunday with or without the Eucharist. And those who wanted to argue for the full validity of the service without the Eucharist, they found it very handy to refer to these two roots, two independent roots of the Christian main service of the Mass. And so with this argument, *man merkt die Absicht und wird verstimmt*—as I guess one says in German—one recognizes the intention and gets a little suspicious!

Cullmann is right, I think, when he says that early Christian worship has to be understood as having as its center the meal, the one single cultic act, around which different elements and certainly also elements from the synagogue service of different kinds and the family services gather, are drawn and organized around the one magnetic center, which is the meal.

The two aspects of this meal which I want to stress are, as I said, the communal and the eschatological. The messianic banquet is an eschatological banquet; it is a meal toward the future; it is a meal which, while celebrated now, points toward the future. And this element, for some strange reason, is not adequately reflected in the basic structure of what you might call the canon of the mass, the words of institution, and so forth. But you do know that in all the four accounts of the institution of the Eucharist, the three synoptic accounts plus 1 Corinthians 11, the act is accompanied by—and this is news to nobody—the statement in different forms of how this meal points toward the time when it is made new in heaven. "I shall not taste of this until it is made new in Heaven"—this you have in different forms in the sayings of Jesus. It is moved before and after in the different synoptic accounts, but the common denominator of this eschatological note is a striking one. And I take it that somehow in some complicated way that very difficult beginning of John 14, about whether he is going to take them with him or whether they can stay where they are and so forth and so on (John 14:1–3), has to some extent the same function. In any case it is clear in 1 Corinthians 11 that this kind of act is one in which or by which or through which the death of Christ is announced *achri hou elthé*—"until he come." (The English in its noble style retains the subjunctive properly.)

This eschatological note which is also found in the *Didache* and which I take it is contained in one of the earliest liturgical outbursts that is retained from the early church—namely, "Maranatha," "our Lord, come!"—is the element which gives to this meal its primary character of an anticipatory meal pointing toward the future. In short, it places this meal in the context of what we call the messianic banquet. Now here I would like to warn you a little because we Christians have an odd way of referring to Jewish material. When I say that the Jews had a concept about the messianic banquet, then in Christian commentaries and in my students' papers it often comes out something like: "The Jewish dogmatics held a view or taught that there was to be a messianic banquet," which to some extent misses the point of the nature of the Jewish playfulness in matters of *haggada*. The rabbis in their general and humorous playfulness pictured "the coming age" under many images, and one of them was the delightful image of the huge banquet in which Messiah would gather together with his people. As a matter of fact in some of these playful rabbinic exercises one had even settled the menu for the messianic banquet. One was going to feed on Leviathan, thereby signifying the destruction of evil at the same time as there would be the great and glorious banquet.

185

Now it is true that this idea of the messianic banquet figures in the teachings of Jesus, as you well know. "People will come from east and west and lay at table together with Abraham, Isaac and Jacob." This is the heavenly banquet (Matt. 8:11). Also Luke 22:30: "and you will eat and drink at my table," in parallelism with the passage which we have also in Matt. 19:28 about "you will sit on the thrones and judge the tribes of Israel." This rather playful language is the one, I take it, which is also to be seen behind that column 2 of the additional material to the Manual of Discipline at Qumran, which we call 1 QSa column 2. In this something is described (and here in rather priestly terms as we said, because it is a priestly community, and that has no parallel in Christendom), for instance, the eschatological banquet, how the blessings are going to be said by the High Priest, and how everything is going to be glorious. Then the whole text ends on the notes: "wherever you are gathered more than ten men" (the "minyan" is present so to speak), "there you do likewise," which means that the actual celebration of the meal at Qumran out in that terrible heat and in those pots and pans which we have found in that place (which we can now reconstruct) one celebrated a holy meal understood to be patterned on the final and conclusive messianic banquet. Now it is in the light of these meals that the celebration of the Lord's Supper has to be seen. And it is interesting to note that it is because of the great holiness of this meal as a kind of manifestation of the holy heavenly community in advance that all the rules and regulations at Qumran as to who belongs, who touches the purity, and who does this and that, are all seen as regulating who can participate, cf. *Didache* 10:6.

With that background I would like to draw your attention to the text from the NT which we know by far the best, and that is the Lord's Prayer. I am interested in the classic problem, and I find this important for our discussion of the Eucharist, of how to translate the untranslatable word *epiousios*—"our *epiousion* bread give us today" (Matt. 6:11).

There has been a long debate and discussion about the meaning of this word. There were claims that we did have this word in pre-Christian Greek texts, but I think it is now true to say that one of them proved to read otherwise, and the only one which can be reported has disappeared from its proper place in the British Museum—nobody knows what that text really said. So we are really here at a point, even if this evidence were available, where we can say: to Greek ears the word *epiousios* was a strange word, and it is a strange word because it tries to say something which was not usually said in Greek. It is a homemade word to translate something. We know from the church fathers that there were Semitic editions of the Lord's Prayer which used the term *machar* which has to do with "tomorrow." "Our bread for tomorrow give us today." But brainy little exegetes could easily rule that out as an improper meaning because in Matthew 6, if you read a little further, it says that we should not worry ourselves about what to eat, and what to put on, and that is just what the gentiles busy themselves about. But we Christians are certainly above such things, so such Christians just could not be allowed to pray to the Almighty "And our bread for tomorrow give us already today." That just does not sound good!

There is a linguistic problem here too. According to all linguistic rules *epiousios* should come not from *ep-einai* (*epi* plus "to be"), but *ep-ienai* (*epi* plus a verb meaning "I shall go" or "I shall come"). Origen, who knows his Greek, I take it, is aware of this problem here, but he likes so much the theological mileage he gets out of reading this as something similar to *supersubstantialis* that he gives all kinds of fancy arguments for that being right. Then when he comes through it he says: of course, now there are those who say that this could not be so, and partly on linguistic grounds, but I just say that this is not the case. He is the one who suggests that there were people in the church already at that time who read this as meaning "our proleptic bread" or "our anticipatory bread give us today." Now in the light of this and other data, I am quite convinced that this prayer "Give us this day our *epiousion* bread" does refer to exactly the meal which certainly in early times was also a meal of sustenance, the meal of the community seen as the eschatological meal. "Give us the anticipatory meal of the kingdom here and now."

You should then note the striking thing that the next prayer in the Lord's Prayer is the one about mutual forgiveness in the community. For we are the ones who have forgiven one another; we are the messianic brotherhood where we have cleared up our issues. As you know the right reading according to all the manuscripts is not "forgive us as we forgive," but "forgive us as we have forgiven" (*aphékamen*, the aorist), or "as we forgave." The *aphiomen* is another of these generalizing tendencies of the prayer taking it out of its concrete messianic and eschatological context, as the Gospel of Luke does in so many other respects with this prayer. "Our *epiousion* bread" then is a reference to this

187

messianic meal celebrated by the community which knows itself to be the mutually forgiven brotherhood and praying that it will survive the last showdown or will not be tempted and tested beyond its power: "And lead us not into temptation, but deliver us from evil." Of course, this prayer is an eschatological prayer through and through, and it is in that context that the meal itself functions.

I have used this as an illustration of how and to what extent the eschatological setting of the meal is at the very root of the Eucharist. And we have seen in our reference to the mutually forgiven community that this eschatological understanding carries with it an extremely high (to say the least) standard of what kind of a community that kind of celebrating community could be and should be, namely—one of full brotherhood, of full mutual forgiveness. And I have argued elsewhere[7] (as all snobbish scholars say, and I do too) that the final terms with which Matthew rounds this off: "If you forgive people their transgressions, then also your heavenly Father will forgive you, but if you do not, then he will not." This sort of rubs in this whole element of the mutually forgiven community as the very community which can take part in and which perhaps even can utter the true "Maranatha," the true eschatological prayer, the crying for the coming of the kingdom. This is a eucharistic mood, as I see it, in an eschatological context.

The other textual illustration which I wanted to cite for my stress on the communal and the eschatological is of course the classic text on the Eucharist in 1 Corinthians 11, the only extended biblical text which describes what is going on at the meals. Of course this is described for a specific purpose. The specificity of the problem, especially of the Pauline epistles should never be overlooked, because everything is ad hoc. So, what is the issue in 1 Corinthians 11?[8] The issue is a breakdown of communality, a breakdown of the community in a very specific way. You come together, says Paul, "but it is not the Lord's Supper that you eat." Why? Apparently the better-to-do, the richer participants in the meal brought their own food to this potluck church supper, and they were eager to start. They started before, if we fill out the picture a little, the slaves could sneak out at night and join. The slaves, who could not bring any food with them because that would be stealing, came late and there was no food left. And Paul says, this is to misunderstand the Eucharist. And this, which in a way is just bad behavior, thoughtlessness, and selfishness, is taken up by Paul on a fantastically high level of theological and eschatological seriousness. It is so serious, says he, so that

188

some of you have gotten sick and some have even died, there referring to the rather straight first century and later concept that there is a very close relation between sin, sickness, and death.[9] So he argues this with great seriousness and he says that this behavior in Corinth, which is "in an unworthy manner" (v. 27), is due to the fact that they have not understood the nature of the Christian meal, a meal which gets its institution and its magna charta, according to Paul, from what we refer to as the words of institution, from the last meal of Jesus with his apostles. And so he says that the one who does not recognize that this meal is the meal for the mutually giving and forgiving community has not *discerned the body*. And therefore he criticizes them.

Now of course the history of this phrase has in the Western tradition, in general, centered around a totally different problem, a problem which I have been unable to find in my study of the NT, and that is the problem of so-called "real presence." That is not the issue. The issue is the one that Paul then comes back to in verse 34, and as you know this chapter ends on a most casual note instead of having a little doxology for the great mystery of the mass, which you must admit would be proper. Paul ends instead by saying: "So if somebody is that terribly hungry, let him eat at home so that you do not fall into this tremendous kind of self-judgment when you get together. For the rest I will instruct you when I come" (au. trans.). The note is this misbehavior about their eating. That is the issue in Corinth. And it is this discrimination, this social dimension which according to Paul is the lack of discernment as to the body.

The other passage which one could draw in here is of course in 1 Cor. 10:16–17 where you have the discussion of this ritual act, this cult act of the meal in relation to idolatry and the different sacrificial meals in the Hellenistic world, especially in Corinth. And there the argument is rather of a different nature. It is just to make clear and sure that the participation in this meal is such a participation in Christ and in the blood and body of Christ so that it excludes any other cultic involvement. It is an argument for cultic exclusivism supported by the argument in verse 18 pointing to the Jewish parallel.

So I would summarize my observations as follows: The Eucharist is primarily the *Banquet*. It is the banquet on the way toward the consummation and toward fulfillment. It is a real meal and it is a joyous meal. In the English popular editions of the Mass now used in many Roman Catholic churches in the United States, it is interesting to see how this banquet idea has taken hold in the rubrics. Time and time again in the canon of the Mass there is banquet language smuggled in, although the highly "sacrificial" language of the canon has no relation whatsoever to the concept of the messianic banquet. It is as if the interpreter has wanted to say to the people, "Now, behind it all, the basic thing is that you celebrate the banquet." And they do it, so to speak, against the grain of the actual text translated. It is of course also expressed in the Roman Catholic practice, for which we all rejoice, of moving the table close to the people, saying Mass behind the table, and so forth. (Finally I guess the Lutherans will be the only ones who hold on to the bad medieval ways. At least when I was in Uppsala at the World Council of Churches, the Swedish church excelled in this medievalism to the utmost. But it is beautiful, or as the Swedes always say, dignified. They should have been in Corinth. I have always loved Corinth. It was a wonderful church, I think. It had all kinds of faults, but it did not have the fault which most of our churches today have: it was never dull. You think about that when you read Corinthians, and you will get a big lift out of it!)

So I note that this meal idea is dominating in a very interesting way practically all the reasonable (and some not so reasonable) experiments in the liturgical field of today. This is due particularly to the fact that the last decades have been a great period of restoration both of primitive Christian piety through the Gregory Dixes and others and toward a deepening of the liturgical understanding.

I have not said anything about *sacrifice* because it is my conviction, though I might be wrong, that at least as far as the primary texts about the Eucharist are concerned in the NT, the sacrificial aspect is not operative. Now I say that quite openly in spite of the fact that the words of institution do refer to the night in which he was betrayed and do refer to the eating and drinking, but the specific sacrificial aspect at no place is made theologically relevant.

I should like to make a remark about the weighty theological concern for the problem of the *real presence* of Christ. I think we are all aware of all the complicated and dated language, "transubstantiation" and otherwise, about the "how," and I do not think we should get involved with that. That can be cleared up, I think. I am asking a much more crucial question: *Why* did one become so interested in the question of the *presence* of Christ? Why would that be so important? When and where does the question about the presence occur? If I read the NT right, Jesus Christ is as solidly on the right hand of God as anything can be; that is where he sits and waits, and what is present is the Spirit. And I am very interested in asking scholars of a somewhat later period than mine whether they can tell me when this tremendous concern for the presence of Christ became an issue. I am also inquiring to what extent it is a real issue in the living piety of our time. Or is it a problematic one which we have carried with our freight? And if we were to discuss the presence further, I would suggest that just as when one discusses authority and other things like that, we should not discuss presence in general, but we should ask: presence *for what?* For what is this presence thought to be significant?

Finally this is a banquet of joy, the *joy of eschatology* which—if Joseph Fitzmyer, the Jesuit from Woodstock, and others are right—is expressed in that odd verse, 1 Cor. 11:10. That is the passage about the women who have to have a "power" (which some people have thought meant a hat) on their heads for the angels' sake. Fitzmyer and others have argued in the light of the Dead Sea Scrolls that the point here is quite simply that now the eschatological fulfillment is so nigh in the church so that the angels are worshiping together with the Christian church, although you cannot quite see them, and hence superdecency is in order. The point is a reference to the fact that the Christian worship —and its very center, the Eucharist—is a worship in an angelic mood, in angelic presence as a sign of the eschatological intensity which gives the note of joy.

NOTES

1. The manuscript of this lecture was transcribed and edited from the recording by the institute staff in Strasbourg.

2. See above, my essay "The Church in Early Christianity," pp. 163–72.

3. Cf. Luke 3:18 where to announce doom is to evangelize (RSV: "preached good news"). There is no "good" element here and *euaggelion* has only the common Greek meaning of authoritative announcement.

4. See above, my essay "Kerygma and Kerygmatic," pp. 45–53.

5. I would guess that the similar use of *baptisma* in relation to Jesus' death and to martyrdom of his disciples in Mark 10:38 is secondary in Mark and must be understood in the light of reflection upon the meaning of baptism in the martyrological sense. If we had time one could go into this in detail. It is one of those places where Mark has more than Matthew. Matthew has only the cup that Jesus has to drink and does not mention the baptism of death. Mark has the baptism of death and martyrdom, and I am inclined to say that this is growth of speculation within the Greek-speaking church. See my article "One Baptism for the Forgiveness of Sins," *Worship* 40 (1966):272–75.

6. Finally, an exegete would perhaps like to draw attention to Mark 16:16, the text which plays a great role in Luther's discussion of baptism and has even made it into the every-Sunday form of the Mass in the Lutheran Church in America. "He who believes and is baptized will be saved," belongs to that longer ending of Mark which is not in the better manuscripts. And it is one of these interesting questions that emerges in the history of theology when we really become convinced that this was not really in the Bible in the first place. Yet, a whole theology has grown up around it. It is perhaps the kind of question for a dialogue between the systematic, the historical, and the biblical theologian.

7. See above, my essay "Prayer and Forgiveness," pp. 115–25, where there is a fuller discussion of *epiousios*.

8. Here I follow some of the insights from G. Bornkamm: Herrenmahl und Kirche bei Paulus, *Zeitschrift für Theologie und Kirche* 53 (1956): 312ff.; also in idem, *Studien zu Antike und Urchristentum* (1959), 138–76.

9. As a footnote one could point out that once you have read verse 30 here, you can understand what a tremendous handicap it was for Paul that he so often fell sick during his travels. You remember how he says to the Galatians: "And in spite of the fact that I was stranded at Galatia for sickness' sake, you took my word as the word of God" (Galatians 4, au. trans.). And that is really remarkable, because a sick apostle in those days must have been somewhat like a one-legged football player, literally a contradiction in terms!

14

Immortality Is Too Much and Too Little

Introductory Note: Gustavus Adolphus College in St. Peter, Minnesota, has hit on a great idea by cultivating its historical ties with Sweden. Since 1965 they have sponsored an annual Nobel Conference, with participation from recent Nobel Laureates.

For the Sixth Annual Conference in 1972 the chosen theme was "The End of Life." I remember Professor George Wald (see below, p. 195) giving a stunning presentation on "The Beginning of Death" (i.e., procreation by intercourse). Since there are no Nobel Prizes in Theology, that field must be represented by lesser lights —and in 1972 I was such a one.

The essay here republished in the original form caused some stir, and I received more angry mail about it than about any other speech or article. I can understand why. But it is my hope that the reader will discern the intention, the pastoral intention of the article. On the basis of cool, descriptive biblical theology I make the suggestion that the original setting of the resurrection faith (Jewish as well as Christian) was in the martyrology of a people and in the grappling with the question of God's chances to restore rightness and justice in an evil world. I further suggest that such a setting has deep relevance for many thoughtful people today—perhaps more so than the long tradition of individual immortality. That is all. I am not a biblicist who wants to say that the long and glorious tradition of hymns and thoughts of immortality is wrong or less "Christian." But there may be an alternative worth expression in contemporary spirituality.

The most common critique of this essay is built on references to the expression "eternal life," *zōē aiōnios*. But I would argue that this concept is quite distinct from "immortality" especially as used in Johannine theology where it refers to a quality of life both in this world and in the world to come. The believer has eternal life already here and now, e.g., John 5:24. See above, pp. 64–65.

The original publication was in *The End of Life: Discussion at the Sixth Nobel Conference organized by Gustavus Adolphus College, St. Peter, Minnesota*, ed. John D. Roslansky (Amsterdam and London: North Holland Publishing Co., 1973), 71–83. I had begun thinking about the topic more carefully when I edited four significant Ingersoll Lectures on Immortality (a Harvard Divinity School Lecture Series) by Oscar Cullmann, H. A. Wolfson, W. Jaeger, and H. J. Cadbury, in *Immortality and Resurrection* (New York: Macmillan & Co., 1958), and I had learned much from G. W. Nickelsburg, *Resurrection, Immortality, and Eternal Life in Intertestamental Judaism*, Harvard Theological Studies 26 (1972).

For a contemporary philosophical and theological approach in which immortality is seen as the irreducible center of religion, see John Hick, *Death and Eternal Life* (New York: Harper & Row, 1976).

Religious man in his faith, in his speaking and singing about God, is actually seeking—and seeking to express—his place in the total universe. He is trying to cope with reality. And religious men and women through the ages have done that within the knowledge of their time, within the science of their time, as well as within other insights and wisdom. The conflict between science and religion has, if I understand it correctly, never been a conflict between science and religion. It has been an unfortunate mistiming or comparing not equal to equal: when religious sanction was given to scientific insights of an earlier time, it often clashed with newer insights in the sciences. Thus the famous clashes between religion and science—theology and science—have usually been clashes between *sciences*. And yet the church has lived through many serious transitions as to world views and scientific insights, and so have other religious communities. There was one such transition in the time of the early church fathers: the change from the three-story universe to the Ptolemaic view of the world. And then there was the Copernican one. And there is a saying in my homeland that in the first generation the church fights new scientific insights; in the second generation we say that those scientific views are adiaphora, that is, they do not really make a difference to the essence of the faith; and in the third generation we write hymns on the basis of the new scientific insight. You all know

194

that nineteenth-century evening hymn which begins "The day thou gavest, Lord, is ended . . . " In it we sing: "The sun that bids us rest is waking, Our brethren neath the western sky. And hour by hour fresh lips are making, Thy wondrous doings heard on high." It is a beautiful Copernican hymn.

Now, there has always been, as that dialogue has gone on, a certain tendency of plucking the flowers from the latest scientific insights, and we had a wonderful flower blooming before us here in George Wald's presentation. In this Wald said that actually the entrance of death into this long chain of development coincided with the sexual mode of pro-creation, which is exactly what it says in Genesis 3, where the aware-ness of sexuality is combined with the entrance of death into the earlier paradise. But that is exactly the kind of example that preachers should not use glibly for it really is two different modes of speaking. A facile mixing of the language of science and the language of the Bible easily gives the believer the feeling that "science proves the Bible," as if the Bible could not speak for itself in its own language.

I happen to believe that the whole long and glorious Christian tradi-tion of speaking about the immortality of the soul is only a period of the Judeo-Christian tradition, and that period may now be coming to an end. I say this with some trepidation, and my trepidation is not for any other reason than that it is always painful to tear into what is very dear to many. And yet there are times in the history of theology and of the Christian community and the church in which such changes take place. I have always loved the example of the apostle Paul who under-stood what theologians have great difficulties in understanding: that sometimes there are new problems and new data. It is very hard for a theologian really to have respect for "new data." Partly he is in tune with the historians who always play tricks on us by showing that new data are really just new little twists of the old data. Having as many old data as the historian has: (a) it's easy for him, and (b) he should have some reward for knowing so many data. So he has a tendency always to minimize the new. But tradition, unless it is just museum tradition, living tradition is just as much a way of change as it is a means of conti-nuity. You remember when Paul discusses matters of divorce and things like that in 1 Corinthians 7. Paul says that there are now certain cases of divorce, and Jesus said that there should not be any. Then Paul quotes a word from the Lord, but then he says, "Now how is it then in special cases?" and mentions certain special cases. Finally, Paul says, "On this one I have no word from the Lord." And I think he was the

195

last preacher in Christendom who had the guts to admit that. But what is really involved in that is a respect for the new. He could just as well—could he not?—have done what we all do: "Now, of course, we don't have exactly a word for that but it follows from what we have—etc. . . . " That way one will always smother the newness.

The new insight, the new experience, is something to be taken seriously, and I happen to believe that this should be our first observation when we think about immortality and the end of life in the perspective of the Christian tradition. Now, to outsiders this kind of speaking about new interpretations does not go over very well, because it always sounds as if: "Oh, those tricky theologians. Of course, they really have lost their faith but they have to somehow make something of it. So they are clever manipulators. Of course, they do not believe but after all they earn their living on belief so they have to do something."

There is an attitude which I always have called "the fundamentalism of the nonbeliever," and that is the worst kind because it is one that takes for granted that "the Christian faith," or "the meaning of the Bible," is always the most sterile, unchangeable orthodoxy that could ever be imagined. That is at least honest, as they say. But as the rabbis already knew, there comes a moment, as they said, when there is time to do something for the Lord, and by that they meant a time for a new interpretation. Now, that is a little arrogant but it points in the right direction.

The question about immortality of the soul is interesting for someone who is primarily a biblical scholar because he specializes in sixty-six so-called books that do not know of immortality of the soul. The word occurs in two places in the NT: once about God "who alone has immortality" (1 Tim. 6:16), and once in a very special setting, where it is perhaps borrowed from other people whom Paul quotes when he speaks of how the mortal nature must put on immortality (1 Cor. 15:53ff.). But perhaps the almost complete absence of the word "immortality" is not really the point. The point is that the whole world that comes to us through the Bible, OT and NT, is not interested in the immortality of the soul. And if you think it is, it is because you have read this into the material. In terms of the OT it is very clear that Abraham, Isaac, and Jacob, and George Wald are one in believing that the only immortality that there is, is in the germ plasm, or they called it "the loins" (e.g., Gen. 35:11). The only immortality that the earlier strata of the OT knows about is perpetuation through offspring. The OT view is a view of man created of dust who is made a human being by God's energizing power, the "spirit," being blown into the dust. That is also what Ecclesiastes speaks about in that beautiful description of aging (which outdoes T. S. Eliot because that is what he tried to copy) that ends on the note, as you know, "the dust returns to earth, whence it came, and the spirit returns to God who gave it" (12:7). Here the spirit is not the individual's little identity spirit, but the life-giving power of God, the *ruach*, the wind which is withdrawn causing man to disintegrate into dust. Dust to dust, ashes to ashes.

Immortality of the soul is not emphasized. The NT in a very interesting way speaks constantly about resurrection as against immortality. The interesting thing with this is not the discussion that has gone through the whole history of the Christian tradition concerning how resurrection relates to immortality and whether immortality is for the soul and resurrection is the way in which the body is added to that soul, or whatever the relations between them are. That is a later question of theological speculation once the Christian message about the resurrection came up against the Hellenistic and secular preoccupation with immortality. We should rather ask why and for what purpose the NT speaks about resurrection—why that is its proper way of speaking.

Learned scholars have found out—and that is not so hard to do—that the origins of this strange language of the resurrection are to be found in thoughts about martyrdom and that the question to which resurrection is the answer is not the question about what is going to happen to man when he dies. The question is not: What is going to happen to little me? Am I to survive with my identity or not? The question is rather whether God's justice will win out. The martyrs and the righteous are suppressed by the establishment—their own or foreign—the rich are fat-eyed and happy and seem to carry the day while the righteous go down the drain. Resurrection answers the question of theodicy, that is, the question of how God can win, the question of a moral universe. Does crime pay? Will evil win? Where is God's promise and power? Will God ultimately come through? Will the kingdom come somehow so that righteousness flows forth and justice is in the midst of us all? That is the matrix, that is the womb out of which the dream and thought and hope and prayer for the resurrection emerged out of the Jewish community in times of martyrdom and suppression. They spoke about vindication of the righteous and the martyrs. They did not affirm so much the fate of such individuals. They were interested in whether God and justice would have the last word.

You can see this in a strange way, if you are a careful Bible reader.

There is a passage in Matthew (27:51–53), where on Good Friday itself, when Jesus dies and there is the earthquake (i.e., the cosmic forces join in the drama), the situation is so jittery, so to speak, so that some of the righteous who had already been suppressed come out of their graves, and the general resurrection that one looked forward to, the ultimate establishment of justice in the world, started to happen.

I am just lecturing you on plain, descriptive biblical studies. It is a simple fact that when Peter said to his friends up in Galilee, "You know, this Jesus whom they crucified and whom we loved so much is risen," the thoughts that went through these people's minds were not, "Oh, that means that there is eternal life for little me." That would be a rather odd way of making such a point. No, to them it meant that there was reason to believe that God's ultimate power of justice, vindicating the oppressed, the suppressed, and the martyred, had manifested itself. Compare Acts 2:22–24, and the way in which Jesus had left his case in the hands of God the just vindicator (1 Pet. 2:23). The kingdom had taken a big step forward as one had been praying, hoping, and dreaming for its coming. So that the issue of the most original Christian way of speaking about the end of life in the sign of the resurrection of Jesus was an issue that did not speak to the question of what is going to happen to my identity, but what is happening in and to the world. Is there reason to believe that justice will win out? It is a concern for where the world is going, not a concern for oneself.

I think about Easter sermons. There is, of course, the type of Easter sermon that capitalizes on the fact that it is spring and nature is coming back to life. It is beautiful, but I guess such preachers should be sent by their mission boards to the Southern Hemisphere for a couple of years. Or perhaps one should be more serious about it and say: no, if Easter means anything in the Christian tradition it means the breaking of the chains of nature, in a certain sense, rather than the affirmation of the cycle of nature. And then, of course, there are those for whom the meaning of Easter is primarily the assurance as to eternal life and the immortality of the soul: the assurance as to the afterlife. I do not know how it is with you or with people you know when the role play between congregations and pastors is broken through, and people say what they really think and are concerned about; but I think it is true to say that an increasing number of men and women are less and less concerned about the immortality of the soul, especially their own. That somehow it is not that obviously attractive and commanding; the glow of the immortality-language has worn off. And why has it, if this is true? It has because that whole way of thinking and speaking, which we, as I said, do not even have in the Bible, is really part and parcel of a whole world view that is basically built on a Platonic view, a Platonic philosophy, and a Platonic understanding of reality—polarity between soul and body. And for centuries and centuries such a Platonic model was not only maintained by the church—and the church never invented it—but it was the lingua franca, the common way of thinking about man and the world. It seemed obvious and self-evident. But now on Easter day the church in many cases has a double duty. On the one hand, it has to convince man that he has that soul so that the message fits because there can be no joy unless he first has the need that the joy is supposed to satisfy. I happen to believe that that whole way of thinking, feeling, and ultimately experiencing oneself in the world is on the way out.

On the other hand, this is not a sign of less human, existential, and ethical seriousness or religious seriousness on the side and part of modern man. What he is concerned about is not so much what is going to happen to him but what is going to happen to this poor world. He is just as concerned with the future of God's plan and creation, the future of justice: Is the kingdom a dream or is it a dream worth believing in, a dream affirmed by God in Christ? That is what the problem is now to many, and as a biblical scholar I must note how that concern is in many ways similar to the concerns of the first Christians as they prayed for the coming of God's kingdom rather than for their own immortality.

In that setting immortality and the concern for immortality appear much *too little*, too selfish, too preoccupied with self or even family, race, and species. The question of prolonged identity somehow does not fit to what is really bothering us as we ask the questions of meaning and we seek the rays of hope. And immortality is *too much* since it has a tendency to claim to know more than may be good for us. It is too much because it is too specific, too tied up with a peculiar way of thinking about man, God, and the world. It is too much because it does not ring quite true to many a man's religious experience. Now, it is a funny thing that whenever something suggests itself to a person, even to a theologian, even to a preacher, and it is not quite as it has always been, then he is always accused of being secular or something, of being influenced from somewhere else. But it is in his religious experience and understanding that he finds that somehow this kind of language does not ring true. Against those who know too much, 1 John 3:2 says:

199

Beloved, we are God's children now; it does not yet appear what we shall be, but we know that when he appears we shall be like him for we shall see him as he is.

The end of life is thus in the mystery of the will of God and in the coming of the kingdom. The issue is not what happens to me but what happens to God's fight for his creation. What it is about is what we pray about in the Lord's Prayer which does not have a single word about little me. That is why it is such a great prayer, and that is why it might even have come straight from Jesus. Have you ever thought about that? When you pray that prayer you really do not pray about yourself, but you just shout: thy kingdom come, thy will be done, and you are just sort of swallowed up in the concern for the victory and coming of the kingdom. And that blows our minds out of preoccupation with ourselves. And it should. It opens up in our time a feeling for the fascination with the billions of years and the galaxies and the possibility of life on other planets. (I have always hoped that there is something like it because it would put us in place, not to be so terribly preoccupied with our own importance.)

The end of life is not in the question of, or the concern for, "my identity." And when I speak about the kingdom and the victory of God and about Jesus then I say to myself: a life like his was a kind of spearheading of the kingdom coming into this world; a life like his was vindicated by God, was resurrected; a life in its weakness, in its death, with a power of weakness, the turning of the other cheek, all these strange things which I like to call the "operation headstart" for the kingdom. I know, the world is just not ready yet for that life style; and we live in a nation that has no respect whatsoever for the power of weakness, or for that whole phenomenon of the coming of the kingdom, of the Christians as the guinea pigs for the kingdom, with what I term the eschatological "itch." You know, it is a very interesting thing that one has always thought about Jesus as teaching people patience and that is partly because of our way of speaking about and thinking about eternal life instead of thinking about the kingdom. Religion has had a tendency of becoming, as Marx rightly said, an opiate for the people, handed out by those in the leading positions: of course, you cannot have it all now, but if you behave you will get it in the yonder somehow. It has given us an image of religion as serving toward patience. But when I read about my Jesus I know nothing less patient—less patient with evil, less patient with sickness, even less patient with death. He went to the attack, he pushed the coming of the kingdom.

Now, what I suggest to you is that the proper image in the center of the Christian life as we look to the end of life is a new one, or rather an older one, one that should come back and engender new theology, new prayer, new faith, new bread and life—the image is the kingdom, the coming of the kingdom. That is what it is about. And that is why the whole concern for individual identity, which is the technical meaning of immortality of the soul, is not to be found in the Good Book because its concern and its focus is elsewhere.

Let me then just observe that in so doing, and especially in using and being inspired by the image of tenderness, love, and weakness in him who came, comes, and will come with the kingdom, we should perhaps also note that one of our problems at this time is not so much our powerlessness, but that we have in a way too much power. We can split the atom, we can manipulate the gene bank, we can make Einsteins galore, we can, we can, we can . . . And we can certainly upset the balance of nature. George Wald has spoken already about the serious ways in which we must be prophets of doom, and I guess both George Wald and I know that a true prophet is one who prays and hopes that he will be proven wrong. I think in a way that applies to Jesus. Jesus expected the end of the world in forty years and the Bible-reading Christians ask, Could Jesus be wrong? But Jesus was a true prophet; he was one of those who prophesied as the Lord had told him and as he saw it but since he was a true prophet, his hottest dream was that his prophecy would not come true. And it did not—but it looks pretty bad now.

Our problem is one of overpower and that is perhaps why we as human beings should take a lower posture. The fighting arrogance of man, even heightened into his projecting his importance into immortality, should perhaps be checked. We have overstepped, and perhaps we should seek to be closer to nature because the kingdom that Jesus speaks about is a funny kingdom. Its prototypes are the children, the lilies, and the birds. And one of the things that is going on right now as you meditate on the kingdom and on Jesus is that we start to understand the importance of seeking ourselves closer to the vibrations of nature. I do not know if you have noticed one of the signs of the generation gap, or whatever you want to call it, but one of them is actually that when my generation spoke about "civilized" the kids speak about "humanized"; and those are two very different things. The kingdom where the child is the ideal is closer to the "humanized" than to the "civilized."

I think that is one of the reasons there is such an attraction, and a

201

sound attraction, toward Eastern religions which have not glorified man by immortality, but rather have seen man finding himself by taking a lower and a lower posture even all the way toward Nirvana. And this has made Eastern religious man sensitive and given him, strangely enough, the tremendous respect for life, for other men's lives, because he did not "up" his own life with a kind of ferocious and arrogant intensity which we might have done. In times of demonic overpower and superpowers and overkill, there is wisdom in the low posture of the East.

So, sisters and brothers, we are very small but we are small in the hands of God. Hence we do not need to increase our importance. George Wald pointed out with striking clarity that man has his immortality in the germ plasm, but man has always liked to have it in his body. And I would add: for a long period of the Christian tradition, he liked to have it in the soul. But perhaps this whole search for identity perpetuation, or immortality, as assurance should be lifted out of the ego and be placed in God. To me it seems that if God is God, I neither care for nor worry about the hereafter; I celebrate the coming of the kingdom by singing hymns and by caressing with words the heaven with angels and saints and the messianic banquet with light and joy and glory. And I know that I paint, but I like to paint and I paint out of love and hope and faith. But when all is said and done I pray that the evil I have put into the world will not cause others to suffer too much, and that my little life will fit somehow into God's plan for the kingdom. The rest I leave. May his kingdom come.

JUDAISM,
CHRISTIANITY, AND
THE WIDER PLURALISM

15

Judaism and Christianity I:
Then and Now

Introductory Note: When I began more serious studies of Judaism in the late 1940s, I gave little or no conscious attention to Judaism as a living, contemporary reality. It now seems incredible and embarrassing to me how that could be so—in the late 1940s of all times. As I recall it, my aim was to achieve a better understanding of Christianity, and I had a strong hunch that the stereotypes which dominated our biblical work were wrong, especially those enforced by the Lutheran model of law and gospel.

But it was not until I came to the United States in the 1950s that I met Judaism as a living tradition. And gradually but rapidly I found that my academic groundwork on the period when Judaism and Christianity parted ways in the first and second centuries C.E. had serious relevance for the dialogue which now became the order of the day and into which I became increasingly drawn.

Thus I chose the occasion of the 1962 convocation at Harvard Divinity School for my first attempt at clarifying my thinking in the context of dialogue between Jews and Christians ("Judaism and Christianity I: Then and Now"). The second essay in this volume grew out of a Colloquium on Judaism and Christianity held at Harvard Divinity School in the fall of 1966, but was not written until after the Israeli victory in the summer of 1967. The original title was "Judaism and Christianity: After a Colloquium and a War."

Thus both essays are clearly dated and much has happened in the fifteen or twenty years since. There are significant milestones in the history of Jewish-Christian dialogue, not least the Vatican Guidelines for such dialogue (1975) and the Ecumenical Considerations on Jewish-Christian Dialogue, "received and commended to the Churches for study and action" by the Executive Committee of the

World Council of Churches (July 1982). Thereby the fruits of dialogue will reach outside the inner circles of the specialists and contribute to the process of consciousness raising in the everyday life of the churches.

Now we need a new generation of scholars—Jews and Christians—committed to seeing the others as they see themselves. We Christians tend to see Jews as playing a part—negative, or more recently positive—in our own scheme of things. That does not contribute to a recognition of the other in fulness and integrity. Or we think that we give honor to Judaism by stressing the similarities. But that often means that we can appreciate others only insofar as they are similar to us. But genuine, lasting, and enriching friendship can only grow strong when it is that which is different from ourselves that we find so lovable and so necessary for a fuller understanding of God's whole world—of which Judaism and Christianity is the part closest to us.

"Judaism and Christianity I" was originally published in *Harvard Divinity Bulletin* 28:1 (1963):1–9. It was reprinted in *New Theology No. 2*, ed. M. Marty and D. G. Peerman (New York: Macmillan & Co., 1964), 153–64; and in *The Death of Dialogue and Beyond*, ed. Sanford Seltzer and Max L. Stackhouse (New York: Friendship Press, 1972), 105–19.

"Judaism and Christianity II" was originally published in *Harvard Divinity Bulletin*, New Series 1:1 (1967):2–9. It was reprinted as "Judaism and Christianity: A Plea for a New Relationship" in *Cross Currents* 17 (1967):445–58; cf. *Christian News from Israel* 19:1–2 (1968); and in *Disputation and Dialog*, ed. F. E. Talmage (New York: KTAV, 1975), 330–42. The Talmage volume is an excellent source book for historical and contemporary studies in Jewish-Christian relations.

In his recent book, *The Meaning and End of Religion*, Wilfred Cantwell Smith of McGill University and, we may say, of Harvard, has drawn to a pointed conclusion the uneasiness which scholars have felt for some time when using the word "religion," not to say "religions." His warnings are much to the point when we try to speak about Judaism and Christianity.

"Christianity" and "Judaism" are abstractions. The given is not a religion but a people, a church, a community with its history, its traditions, its claims, its witness, its attempts to relate itself to an ever-changing world. If we were to use a not-too-attractive image we could say that the abstraction "Christianity" is just the skin that the snake sheds every so often. It can be handled and studied in many ways. But the living reality is the church, the people with its organic continuity and the complexity through the ages. And the same applies of course to Judaism. To speak about Christianity and Judaism as two religions already forecloses many of the possibilities to understand what happened, happens, and might happen.

At the present time the popular image of the relationship between Judaism and Christianity is well expressed in two distinct habits of speech. On the one hand, there is the reference to the Three Faiths of America: Catholicism, Protestantism, and Judaism. On the other hand, there is the more academic construct the "Hebrew-Christian Tradition." Both of these "models" exert a powerful influence on our culture and our thinking. While theology is to many a highly technical and suspect term, it is evident that such expressions harbor whole theologies, partly conscious but mainly unconscious. It is reasonable to ask whether these theologies are well-founded, sound, and honest.

To speak about the Three Faiths is perhaps dubious already since it suggests that a Hindu, a Buddhist, a Muslim, an agnostic, or an atheist could not be a true American. But it is not necessary to draw that arrogant conclusion. More serious is the implicit suggestion that the relation and the distance between these three faiths is somehow of the same order. This is further complicated by the fact that, due to the given majority/minority ratio in a community, we often get a constellation of Protestants and Jews versus Catholics. Yet, from many points of view, Catholics and Protestants would be expected to have a great deal more in common than such a pattern suggests. And also Judaism has *its* catholics and protestants. It becomes increasingly clear that the pattern of the Three Faiths is a construct in which the nontheological factors easily gain the upper hand. That does not diminish its significance. But it makes us anxious not to extend this significance beyond its own limitations.

The expression the "Hebrew-Christian Tradition" is more at home in colleges and universities, in the survey courses of the humanities. It sees this tradition as having furnished the Western world with certain indispensable ideas and ideals, often epitomized as justice and compassion. It presupposes that the significant elements in Judaism and Christianity are those which they have in common, not those which divide them. If

207

the Three Faiths are nontheological in the direction toward the sociological, the Hebrew-Christian Tradition is nontheological in the direction toward the philosophical and ethical. It should also be noted that the Christian imperialism exerts its pressure on how this tradition is usually handled in higher education. The component "Hebrew" often stands for what Christians call the OT, and once Christianity is on the scene this "Hebrew" element is absorbed in the Christian tradition. Little or no attention is given to Jewish history and thought after 70 or 135 C.E. Maimonides may be a footnote to Thomas, the Jewishness a footnote to Spinoza, and Hasidism is not mentioned at all. Thereby the expression the "Hebrew-Christian Tradition" becomes more manageable, but the term pays little more than lip service to the actual relationship between Judaism and Christianity. It does not need to be that way, of course, and it may well be that the formula the "Hebrew-Christian Tradition" could function more adequately in our search for a viable understanding of the relations between Judaism and Christianity. Even so, we should not forget that it of necessity puts a premium on similarities rather than differences, thereby prejudging the case before us.

Whatever the respective and relative assets and liabilities of these two models, habits of speech, or even slogans, we cannot stress too emphatically that they are good and highly significant signs of a positive climate; a climate which the Western world has seldom known, and the Christian majority has seldom allowed; a climate in which we may be able to take a new look at the relationships. Without sounding more prophetic than we have the right to be, we could see the present situation in America as a unique and fresh challenge to our own generation of theological scholarship. The Jewish and the Christian communities find themselves side by side without many of the man-made walls which earlier separated them socially, culturally, intellectually. In both communities this proves to be a blessing, and it has driven us to a deeper grasp of our separate identities as believers. This is the time and the place and the climate in which we dare to, and we must, question these models. We can and we must ask whether they are as well conceived as they were well-intentioned and have proven pragmatically beneficial.

It is my contention that, in the long run, a one-sided stress on the common elements, or a nontheological acceptance of a sociological status quo with its mutual and, hopefully, increased respect for one another, cannot be the final chapter. That climate constitutes rather the first pages of a new volume in the history of the debate out of which the Christian church was born. The time has come for resuming that debate which was cut off prematurely and transformed into an unusually grim history of everything ugly from name-calling to pogroms and holocaust.

I am not sure that the image is a happy one, but for whatever it is worth, we need a certain type of historical psychoanalysis, by which we are made aware of what happened in that most early infancy when the nascent church emerged out of its Jewish matrix and when the first steps were taken. Without serious attempts to recapture that most significant stage in the life of the Christian church, new and free and fearless action may well be impossible.

We know a good deal more about those early years than we did a hundred years ago. But such knowledge is slow in affecting the sentiments and the systematic thinking of the present. Contemporary biblical and Jewish studies may have many weak points, but they have developed a very impressive ability to distinguish the actual issues of the past from the ways in which these issues appeared to later generations, our own included.

Let us then turn to a few areas where I think a changed picture of the past might affect the questions of the present and rectify the future debate between Judaism and Christianity.

1. The understanding of Jesus depends heavily on how one reads what we Christians call the OT. In a time when the red thread through that OT was seen to be ethical monotheism and where the prophets were hailed and measured by that canon, Jesus became to the Christians the superprophet. His greatness was asserted by demonstrating—often on shaky grounds—that his ethic was higher and his monotheism was purer and warmer than ever before in Israel or in the world at large.

We are now very much aware of how such a perspective on the OT, while congenial to the nineteenth century in the West, is alien to the perspective of the Scriptures. We have learned to see the OT centered in the people of the covenant, with its Torah, its cult, its psalms, its wisdom and proverbs, its prophets and their promises. We see an OT that points toward an age to come, an OT that leads to eschatology and messianism.

2. This new picture was mainly drawn on the basis of a better analysis of the OT texts in their historical context, but it was highly confirmed and corroborated by the increased concern for, and knowledge about, the so-called intertestamental literature with its apocalyptic intensity and religious vitality. All this came to the attention of a wider

public with the much-celebrated find of the library of the Qumran community, the Dead Sea Scrolls. Here was a Jewish community in which the strict obedience to the law was an integral part of its eschatology, even to the point of an anticipatory realization of the new covenant. Their common meal was a foretaste of the messianic banquet.

3. Different in structure and yet not unrelated to the sentiments of the age, pharisaism can be understood in categories that had been utterly submerged in the anachronistic alternatives of legalism and grace. Pharisaism becomes a serious and honorable way of living in expection and obedience, an obedience that is motivated and warmed by the expectation and an expectation that is made realistic and practical in concrete and flexible obedience.

4. In such a setting all that is said and came to be said of Jesus has its genetic center in the claim that he was the Messiah, that with him or through him the messianic age had drawn nigh. His teaching, his actions, his gracious and his harsh words all relate to this one claim. It would be wrong to say that he came to teach a better concept of love, a deeper concept of repentance, a more spiritual concept of the kingdom. All these concepts were there, warm, deep, and spiritual enough. But, to him, so close was the kingdom, so closely did he believe himself related to its coming, that he dared to apply its glorious gifts and standards here and now. And often—I think to his own surprise—the publicans and the sinners were more willing to listen and follow than were the professed religious. Thereby both the grace and the judgment were heightened immeasurably in the very structure of the gospel.

5. There is increasing evidence that the role of Pilate was considerably greater in the execution of Jesus than the tradition and even the gospels lead us to think. The precise role of the Jewish leaders we cannot assess. The nature of the sources makes it unlikely that we ever will. The crucifixion—a Roman execution—speaks its clear language, indicating that Jesus must have appeared sufficiently messianic, not only in a purely spiritual sense, to constitute a threat to political order according to Roman standards. At this very point we can discern one of the earliest signs of how tensions between Judaism and Christianity have affected the writing of history. Already in the gospels two tendencies are at work. The role of the Roman official, Pilate, is minimized—it was not easy in the empire to have a founder who had been crucified by a Roman procurator; and the "no" of the Jews was the theological basis on which Paul and other missionaries claimed the right to bring the gospel to the gentiles. "He came to his own, but his own received him

not . . . "—". . . and the vineyard will be given to other tenants who will deliver to him the produce when the time comes." Under the pressure of these two tendencies, one political and one theological, the exact events of history have been lost, as to the interplay between the members of the Sanhedrin and Pontius Pilate. But it is reasonable to see the latter as the key figure.

6. Thus the messianic issue in all its Jewishness stands in the center of Christian origins. What else could we expect when "Christian" is actually only the Greek for "messianic." I do not consider it an overstatement to say that the whole christological development of Christianity, even to that famous intensity of the fourth century, should be seen as a development from its original and Jewish nucleus: Jesus Christ. That is the creed: I believe that Jesus is the Messiah; and its chiastic correlate: the Messiah is Jesus.

There is one point in the early stages of this christological development that needs special attention. If we were to say, as we often do, that the Christian believes that the Messiah has come, while the Jew still lives in expectation, then we use at least highly imprecise language.

In one of the earliest christological expressions found in the NT we hear Peter say: Repent . . . that times of refreshment may come from the Lord and he may send the Messiah who was appointed for you, that is, Jesus, whom heaven must keep until the time of consummation (Acts 3:19–21). Here the coming of the Messiah Jesus is still future. Peter here shares with the Jewish community the faith in the Parousia, which is the consummation, the age to come. He announces that their Messiah will be this Jesus. While later Christians came to assert the "first coming" of Jesus in his earthly ministry but had highly divided opinions about the so-called "second coming," the earliest Christians were clear about the coming, the Parousia, which they looked forward to, together with their Jewish brethren. *Their* problem was to find the right answer to the question: In what sense and to what extent were the life and death of Jesus a coming of the Messiah? This is the problem to which the different gospels, and the traditions underlying them, give their answers, some tentative, some increasingly clear.

In the earliest stages of this development the claim that the messianic age had come and was truly inaugurated, that its powers were at work in the world through the church, centered around the resurrection and the Spirit. These were the decisive signs that the new age was here. The general resurrection had begun, Jesus being "the first fruits from those who have fallen asleep," and the Spirit was at work as the prophet Joel had promised. The Messiah was now enthroned in heaven, and one prayed in the Lord's Prayer: let your will become manifest on earth as it is now manifest in heaven. Maranatha.

It may be suggested that this and similar layers of Christian thought, piety, and experience will prove significant to keep in mind as we resume the debate between Judaism and Christianity. No one could or should claim that such language is a complete witness to Jesus as the Christ. Nor is it easier to take than much of the later christological or trinitarian development. But it is a language cut out of the same cloth as that of Judaism. And Judaism, in turn, has had its own developments. Yet one point at which to start is where the communications broke off, perhaps for extraneous reasons. This is not to turn the clock back; that neither should nor could be done. But since the picture of that early history has been one of the alienating and agonizing factors in the later developments of our relations, let us at least get the record straight. And let us compare similar things, that is, first-century Judaism with first-century Christianity. To compare Buber to Paul, and Tillich to Akiba or Philo is nonsense from many points of view. And so it is to compare Jesus to Maimonides, and Hillel or Qumran to Origen or Chalcedon.

7. But what about Paul? In the more recent phases of Jewish studies of Christian origins there has been a tendency to recognize Jesus as somehow within the pale of Jewish tradition: Jesus as one of the great teachers in the prophetic tradition. Such an *Ehrenrettung* of Jesus has usually taken place at the expense of Paul. Paul the Jewish renegade is then blamed for having transformed and distorted the teachings of Jesus into a sacrilegious Hellenistic mystery religion in which the properly Jewish sentiment of monotheism yields to claims of the divinity of Jesus. Or we hear about Paul's willful or inadvertent misunderstanding of Judaism and its understanding of law, mercy, repentance, and forgiveness.

It is striking that such assessments of Paul depend heavily on an understanding of Paul that was set forth by apologetic and tendential Christian interpreters. In such studies Paul's words and attitudes have often lost their connections with the specific issues that were Paul's primary concern. "Judaism" and "Judaizers" became symbols of self-righteousness and legalism as discussed in the controversies of the Western church by Augustine, Luther, and Harnack. One could perhaps have expected Jewish scholars to be more sensitive to the primary setting of Paul's arguments than were their Christian contemporaries. Only recently, through the work of men like Johannes Munck, have we

212

begun to see more clearly how Paul was positively related to Judaism even in his sharpest arguments in favor of the inclusion of the gentiles into the people of God. And Paul's doctrine of a justification by faith without the works of the law was primarily a scriptural argument, according to the exegetical principles of Judaism, in defense of his mission to the gentiles. It was not a promulgation of a superior religion or of a deeper insight into the nature of grace, superior to that of "benighted pharisaic legalists."

Thus Paul's epistle to the Romans reaches its climax in chapters 9—11, where he gives his most explicit views on the relation between the Jews and the gentile Christians. He, the apostle to the gentiles, is not only full of what could have been a condescending concern for his "kinsmen according to the flesh"; as he looks toward the consummation of history, he cannot imagine that end without the final salvation of the Jews. He goes as far as to consider the mission of the gentiles and the success of that mission in the name of the Messiah Jesus only as a detour which ultimately must lead to the point where the Jews accept this same Jesus as their Messiah.[1] To him this is necessary; otherwise God would not be the God of Abraham, Isaac, and Jacob. He reminds his gentile Christians that they certainly have no reason to boast and to feel superior to the Jews. On the contrary, they should remember that they are wild branches, only engrafted on the true olive tree of Israel. "So do not become proud, but stand in awe."

It is of interest to note that Paul does not think about this final return of the Jews to their Messiah as the result of a mission from the gentiles. At least he nowhere admonishes his congregations to such efforts. Nor does he intimate that it will come about by a spectacular display of virtue on the part of the gentile Christians. In accordance with his good pharisaic training he looks toward this return as a mystery that lies in God's hands and that will happen in God's own time. But without such an end the gospel could not be the gospel, and Jesus could not be the Messiah.

The Pauline panorama suggests to us and to our concern for the relations between Judaism and Christianity that these two are far more closely connected than we are apt to think when we speak about them as two religions. It suggests even that the gentile Christian is what we might call "an honorary Jew." As Christians we speak to our Jewish friends and ask them to consider our claim to be fellow heirs to their promises. We claim that right by faith in Jesus the Messiah and for his sake. Such a claim appears to be well in accordance with the image that has emerged from our reconsideration of some of the earliest facets of our common and divided history.

Such a view has a strange effect on the present situation. First, it reminds us that the NT has something to say about our relation to actual Jews. There are many good Christians who know their NT and Romans 11, in particular, quite well. But, to them, the "Jew" has ceased to be a real Jew; it has become that negative symbol for legalism and self-righteousness. The church has so spiritualized its Scriptures that they have lost their original and concrete meaning. While this at times has a beneficial effect, it has also been impoverishing and misleading. The present discussion at the Vatican Council seems to follow a spiritualizing course when it expresses the conviction that all mankind shares in the guilt of Jesus' condemnation. The validity of such a *theological interpretation* of the gospels can hardly be denied by any Christian. It should become a cornerstone in our catechisms, and it will prove highly beneficial. But such an interpretation should not deprive Israel of its particular role in God's history, nor should it absolve the churches from listening obediently to Paul's warnings against Christian boasting and superiority feelings.

What is far more important is, however, the way in which Paul's vision somehow reverses the present sentiment of many Christians. The gentile Christian now finds himself in need of defending his right and his claim to be one with his Jewish brother. With that attitude the debate which was drastically interrupted can be resumed. For the Christian there is an inner necessity to resume it. Not for the benefit of the Jews but for the sake of his own faith and identity—and that at the very center of the faith.

What good could come of such a resumed debate? The history of the debates between Judaism and Christianity has many chapters which make such encounters the last thing to be encouraged. *Vestigia terrent.* But if the general climate from which we took our point of departure is what I think it is, and if the attitude of which we have just spoken in the context of contemporary biblical studies is a valid one, then the debate is not only necessary for the reasons given but holds much promise. Not that we know where it will lead, but it should at least bring us to the point where we differ and disagree for the *right* reasons. In the atmosphere of the university such a result is a great and purifying achievement; in the hands of God it may prove fruitful and significant beyond our planning.

Our plea for such an approach should, however, never lead us to forget or belittle the unity of our common humanity. That unity is all the more significant for Jews and Christians since as human beings we have more things in common than many: the faith in God, a God who acts in history; the glorious and demanding values of what could be called the Hebrew-Christian tradition; with these we share in the common responsibility to our fellow men near and far. All these things bind us together in an all-embracing brotherhood with truly universal ties. And yet the future does not lie only in the attempts at letting all that is particular to each of us be swallowed up in an ever-growing universality.

It seems that the power of religion in men's lives and in human culture lies in the specific, the particular, that is, that which divides. Here philosophy and religion part ways and reach their intensity and identity in opposite directions. Worship and faith reach truth and creativity by intensifying the specific, the particular. I guess that is why we are apt to speak about a personal God, and that is why the language of worship must always be closer to myth and poetry than to philosophy. Thus the particular—which is the divisive—is of the essence to our two traditions. We can only proceed by purifying our understanding and intensifying our grasp of the particular, even toward the point of transcending it; and yet we retain the specific, lest those who come after us be deprived of that transcendence.

NOTES

1. I think I was wrong in this interpretation of Rom. 11:26. The expression "And so the whole of Israel will be saved," *sōthesetai*, does not indicate any acceptance of Jesus as the Messiah. See now below, p. 243; and my *Paul Among Jews and Gentiles* (Philadelphia: Fortress Press, 1976), vi.

16

Judaism and Christianity II:
A Plea for
a New Relationship

For *Introductory Note*, see above, pp. 205–6.

In 1963 the Harvard Divinity School arranged for a Roman Catholic–Protestant Colloquium. Many factors converged into that decision and invitation. Some of our faculty had served as observers at the sessions of the Second Vatican Council and were closely following its further developments. In 1958, the Charles Chauncey Stillman chair for Roman Catholic Studies had been established at Harvard University, and it had been decided that this chair should be in the Divinity School rather than in the Faculty of Arts and Sciences. For the academic year 1962–63, we were granted permission to use the funds for this colloquium in lieu of the visiting professorship envisaged. And, above all, it was the right moment to highlight and scrutinize the new spirit of ecumenism by placing it in the crucible of academic inquiry. For all of us who participated in the seminars, the colloquium was a stimulating and reassuring experience. Our scholarly deliberations indicated that the image of an ecumenical breakthrough—as pictured by the press coverage of the Vatican Council—was, indeed, a well-founded one, and we could push beyond what was already achieved. In addition, there were the symbolic effect of Cardinal Bea's lectures and the demonstration that Roman Catholics were not guests but coworkers in the theological enterprise of the Divinity School.[1]

In some ways things turned out differently with the Jewish–Christian Colloquium to which the Divinity School invited an equal number of scholars in the fall of 1966. And these differences are symptomatic of the present state of Jewish–Christian relations. The outward arrangements were similar. A wide range of such consultations had taken

217

place, the press coverage of which usually highlighted a new "ecumenical" spirit. It was deemed timely to choose this topic for the major scholarly celebration of our one hundred fiftieth anniversary year as a divinity school. Names like those of George Foot Moore and Harry A. Wolfson indicated Harvard's substantial part in the serious academic study of the topic. The present faculty had played its part in these areas, both in the United States and in the Middle East. The generous interest of the American Jewish Committee allowed us to plan on strong international participation. The aim was the same as three years earlier. We wanted to test, in the sober and sharp light of academic inquiry, where the cutting edge was in studies significant to the widespread dialogues of Judaism and Christianity. We wanted to test how well founded the publicized spirit of brotherhood was, and hopefully, to suggest lines for further progress. I think it is fair to say that we did not come very far. We did not do very well. But this was also important, since it indicates how mandatory it is to work harder. Thus it may be useful to have me, as one of the participants, reflect in writing on some of the reasons for such a state of affairs.[2]

Here we must consider a basic incompatibility between Judaism and Christianity. We are used to treating them as two "religions" or two "traditions" contributing to Western culture. But in doing so we may well overlook elements that are constitutive. Both as religions and as traditions, Judaism and Christianity are related to each other in ways that make it difficult for them to be merely parallel phenomena. On the one hand, Christianity grew out of Judaism with a claim to be the fulfillment thereof, and, on the other hand, in the history of ideas they are intertwined beyond disentanglement. It could be argued, for example, that the beneficial contribution of Christianity to Western culture was exactly its function as the vehicle for the Jewish component in Christianity, while some of the less attractive elements of Christian ideology are the properly "Christian" ones. Or—as is often done in Christian circles—such an argument could be put forward in its absolutely opposite form. So complex is the matter when considered in the history of ideas.[3]

When we think of Christianity and Judaism as communities of faith, as church and synagogue, the incompatibility is perhaps most obvious in the fact that the church is by definition set on mission and conversion, and that this missionary thrust includes the hope that Jews accept Jesus as their long-awaited Messiah. Judaism, on the other hand, has no *equivalent* urge toward evangelization among the gentiles.[4] While this difference in the theological structure of the two has led to gruesome things where the Jews constituted a minority placed in a so-called Christian society, the problem itself is not dependent on a minority/majority situation. While it can be alleviated in a secular and pluralistic situation, it remains a problem at any direct confrontation between church and synagogue. It is a problem that works both ways. The "pressure" from the Christian side heightens the fear on the Jewish side, and leads to frequent pleas that the Christians declare a nonmission stance, in conformity with that of Judaism. If *we* do not, why do *you*? The incompatibility is a basic one, and is one of the most serious factors in the Jewish dispersion with its concern about assimilation.

This leads us to another factor which troubles a dialogue between Judaism and Christianity: the whole web of guilt and fear which the two thousand years of our common history has made us inherit. It could perhaps be said that one issue in our colloquium as an academic enterprise was whether the scholarly approach should attempt to stand above this factor and achieve a nonemotional detachment therefrom. Were Auschwitz and Belsen to be considered admissible evidence in our court of discussion, or not? The problem reminds me of a discussion about whether nuclear warfare is just another quantitative development of weaponry, or whether it changes the ethical problems of the world in a qualitative fashion so as to make many earlier forms of argumentation obsolete.

Such discussions can often turn cynical. It seems that the attempted genocide of the 1940s, even if considered "only" a quantitative intensification of the pogroms, is a valid reason to ask new and more drastic questions about Christian responsibility, and exactly in that academic fashion. Christian theologians, preachers, and lay people all tend to make a most convenient distinction between Christianity as an ideal phenomenon—a priori beyond suspicion of any guilt in these matters —and bad "Christians" who in their lack of true Christianity have committed heinous crimes. But after two thousand years, such a facile distinction becomes rather suspect. It is a striking example of the most primitive mistake in the comparative study of religions. One compares one's own religion in its ideal form with the actual form and manifestations of other faiths. We must rather ask openly and with trembling whether there are elements in the Christian tradition—at its very center—that lead Christians to an attitude toward Judaism which we now must judge and overcome. It is an odd form of anti-intellectualism to believe that the theology is all right but the practice and sentiments of individuals are to blame. It may well be that we should be more responsible for our thoughts and our theology than for our actions. To trust in "men of good will" and to leave the theological structures unattended is bad strategy.

The Harvard Colloquium had its challenge exactly at this point. We could take for granted that we were all for brotherhood and against bias and discrimination. We had all done our part at community activities to the betterment of social and personal relations between Christians and Jews. But now we were to test the theoretical bases for such desirable attitudes. And here we found that little had been done that could constitute a consensus. And even less had been done so as to intimate a new starting point.

It could perhaps be argued that this was partly due to a more accidental incompatibility at our colloquium. We were fortunate in having a wider spread of theological and philosophical opinion among the Jewish participants than was perhaps the case with those who spoke out of a Christian tradition. In the future, this should be corrected by widening the Christian spectrum. The main threat to ecumenical work is that more and more significant voices are frozen out, while those who remain in conversation pride themselves on their increasing agreements. Neverthelsss, the radical nature of our problem can perhaps be well exemplified by two publications which have appeared since the colloquium.

On my desk is an edition of the Gospel of John, of which the title page and dust jacket state—partly in reassuring Gothic print—that here is "The Gospel according to Saint John, in the words of the King James Version of the year 1611. Edited in conformity with the true ecumenical spirit of His Holiness, Pope John XXIII, by Dagobert D. Runes. The message of Jesus is offered here without adulteration by hate and revulsion against the people of the Savior."[5] In this edition, some twenty shorter or longer passages of the fourth gospel are deleted,[6] and at other points references to the Jews are exchanged for general terms like "the people," "the crowd(s)," and so forth. In 7:13; 19:38; and 20:19 we read that those friendly to Jesus acted out of fear of the Romans—not of the Jews, as the text says. Such an edition is based on a laudable sentiment. And many of us would prefer a NT without the marks of bitter feelings between church and synagogue. But it is hard to believe that the production of a fraudulent text can help anyone. There is no manuscript basis whatsoever for these deletions and changes.[7]

I have not brought up this type of pious fraud in order to ridicule what is intended as a positive attempt toward bettering Jewish-Christian relations. Rather, it points toward the serious fact that the Christian Bible itself contains material about the Jews that must strike the contemporary reader as offensive and hateful.

It is well known and a commonly accepted fact that such and similar NT sayings have functioned as "divine" sanction for hatred against the Jews. The most crucial question is whether they should not be defined as having in themselves, and in their very biblical context, that element of bitterness and hateful zeal.

This issue is well and tragically demonstrated in a recent book by Cardinal Bea.[8] It had been his eager expectation to have the Second Vatican Council make a strong statement which in effect would condemn all anti-Jewish sentiment, social and theological, as sin against God and his Christ. Much attention has been given to the ways in which this statement was finally toned down to a far more guarded and general one and placed in the context of the council's "Declaration on the Relation of the Church to Non-Christian Religions." By his book and by its very title, Bea tries to salvage his original intention and to give as positive an interpretation as possible to what finally was decreed. In that sense the book is a moving personal document. We should, however, not blame the outcome at the council only on political pressure from the Arab world—Christian and Muslim—nor on an ill-intentioned conservatism among the bishops. Bea's own presentation makes it perfectly clear that the theological structure of the NT material cannot so easily be brought into harmony with a spirit of love and humility on the side of Christians. First Thessalonians 2:14ff. stands out and bothers Bea continuously (e.g., 74, 87, 158, 165), and he can only counterbalance it with the Pauline sentiment in Rom. 9:1ff. Much attention is given to the fact that the gospels often confine the responsibility for the death of Jesus to the Sanhedrin or to inhabitants of Jerusalem; hence it is not tied to all "the Jews" of that time, let alone of later generations. This is not the place to argue whether such an interpretation can be defended. If it is, it is a fine point, immensely difficult to retain, in the future development. Nor does it quite suffice to stress the love of Christ as an antidote to the bitter language about the Jews to which the Christian Bible reader is exposed. At least history shows that, so far, that has not been enough. In short, one reason for the defeat of Bea's intentions at the council was that too many texts from the NT were against him. This is the really serious level of Christian anti-

221

Semitism: Can the church admit to the tinge of anti-Jewish elements in its very Scriptures?

Much of recent discussion, especially the one related to the Vatican Council, has centered around the question of the "guilt" of the Jews for the crucifixion of Jesus and the so-called deicide. It may be that this specific issue is the natural one to focus upon within the Roman Catholic tradition, and within that context the council's declaration achieves a certain corrective when it declares that "what happened in his (Jesus') passion cannot be charged against all Jews, without distinction, nor against the Jews of today."[9]

But there is a more subtle and, I think, more powerful form of the anti-Jewish element in Christian theology to consider, especially in Protestantism and then most prominently in Lutheranism.[10] I refer to the theological model "law and gospel." According to this model, this habit-forming structure of theological thinking, Jewish attitudes, and Jewish piety are by definition the example of the wrong attitude toward God. The Christian proposition in the teachings of Jesus, Paul, John, and all the rest, is always described in its contrast to Jewish "legalism," "casuistry," "particularism," ideas of "merit," and so forth. This whole system of thinking, with its image of the Pharisees and of the political messianism of the Jews, treats Jewish piety as the black background that makes Christian piety the more shining. In such a state of affairs, it is hard to engender respect for Judaism and the Jews. And the theological system requires the retention of such an understanding of Judaism, whether true or not.[11] Even when the seriousness of Jewish piety is commended, it is done with faint praise: it may be admirable in its sincerity but just for that reason it is more off the mark.[12]

All this adds up to a deep-rooted tension between Judaism and Christianity. In a historical perspective there is little surprise that that should be so. The early Christian movement was a distinct and vigorous sect within Judaism, fierce in its critique of other segments of Jewish religious life, just as was the Qumran sect at the Dead Sea, the writings of which are filled with scathing and even hateful comments about the Jewish establishment in Jerusalem.[13] The prophetic tradition within Judaism reaches equally fierce expressions, "for the Lord reproves him whom he loves, as a father the son in whom he delights" (Prov. 3:12; cf. Heb. 12:5ff.), and the prophet did his part of that reproving. In a prophetic tradition, this is the natural discourse.

The focus of the problem for Christianity versus Judaism is that this prophetic language fell, so to speak, into the hands of the gentiles. It should not be forgotten that perhaps all of our literary remains from the earliest period of the Christian movement are not only in the Greek language (which was used at that time also by many Jews—even by the majority of the Jews), but was shaped in its present form by churches which were predominantly gentile in their constituency. In seeking its identity, this primarily gentile church found its rationale partly in the "no of the Jews" to Jesus Christ. To Paul the Jew, this "no" was a mystery that he treated with awe, and that, according to him, should create even greater awe and reverence in gentile minds (Rom. 11:20). Nor does he suggest a gentile mission to the Jews. As a good Pharisee, he leaves the solution in the hands of God (11:25–36).

But once this Jewish context and identification were lost, the words of Jesus and the earliest witnesses of the apostolic period received a new setting. They were not any longer operating within the framework of the Jewish self-criticism. They hardened into accusations against "the Jews," the synagogue across the street, and against the people who claimed the same Scriptures, but denied their fulfillment in Jesus Christ.

The drastic consequence of such form-critical observations could perhaps be stated somewhat like this: The Christian church has no "right" to the use of these prophetic statements, once it has lost its identification with Judaism. Even if we repeated the actual words of Jesus, preserved by tape recordings, these very words would mean something else, something contrary to his intention, once they were uttered from without instead of from within the Jewish communities.[14]

The compassionate sorrow of Jesus as he placed himself in the succession of the prophets and wept over Jerusalem (Matt. 23:37–39) hardened into a self-righteous reassurance in the church; and the way in which Jews chose to remain aloof to Christian claims angered the frustrated missionaries and theologians so as to make the Jews the primary example of the enemies of Christ. Such sentiments color practically all expressions of Christian theology, from NT times (including the gospels) to the present.[15] There is little reason to wonder about the fear and tensions in this area. The question must be asked—as it was at our colloquium—if the present attempts to purge Christian liturgies, catechisms, and hymnals from overt anti-Semitic elements are not only coming too late, but are primarily too timid and totally insufficient. The church is not only responsible for its intentions, which may be honorable, but also for what *actually* happens in the minds of its *actual* members and half-members as they have been and are exposed to its Scriptures and message.

What should and could then be done? It is clear to me that Christian theology needs a new departure. And it is equally clear that we cannot find it on our own, but only by the help of our Jewish colleagues. We must plead with them to help us. And as far as we are concerned, it is not a dialogue we need; we are not primarily anxious to impart our views as they impart theirs. We need to ask, in spite of it all, whether they are willing to let us become again part of their family, a peculiar part to be true, but even so, relatives who believe themselves to be a peculiar kind of Jew. Something went wrong in the beginning. I say "went wrong," for I am not convinced that what happened in the severing of the relations between Judaism and Christianity was the good and positive will of God. Is it not possible for us to recognize that we parted ways not according to but against the will of God?

I know that this is a strange way to speak. I know that it may be branded as historical romanticism, an attempt to turn the clock back. But why call it "to turn the clock back"? Why not say instead that the time has come for us to find the alternatives that were lost at that ancient time, alternatives which are the theological expressions of our repentance and of our understanding as they force themselves upon us today?

In this respect the parallel to the ecumenical movement is highly instructive. After a period of improved relations between the churches, Christians came to a point where the parting of ways in the past appeared to have grown out of diverse concerns within the one church. Many of these differences—some of them prefigured already in the rich variations within the NT itself—are serious, but none serious enough for the divisions which hardened into distinct "churches" and "sects." And, to be sure, no excuse could or should be found for the way in which this "hardening" developed into walls of suspicion and wars of suppression. So began a new attempt to find ways of growing together again—not a syncretistic compromising of conflicting views, but a strategy developed by which actual churches begin to express the once-lost unity. This is not a romantic way to play the fourth, or eleventh, or sixteenth century. It is a way to respond to one's own faith and understanding in the twentieth.

There are good theological reasons for a similar movement in the relation between Judaism and Christianity. Needless to say, there are differences, too. But if it be true that "something went wrong" in their parting of the ways, we should not elevate the past to an irrevocable will of God, but search for the lost alternatives.

What they are, it is too early to say. There may be many. The important thing is to accept the possibility that there are such. My own thinking is naturally influenced by my studies of the first century of the Common Era. In the colloquium, strong arguments were given by Jewish and Christian scholars of that period to the effect that *both* "Judaism" as we know it and "Christianity" have their respective beginnings in the first century. Out of the varied and rich religious life of postbiblical Judaism prior to 70 C.E., there emerged two main traditions. One was Rabbinic Judaism as codified in Mishnah and Talmud, the other was Christianity. *Both* claimed their continuity and authenticity from the Scriptures and the ongoing postbiblical tradition. Each came to brand the other as unfaithful and heretical in its respective teaching and practice. Such an admittedly oversimplified model has much to commend it as far as historical scholarship is concerned, and it serves to question many of our traditional views.[16]

It is obvious that a Christian plea for a new relation between Judaism and Christianity of the kind we have wished for here must raise serious questions in the minds of the Jewish community. Even if it were granted that our intentions are serious when we describe our plea as one born out of repentance and humility—for we are the ones to ask that we be recognized as a peculiar kind of Jews, and it is up to "Judaism" to see if that is possible—it must be recognized that such a question is a new one, and utterly unexpected from our divided and common history. We Christians must be prepared to face "conditions," and that will be the time when the seriousness of our repentance will be tested. Such "conditions" may be interpreted by some as a compromising of our faith. At that point, it will be of utmost importance for Christian theology to see clearly what "our faith," is, and what must be judged to be expressions of that faith which were conditioned by our division, rather than by the revelation in Jesus Christ and by the will of God.

Obviously Judaism, on its side, will have to face similar searching questions. But rabbinic *halaka* knows how the time can be ripe for something new, and this, if any situation, is one "when it is a time to do something for the Lord" (Gittin 60a; cf. MBer. 9:5).[17]

It should be noted that our thinking here is openly informed by a theology of history. That is we do not think about religious matters in terms of timeless truths, revealed in a form unrelated to the situations in which they are given. Both their original form and their continuous interpretation depend on the situations to which they speak. And the religious communities that listen and interpret are organic bodies which must find out what God wants now, as he governs his people and his world. Without attention to that *now*, our interpretations can never be true, although they may sound orthodox in a literal sense.[18]

In such a context, a comment that was made repeatedly at the colloquium deserves attention. When Christians take for granted that their faith and theology are superior to Judaism, they often do so for the very simple reason that Christianity followed upon Judaism as a new and hence superior "philosophy." Or an argument of *Heilsgeschichte* makes it easy to see the later stage as superior to an earlier one. If that be so, we should take the emergence of Islam far more seriously than we usually do, for here is a tradition that makes the reasonable claim of having superseded both Judaism and Christianity, and of doing so according to the will and plan of God. We should at least not close our minds to the suggestion that future theological reflection, Christian and Jewish, will cut through the immense historical barriers against bringing Islam into our serious consideration.[19]

It may seem almost ironical to bring up such a matter at the present time. Just as centuries of Western history were marked by hatred between Christians and Muslims—while the Jews were treated far better by the latter than by the former, first in Spain and then under the Turks—so today the tension between Muslims and Jews is one of the concerns of the world at large. It should not be forgotten, however, that the Arabs most involved in the present crisis are not to be identified with the Muslims since a sizable number of them are Christians. Also for that reason I find it important to close my reflections about Judaism and Christianity with some observations on the situation after the military victory of the Israelis in the summer of 1967.[20]

It is clear enough from what we have said already that current events and theological work are not unrelated. Theology—be it academic or unconsciously embedded in piety and spontaneous reactions—does inform man's actions, for better or for worse.

The relation between Judaism and the State of Israel is naturally quite complex. It would be wrong to identify the two, both in terms of Israel itself, and in terms of the vast majority of Jewry living in other parts of the world. But it would be equally wrong to consider Israel a purely secular state. To be sure, its constitution guarantees freedom of religion, and retains the religious courts for Christians and Muslims in matters of marriage, and so forth, according to the ancient system inherited from the Turks and the British. But Israel is a Jewish state, and its religion is Judaism. Without getting involved in the difficulties of defining "Jew," "Judaism," and "Israel," it is important for Christians and Westerners to realize that a certain kind of "clean thinking" does not work here, although it would be convenient. I refer to the view—expressed also by some Jews—that Israel is a political and secular phenomenon, while Judaism is to be defined in spiritual terms as a religion or a tradition. At this juncture in history, at least, that is not so. The driving forces which made Palestine—rather than Uganda—the goal for Zionism[21] are reason enough for the intertwining of Jewish faith and the State of Israel. That force was rooted in the Scriptures and the tradition. Our evaluation of the present situation must take that into account. Whether we like it or not, when we speak and think about the State of Israel, we are speaking about a very substantial element of Judaism. Not only in terms of so many Jews, but also in terms of Jews who see the State of Israel as the fulfillment of God's promises.

We began our reflections by pointing to the incompatibility of Judaism and Christianity. This is not only a "difficulty" in dialogue. It is also necessary to grant to Judaism its right to work out its own problems according to its own understanding of its Scripture and tradition. It is not for us to impose on Judaism our understanding of what are the "true insights of the best of the prophets." It is not for us to prescribe for Judaism that its religious aspirations should not be tied to a land or a city, "to a piece of real estate" as one Christian writer chose to express it. It is true indeed that Judaism has lived and flourished in the Diaspora for two thousand years, but it did so because somewhere in its soul was the hope for the return. That hope became spiritualized at times, but never really so. Judaism as we know it today is related to the Land, the *Eretz*. Its rabbis and its believers may differ widely in their interpretations of this fact and its foundations,[22] but it is hardly our task as Christians to lecture the Jews on how they as Jews should read their Scriptures.

For this reason, I am inclined to think that some of the present discussion about the possibilities of an international Jerusalem overlook one important point. The discussion often centers on the access to the sacred sites. For Christians and Muslims that term is an adequate expression of what matters. Here are sacred places, hallowed by the most holy events; here are the places for pilgrimage, the very focus of highest devotion. It would be cruel indeed if such places were not available to all the faithful.

Judaism is different—although the Wailing Wall came to take on much of that same sacred character, partly under the influence of the

Christian example. The sites sacred to Judaism on the Israeli side have no shrines. Its religion is not tied to "sites," but to the Land, not to what happened in Jerusalem, but to Jerusalem itself.

I would not argue that this settles the matter in favor of Israeli rule in Jerusalem. But I would argue that we as Christians concerned about the right relation to Judaism must recognize the difference between the access to Christian and Muslim sites, and the Jewish attachment to the city. To overlook that is another form of a patronizing *interpretatio christiana*. To Christians, Jerusalem is a holy city by virtue of its shrines. For us it would be more than natural to worship at them in a Jewish city; one could even say that such a situation would be preferable, since that is how it was when it all happened.

In the months and years to come, difficult political problems in the Middle East call for solutions. Christians both in the West and in the East will weigh the proposals differently. But all of us should watch out for the ways in which the ancient venom of Christian anti-Semitism might enter in. A militarily victorious and politically strong Israel cannot count on half as much good will as a threatened Jewish people in danger of its second holocaust. The situation bears watching. That does not mean that Israel is always right or that its political behavior and demands should always be supported by all who as Christians would like to be considered honorary Jews for Jesus Christ's sake.

Our stance, rather, presupposes our trust in Judaism's capacity to find its own way as it seeks viable structures for the relation between its faith and the political realities of the State of Israel, and of the global community of nations and men. The Christian West has learned far too slowly and reluctantly that a close interplay between religion and politics has dangers so insurmountable that our best choice must be an acceptance of pluralism and the secularization of political decisions. The progress in that direction has also paved the way for many of the improvements in Jewish-Christian relations in the West. For that reason, it is only natural that we hope for similar developments within the Jewish state. To most of us, such a development is the only one in which we can put our realistic hopes for peace and coexistence. When we as Christian theologians want to defend the freedom of Judaism to find its own answers, we cannot help hoping that such answers can be aided by the negative experience we—and they as a minority in Christian societies—have had, experiences that have taught us to fear rather than rejoice in religion as a political factor. In politics the theologian, Christian

228

and Jewish, must recognize that he is an amateur, and his professional concern for the ways of God should not cover over that simple fact.

I have no doubt that Judaism has the spiritual capacity to find its own solutions to the problems at hand. The present political situation may well unleash a type of Christian attitude that identifies Judaism and Israel with materialism and lack of compassion, devoid of the Christian spirit of love. Even a superficial knowledge of Judaism on its own terms makes it abundantly clear that such is not its nature. And an even more superficial acquaintance with church history suffices to silence such a patronizing attitude. Our hope for Israel should rather be for political wisdom in accordance with the riches of the long and varied tradition of the Jewish faith, a faith rich in compassion, as it always remembers the words " . . . for you were strangers in the land of Egypt" (Exod. 22:21).

As we look and work toward a new structure for our common trust in the God of Abraham, Isaac, and Jacob—and of Jesus of Nazareth— that trust includes our personal confidence in Judaism as a force for peace and justice.

NOTES

1. For the material see Samuel H. Miller and G. Ernest Wright, eds., *Ecumenical Dialogue at Harvard: The Roman Catholic–Protestant Colloquium* (Cambridge: Belknap Press, Harvard University Press, 1964).

2. My perspective is limited, especially by the fact that our work was divided into three seminars, and I took part in Seminar II, devoted to biblical and theological questions, subsumed under the title "Torah and Dogma."

Seminar I dealt with the period of the sixteenth-century Reformation, and especially with the question about whether the Calvinistic emphasis on the OT and covenant leads to a difference in the Jewish-Christian question, as compared with the Lutheran and its pattern of Law-Gospel theology.

Seminar III addressed itself to the social dimensions of the problem and focused on "Secularism: Threat and Promise."

3. Hans Jonas's lecture—"Jewish and Christian Elements in Western Philosophical Tradition—at the Colloquium argued impressively that the Christian contribution to Western *philosophy* was in matters relating to creation, and thus "Jewish," while Christology and trinitarian speculation had fostered little of significance.

4. For the evidence of Jewish missionary activity in the period before the Crusades, see B. Blumenkranz, *Juifs et Chrétiens dans le monde occidental, 430–1096* (Etudes juives 2; Paris, 1960), 159–212.

5. New York: Philosophical Library, 1967.

6. Major deletions: 2:12–22; 5:15–18; 7:19–23, 32–36, 43–52; 8:37–59; 9:22–23, 27–29; 11:52–57; 12:10; 18:14, 19–24, 32, 35–36; 19:4–8, 15–16, 31–37.

7. In his *The Jews and the Cross* (New York: Philosophical Library, 1965), Runes gives what seems to be the rationale for his "editing." There he speaks of the gospel accounts as "set down by the evangelists of the Bishop of Rome in the fourth century" (25); cf. "the scribes of the Bishop of Rome" (26). It so happens that the oldest papyrus to any NT book is a fragment to the Gospel of John which begins with the words "the Jews" in 18:31, where Runes pretends to bring us back beyond the anti-Jewish papal scribes of the fourth century by reading "the people." And the whole fragment contains 18:31–34, 37–38, i.e., exactly some of the verses deleted by Runes. But the papyrus fragment is from ca. A.D. 125.

On the other hand, 7:53—8:11, the moving story about the woman taken in adultery, is included in Runes's edition, although all significant manuscripts indicate that it was added by Christian scribes, perhaps just in the fourth century!

8. Augustin Cardinal Bea, S.J., *The Church and the Jewish People* (New York: Harper & Row, 1966).

9. Ibid., 152. On the Jewish question at the council, see also G. H. Williams, *Dimensions of Roman Catholic Ecumenism* (IARF Papers on Religion in the Modern World 1; 1966), 30–34.

10. And it should be noted that Lutheran theologians, and historians unconsciously shaped by a Lutheran tradition, have played a disproportionately great role in contemporary NT studies. Names like Jeremias, Bultmann, Käsemann, etc., appear on the American scene as "highly critical scholars," but they are all Lutheran in background and commitment.

11. See my article on "The Apostle Paul and the Introspective Conscience of the West," in which I try to show how this image of Judaism is not that of Paul, but of the Western tradition from Augustine, via Luther, up to the present, *Paul Among Jews and Gentiles* (Philadelphia: Fortress Press, 1976), 78–96. Also D. Georgi, "Der Kampf um die reine Lehre im Urchristentum als Auseinandersetzung um das rechte Verständnis der an Israel ergangenen Offenbarung Gottes," in *Antijudaismus im Neuen Testament*, ed. Stoehr (Munich: Kaiser Verlag, 1967).

12. It has been argued that many articles in the great *Theologisches Wörterbuch zum Neuen Testament* (ed. G. Kittel et al.) contain anti-Semitic elements, especially some of those produced during the 1930s and 1940s. It is true that it even contains some seriously meant references to, e.g., A. Rosenberg's *Der Mythos des 20. Jahrhunderts*. Such details can be easily corrected. More serious is the fact that, by and large, it labors under the above-mentioned model, according to which Judaism is an inferior and erroneous approach to God. This question is the more significant once this indispensable tool for NT studies is in the process of publication in English translation, four volumes having been published so far (*Theological Dictionary of the New Testament* [Grand Rapids: Wm. B. Eerdmans, 1964–]). While the use of this impressive work is to be highly recommended, its readers are advised to keep the above-mentioned problem well in mind.

For recent developments, see A. Roy Eckardt, "The Jewish-Christian Dialogue: Recent Christian Efforts in Europe," *Conservative Judaism* 19:3 (1965): 12–21; cf. also, in fuller form, *Journal of Bible and Religion* 33 (1965): 149–55.

13. Paul's idea of collecting coals of fire on the enemies' heads (Rom. 12:19) has its perfect parallel in the Qumran community. Its members are taught to practice secret hatred against their opponents, assured of their future punishment through God's righteous judgment. See K. Stendahl, "Hate, Nonretaliation and Love: 1QS x. 17–20 and Rom. 12:19–21," see above, pp. 137–50.

14. Without these hermeneutical consequences, this question is well exemplified by Joseph A. Fitzmyer, "Anti-Semitism and the Cry of 'All the People'" (Matt. 27:25), *Theological Studies* 26 (1965): 667–71.

15. At the colloquium, John Dillenberger, in his paper on "Judaism and Protestantism: Some Historical Patterns of Understanding," stressed the significance of Ch. Y. Glock's and R. Stark's inquiry into *Christian Beliefs and Anti-Semitism* (New York: Harper & Row, 1965). This sociological study of contemporary Christian attitudes makes it abundantly clear that anti-Semitism can hardly be considered unrelated to Christian belief.

16. See now also E. Bammel, "Christian Origins in Jewish Tradition," *New Testament Studies* 13 (1966/67): 317–35. This article is rich in historical information, but one must question the way in which we finally are told, in the tone of Christian evangelism, that the Jews "had no appropriate scheme to cope with this phenomenon [the person of Christ]" (335).

17. As was the case in our colloquium, the views of Jewish thinkers differ greatly as to the possibilities of going beyond the status quo. Here are three able and representative presentations: S. Siegel, "Jews and Christians: The Next Step," *Conservative Judaism* 19:3 (1965): 1–11: J. J. Petuchowski, "The Christian-Jewish Dialogue: A Jewish View," *The Lutheran World* 10 (1963): 373–84; J. B. Soloveitchik, "Confrontation," *Tradition* 6:2 (1964): 5–29. Note the often recurring quote from Maimonides: "The thoughts of the Creator of the world cannot be comprehended by man, for His ways are not our ways, and His thoughts are not our thoughts. All the matters of Jesus the Nazarene and of Muhammed were done for the purposes of preparing the way for the Messiah and to perfect the world so that it will serve the Lord" (Mishneh Torah, Hilkhot Melakhim 11:4).

18. In Rabbi Soloveitchik's article (see note 17), Judaism is seen as an ahistorical, metaphysical entity. Thus our approach would find special difficulty in relation to such an understanding of Judaism—and its equivalents in Christian theology. The same difficulty loomed large in our colloquium. But this could not be considered a distinction between Judaism and Christianity. It rather cuts across such lines, as it is rooted in different philosophical frameworks of religious thought.

19. It is important to note that our observation here differs from the way in which the Declaration of Vatican II deals with Islam. There the relations between Judaism and Christianity are seen in the light of divine economy (*Heilsgeschichte*) and "common patrimony." But Islam is treated in terms of its doctrinal structure. See, Bea, *The Church and Jewish People*, 150.

20. For a fair statement of Jewish reaction to Christian attitudes in this set-

ting, see now S. Sandmel, *We Jews and You Christians: An Inquiry into Attitudes* (Philadelphia: J. B. Lippincott, 1967), 51–56.

21. See J. Neusner, "From Theology to Ideology: The Transmutation of Judaism in Modern Times," in *Churches and States: The Religious Institutions and Modernization,* ed. K. H. Silvert (New York: American Universities Field Staff, 1967). Neusner's article is of special interest since it applies consciously to the study of Judaism the methodology urged by our colleague, Wilfred C. Smith, as stated in his *The Meaning and End of Religion,* and his paper "Traditional Religions and Modern Culture" at *The XIth Congress of the International Association for the History of Religions* (1965).

22. See R. J. Zwi Werblowsky, "Israël et Eretz Israël," *Les Temps Modernes* 253 (1967): 371–93.

17

Christ's Lordship and Religious Pluralism

Introductory Note: The last piece in this collection of essays opens up a problem that has come to occupy me increasingly: How can I sing my song to Jesus fully and with abandon without feeling it necessary to belittle the faith of others? I believe that question to be crucial for the health and vitality of Christian theology in the years ahead. Our inherited language of missions does not quite seem to ring true to what is actually going on. Such a crisis of language often creates a loss of joy and clarity in our gratitude to Jesus Christ.

It is often taken for granted that a biblical theology must by definition be inimical to an acceptance of religious pluralism. Or that the only theological way open is to speak of "anonymous Christians"—a doubtful idea since it suggests that the only way for a Christian to recognize worth in others is to claim that they have performed something "hiddenly" which we have done "openly."

In this essay I try to open up some biblical avenues, less travelled but truly authentic. It was part of a symposium and a book entitled *Christ's Lordship and Religious Pluralism*, ed. Gerald H. Anderson and Thomas F. Stransky, C.S.P. (Maryknoll, N.Y.: Orbis Books, 1981), 7–18.

A BIBLICAL VISION

Whatever question that I have to ponder as a reader of the Bible, it is important to consider it in the total setting of the biblical panorama. When we are to ponder together "Christ's Lordship and Religious Pluralism," the wider setting of a biblical vision may well be what we need first—the whole spectrum from the creation of the world to the redemption thereof.

233

Thus I begin with the obvious question, cast in simple language: What is it all about—from Genesis to Revelation? Let me sketch a biblical vision in the playfully poetic language of biblical theology.

God created the world—cosmos out of chaos. We do not know why God did so. We may humbly guess. God was lonely. Or, in other words, there is something in the very nature, the very heart of God that longs for communion, for company. In any case, God created the world. And as the crowning feature of that world it was God's dream that there be a type of creature that would serve God in perfect freedom, not out of nature's necessity. And human beings were made in God's image—male and female God created them.

There are many details here that are good to remember. First, humans are obviously important, but lest they brag too much, or lest they come to think that I-Thou relationships and individual salvation are the only things that count (or lest they come to fear Charles Darwin), they do not have a day of their own in the scheme of creation, but share the sixth day with "cattle and creeping things and beasts of the earth."

Second, the whole story in Gen. 1:1—2:3 is told as if the most important lesson to be learned from it is that we keep the Sabbath. The Sabbath rest on the seventh day is part of the cosmic order, not an arbitrary convention. This, I guess, to protect the creation against the tendencies of overzealous efficiency of a greedy humanity.

Third, there is the delight of Adam in finally—after having named all the animals and found no equal—finding a true and absolute equal "at last bone of my bone and flesh of my flesh" (Gen. 2:23), although our male cultures made that saying a symbol for the derivativeness and subordination of woman, instead of a word of total identity and equality.

It was God's dream that humans would serve God freely. It was a beautiful dream—and risky. And it went sour already in chapter 3 —Adam, of course, blaming it on Eve, as he has done through the ages (cf. 1 Tim. 2:13–15), initiating the well-known pattern of blaming the victim.

Since that day God has been at work toward the mending of the creation. Once he tried to flood the whole world, but that proved to be not so good an idea; and we have the rainbow as the sign of God's promise never to try that again—the only nonconditional covenant in the Bible.

So God decided to set up a laboratory toward the redemption of the creation and concentrate the efforts, according to the wise and holy laws given to Israel on Sinai. And God sent prophets and prophetesses of judgment and of hope. And there were great achievements and sad setbacks, and a growing hope for the day when the law would one day be written in the hearts of people. That would be the mending of the creation, the redemption of the world.

In due time God took a bolder step, the new move in Jesus Christ. Through the ages Christians have reflected on the significance of that move of God's, and rich languages of confession and reflection have developed among us—"the Lordship of Christ" being one, and the one chosen for our consideration in this study.

But in the sweeping vision of God's total work, I think it is of importance to note that when Jesus came, he chose to express his mission and his message in terms of the kingdom (Mark 1:14, parr.). Of all the some hundred themes that he could have lifted up from the Jewish tradition (biblical and postbiblical), and of all the infinite number of themes available to him in his divine fulness, he chose this one: the kingdom. How come? Again, we may guess.

And my guess is that this very term expressed the continuity with God's old and eternal dream for a mended creation, for a redeemed world. Kingdom is more than a king and a lordship, and reign. The kingdom of God, the kingdom of heaven, stands for a mended creation with people and things—a social, economic, ecological reality. Thus Jesus' miracles were not primarily signs of his power but acts of mending the creation, pushing back the frontier of Satan, healing minds and bodies, feeding, even counteracting the devastation of the premature death of the young and needy. The kingdom with its justice is for the wronged and the oppressed; the little people who hunger and thirst for bread and for justice; the peacemakers who are so easily liquidated.

Such, it seems, were the mission and messsage of our Lord, the new Creator, one with the Father "before the foundation of the world." And we should be deeply grateful to the evangelists that they have preserved for us this vision of Jesus and the kingdom. That is quite remarkable, for the kingdom-language tends to be replaced by other languages in the life and teaching of the church. A glance in a concordance to the New Testament makes that clear. Its dominant and crucial role in the synoptic gospels stands in stark contrast to its relative absence in the other twenty-four writings of the NT (including Acts and John).

It is not difficult to guess how that happened. In blunt language we would say that the kingdom did not come—a fact as obvious to us when we look around in the world as it was to the early disciples. But the Redeemer, the Savior, the King, the Messiah *had* come (note, however, Acts 3:20, where the Christ is to come, not as a second coming, but as *the* coming). And so the focus shifts from the kingdom to the

235

King, from the realm to the reign, from the redemption of the creation to the relation between the believer and the Lord. An outside observer might well interpret this development as "a solution out of embarrassment." For the church it was certainly not felt to be such. On the contrary, there was the enormous gratitude and joy over the gift of Jesus Christ.

But it remains a fact worth pondering that Jesus had preached the kingdom, while the church preached Jesus. And thus we are faced with a danger: we may so preach Jesus that we lose the vision of the kingdom, the mended creation.

Much has been made of various types of eschatologies: realized, anticipatory, future, otherworldly, transcended, and the like. As for the Jesus material, I wonder if his ministry is not best understood if we surmise that there were days when he was hopeful that God's dream could be realized within space and time, and there were days when he felt that the only possibility was the apocalyptic one, "a new heaven and a new earth." Scholarly and theological debates on this matter tend to overshadow the more important issue: be it here or there, the matter that matters is the kingdom—and we are called to be guinea pigs in God's new laboratory for the kingdom. The church is such a laboratory.

In the final book of our Bible the old vision, the old and persistent dream of God's for a mended world, emerges in all its visionary splendor, out of the final spasmodic desperation of evil. It emerges as a new creation with people and trees and cities, lest we forget the total vision.

Nor should we forget that *the* prayer of the Christian church—the Lord's Prayer—is an extended cry for the coming of the kingdom. In that prayer we cry out for the time when the whole creation recognizes God as God, when the kingdom comes, when the will of God is realized on earth as in heaven. We pray for a community gathered and fed by the messianic banquet, a community of mutually forgiven people who trust in God's power to rescue them from the powers of pain and evil—in short, for the victory of one who brings the kingdom and the power and the glory, finally and fully.

An observation about the Lukan setting of the Lord's Prayer may be helpful. Luke tells us that the prayer was given to the disciples in response to their request (11:1). John the Baptist had given his disciples a special prayer. Now Jesus' disciples wanted one also; a prayer that would be their "badge," their distinctive symbol. Jesus answers by giving a prayer that grows out of the themes familiar from Jewish prayers.

Actually, there is nothing in the Lord's Prayer that could not be prayed wholeheartedly by a faithful Jew—then or now. (That does not mean that we should urge the Jews: "Let us say the Lord's Prayer together." Prayers gather unto themselves symbolic meanings, beyond the meaning of the words, and this is *the* prayer of the Christian church.) The point is this: when the disciples desired a prayer to set them apart, Jesus gave them a prayer that constitutes our bond with Israel, as Israel prays for forgiveness from "our Father . . . who art gracious and dost abundantly forgive" (from the *Amidah*); as Israel prays "Sanctified be his great Name in the world which he has created. May he establish his kingdom . . . even speedily and at a near time" (from the *Kaddish*).

IN NO OTHER NAME . . .
ACTS 4:12

The book of Acts pictures the apostles as wonderworkers. This is in continuity with the praxis and the beliefs, especially populist, both in Judaism, which had a strong tradition of wonderworking, and in the Greco-Roman culture. There is no other writing in the NT that is so colorful in its descriptions of Christian wonderworking as is the Acts of the Apostles, and if you want a treat, go to Acts 19:11ff. with the seven sons of Sceva and other colorful stories, which most of us do not like to think about too much. We may be embarrassed to find that magic worked wonders for the Lord. What is wrong with Simon Magus (8:10) is only one thing, namely, that he tries to *buy* the power of Christian magic, not that there is such a power. Acts is a book rich in vividly religious behavior gloriously practiced by the early Christians, and it is all in the name of the "name." The phrase "to do something in the name of Jesus of Nazareth" is in all these passages related to the working of miracles. It is in the relation to the miraculous name-use, not in relation to the Shema (Deut. 6:4) that we must primarily read Acts 4:12—by this name is salvation. Luke uses the name more than any other NT writer. The name is Luke's special term for expressing the Christian gospel at work. It is also worth noting that in these passages the faith of those healed is seldom stressed. Thereby the wonder-working effect of the name is the more striking. For a study of how Jesus and the apostles were perceived as wonderworkers in the Greco-Roman world, see Morton Smith's *Jesus the Magician* (New York: Harper & Row, 1977).

To what question is "In no other name" the answer? That question is found in Acts 4:7. It is the question of the Temple authorities: "By what power or by what name did you do this?" "This" seems to refer back to the healing in chapter 3, although it could include the speech in the court of the Temple. The answer does, however, refer back to the healing. As we know from other such accounts, it was very important for these Christians to stress that they did not do such miracles in their own name, but in the name of Jesus. See for example Acts 3:12: "not as if we had done this in our own name" (au. trans.).

Thus the primary and the simplest, the most obvious context of the words "In no other name is there salvation but in the name of Jesus" is: in the name of Jesus, and thus not in our own name. Pointing away from themselves, they made clear that they were not magicians with their own inherent powers. The power was in the name of Jesus. So that instead of answering all the questions of relations to other religions, the Jews, and all kinds of other things, the simplest level of this verse is: we did not do it in our name but in the name of Jesus!

We may find such a minimalist exegesis almost unbelievably naive. We are all theologians and prone to milking the words of the Scriptures of their last drop of potential. However, in listening to a story as Luke tells it, one should never miss that primary level, the light and quick meaning.

But there is a second context, and that one is obviously the Jewish people. Here, as in chapters 2, 3, and the rest of 4, the addressees are Jews, and in chapter 4 they are most specifically the Temple authorities. Nowhere in these chapters enter any questions about gentile gods, gentile cults, or gentile religion. Thus there is no way of knowing whether Luke, who wrote this, would consider this saying relevant to a discussion on Buddhism—if he knew anything about Buddhism, which is most doubtful. The setting is intra-Jewish and inter-Jewish. The "no other name" has no extra-Jewish referent, nor would I consider it proper to "smuggle in" such by supposing a flashback to the Shema, the confession that Yahweh (the Lord) is one.

The intra-Jewish and inter-Jewish setting highlights instead the distinction between the leaders and the people, a theme that Luke lets dominate the picture of the early days in Jerusalem and beyond (e.g., 4:21). That pattern is familiar to us all in contemporary terms: the Kremlin always thinks the American people are on their side as over against the capitalist and imperialist leaders and establishments. And vice versa. As a matter of fact, it is a timeless apologetic model for

238

struggling revolutionary movements—of which the Jesus movement was one.

Thus we note that Peter here speaks within Judaism, fully identifying with Israel. Such an identification is of great importance for any interpretation. Jesus and the apostles are seen in the honorable and hard role of the OT prophets. It is important to remember that with that role goes the identification with the people and its lot. But when such prophecies and words of warning and doom are not spoken any longer within Israel, from and to Jews—when such prophetic words fall "into alien hands"— then they lose their original meaning, even if they are quoted verbatim. When gentile Christians hurled Jesus' words at the Jews, something went seriously wrong. But here in Acts 4 the "debate" remains inter-Jewish. There is not a Jewish-Christian tension, but primarily one between the establishment and the people, the latter being impressed by God's mighty deeds in Jesus' name.

To the Jewish establishment, Luke here gives—through Peter's speech—the confession to Jesus Christ, apologetically sharpened by the reference to Psalm 118, used also elsewhere, including by Luke (20:17) in the parable about the vineyard. It is important to note what I have called an apologetically sharpened confession. Peter speaks when accused before the court. We should note that Peter has the Holy Spirit especially assisting him in making *this* speech (4:8), but not so in chapter 3. There is only one situation according to the synoptic gospels in which one can count on the assistance of the Holy Spirit and that is when one is brought into court, because the *martyrs*, the witness, is a witness before the powers, before the authorities. That is why we find that phrase "and Peter, filled with the Holy Spirit . . . " (Luke 4:8). He is in court (cf. Matt. 10:19–20, parr.). And in that situation the defense of the accused is a confession.

What is, then, the nature, the genre (*Gattung*), of such a statement as "In no other Name"? It is a confession. What is the nature of such a confession? And now comes the shocking thought: it should be seriously asked if religious language, either confessional, hymnic, or liturgical, that is to say, religious language that we call primary religious language, the language of religious experience, should not be considered as love language, as caressing language. That is why Protestants often have difficulties in understanding what liturgy is about. Liturgy is play, liturgy is repetitious; when you play, when you worship, you use language in a caressing manner. It has the same sort of expression as that kind of language by which one caresses the person dear to one. That is proper, since the ultimate aim of our whole existence is to praise God, glorify and enjoy God forever. Liturgy has a caressing function; its language is a love language.

Or let me make my point differently: if a husband were to say that his wife was the only one for him, and he were telling the truth and nothing but the truth, then that is good and true. But if he were witnessing in court and was under oath and the judge asked him whether he could be sure that nowhere in the world could there be another woman about whom he could have come to say the same thing, then he could not take such an oath. For in that other setting the very same words would take on another meaning, just as would the words of Peter's confession if treated as an axiom of dogmatic theology.

Now most of you would say that such an interpretation is too subjective. I find, however, subjective/objective distinctions far too blunt an instrument here. The issue is, rather, that of different languages and intentions, and I think we should seriously ask one another whether the nature of religious language is not, rather, to be seen in the general direction here outlined.

Such love-language is far from innocent or less threatening to the establishment, as we can judge from this story. (And those of us who were part of the establishment during the student revolution can witness to the power of the emotionally charged language that was spoken against us in those days. It was not harmless, not mere words, nor was it "objective" language, as everyone might remember. It was a powerful witness, spoken with the power of the powerless.)

The foregoing observations suggest to me that Acts 4:12 is not a good basis for an absolute claim in an absolute sense, but that it is a natural confession growing out of the faith, growing out of the experience of gratitude. It also grew out of apostolic humility, that is, the awareness by Peter and John that they did not do it themselves, but that it was all in the power of the Lord. They thereby pointed away from themselves. Just as any reference to election indicates that one cannot understand how it could happen. Here is a confession, not a proposition. It is a witness, strangely enough not actually an argument, but just exactly a witness.

All thoughtful believers and believing communities that have taken monotheism seriously must sooner or later reflect upon how their *different* absolute claims somehow must fit together in God's mysterious plan. In stating this thesis it is clear that I move from the level of primary religious language (prayer, confession, hymn, liturgy) to the level of reflection, afterthought, namely, to theology.

They will do so "sooner or later." It would be a little much to expect that such reflection would loom large in the NT or in the first exuberant generations of the Jesus movement. And yet, as we shall see in the next study, that reflection happened already in the middle of the first century, in the mighty thoughts of the great missionary Paul.

THE PITFALLS OF UNIVERSALISM

Most of us take for granted that universalism is superior to particularism. Christianity is a universal religion, transcending the shackles of particularism. As a matter of fact, we say, here lies one of the decisive differences between Judaism and Christianity. We might even argue that the very essence of monotheism requires a universalist stance.

I would like to take a second look at this comfortable and respectable model of Christian thought and teaching, as to both the Jewish and the Christian sides of the ledger. I would like to do so since I have been struck by the gruesome thought that universalist claims have often led to various kinds of imperialism and crusades. The connection is very simple. If my faith is universal in its claim, then woe unto those who do not see the world as I do.

As a student of Judaism in the time of the second Temple, I know that the Hellenistic rulers were universalists, convinced that their culture was true culture. They could not stand people who did not accept it—hence, the Maccabean revolt. Cultural imperialism—the UNESCO approach in its early forms—builds on a universalism with little patience for the particularism of people and cultures. If that be so about cultures, how true it is about religions, where the one and true understanding of God is claimed in universalist form.

Now it is true that Israel's faith is particularist, resting in the grateful and humble conviction that it is called to a special faithfulness to God. But it is equally true that this particular and peculiar faithfulness is only part of God's universal work in the creation. At least from Second Isaiah's time it becomes crystal clear that Israel has a universal mission: to be a light for the nations, the gentiles (Isa. 49:6, et al.). But not by making them Jews, but by being a faithful witness to the oneness of God and the moral order—toward the day of a mended creation.

This witnessing particularism within a universal perspective led Jewish thinkers like Maimonides to the view that Christianity and Islam were "bearers of Torah"—bearers of the witness to the oneness of God and the moral order—to the gentiles. Such a model is remarkable in the history of religion, since it is rare indeed that one religion assigns a positive role to other religions, especially to religions that are hostile to one's own. But the greatness of this model consists perhaps in its concern for "the kingdom" rather than for oneself. It is the Eldad and Medad spirit from Num. 11:26–29 (echoed in the teachings of Jesus in Mark 9:38–40).

So let us move on to the NT. I would suggest that the image that emerges out of the NT is in more continuity with the OT and postbiblical Judaism than we usually recognize.

It is obviously correct to speak of Christianity as a universalistic religion. The membership of the church is based on faith in and allegiance to Jesus Christ, and in Christ there is neither Jew nor Greek, neither slave nor free, neither male nor female. In that sense its base is universal. But as a new witnessing community the church understands itself as a minority community with a mission. And what—according to the NT—is the aim of its witness? Is it the Christianization of the world, the dream of the Christian century? Or could it be something else? Something less self-glorifying and more centered in God's mysterious plan for a mended creation. A mission more in tune with being a light for the gentiles?

We all know that phrase from the NT, both from the Song of Simeon (Luke 2:32) and from the Sermon on the Mount (Matt. 5:13ff.). The images of salt and light are minority images. Who wants the world to become a salt mine? And note the saying: Let your light so shine before people that they see your good works *and give glory to your Father who is in heaven*—not: . . . and become Christians. And the Magi (Matthew 2) did not start a church in Iran; they just received the uplifting experience of their lives. And the one who gives a cup of cold water to you, since you are a disciple, that "outsider," shall not lose the reward (Matt. 10:42), a word that in Mark is part of Jesus' scathing critique of the cliquishness of the disciples (Mark 9:41). And the whole world will be judged by how they have treated this little, witnessing community (Matt. 25:31–46).

This all indicates that the world is not divided between those who accept Jesus and the *massa perditionis*. The church is a new witnessing community, a minority whose witness somehow God "needs" in his total mission, the *missio Dei*.

It is urgent for us now—in a pluralistic world—to find our right place, our peculiar and particular place as faithful witnesses to Jesus Christ, leaving the result of the witness in the hands of God.

A significant event in the history of Christian reflection about how the Christian mission might fit into God's wider plan for the world is to be found in Paul's letter to the church in Rome. At a crucial juncture in his apostolic ministry Paul reflects on how his mission to the gentiles fits into God's total plan (Romans 9—11).

Paul begins by making clear that he certainly would like the Jews to accept Jesus as the Christ, yea, he swears that he is willing to be "accursed and cut off from Christ" if that would help to that end (Rom. 9:1; cf. 10:1). But before he is through, he will lecture the gentile Christians (11:13) that they have no business in trying to convert the Jews. Paul seems to have discerned two things: (a) an attitude of superiority and conceit in the gentile Christians (11:25), which makes them unsuited for such a mission; and (b) that the Jesus movement is to be a Gentile movement—apart from the significant remnant, the link by grace (11:5). That *is* quite perceptive in the mid–first century—but we know that that is roughly what happened.

For Paul these insights lead to a stress on the mysterious nature of God's mission: "Lest you be wise in your own conceits, I want you to understand this mystery . . . " (Rom. 11:25). And the mystery is that the salvation of Israel is in God's hands, and that the "no" of Israel was not toward her rejection (" . . . have they stumbled in order to fall? By no means!") but in order to open up the salvation for the gentiles (11:11).

Consciously or unconsciously Paul writes this whole section in Romans (10:18—11:36) without mentioning the name of Jesus Christ, and his final doxology has no Christ-language—as do all his other doxologies. It is pure God-language (11:33–36). It is as if Paul did not want them to have the Christ-flag to wave, since it might fan their conceit.

Here the most zealous of all missionaries, the very apostle Paul, has given us his reflection on the dangers of thoughtless universalism, his mature thought about how mission without mystery becomes oppressive. Perhaps he had been burned once by a religious zeal that took for granted that God's hottest dream was that all people believed like him—on the road to Damascus, set on bringing the Christians into line.

The issue at hand here is the church and Israel. But there is also the wider issue of a missionary style in which the mysterious *missio Dei* may call for new ways for us to sing our song to Jesus Christ without

243

conceit. Not that Paul's Christians *felt* that conceit. They thought they were witnessing to the truth. And they were—but in a manner that suggested that God's only way was that everyone become like unto themselves. They did not understand their mission as a particular witness of the peculiar community in a world of communities. And in that, said Paul, they were wrong. They became proud, they did not "stand in awe" (Rom. 11:20).